Knowledge Management and Higher Education:
A Critical Analysis

Amy Scott Metcalfe
The University of British Columbia, Canada

Information Science Publishing
Hershey • London • Melbourne • Singapore

Acquisitions Editor: Renée Davies
Development Editor: Kristin Roth
Senior Managing Editor: Amanda Appicello
Managing Editor: Jennifer Neidig
Copy Editor: Jennifer Young
Typesetter: Larissa Zearfoss
Cover Design: Lisa Tosheff
Printed at: Integrated Book Technology

Published in the United States of America by
Information Science Publishing (an imprint of Idea Group Inc.)
701 E. Chocolate Avenue
Hershey PA 17033
Tel: 717-533-8845
Fax: 717-533-8661
E-mail: cust@idea-group.com
Web site: http://www.idea-group.com

and in the United Kingdom by
Information Science Publishing (an imprint of Idea Group Inc.)
3 Henrietta Street
Covent Garden
London WC2E 8LU
Tel: 44 20 7240 0856
Fax: 44 20 7379 3313
Web site: http://www.eurospan.co.uk

Library of Congress Cataloging-in-Publication Data

Knowledge management and higher education : a critical analysis / Amy Metcalfe, editor.
p. cm.
Summary: "Using various social science perspectives, this book provide critical analyses of knowledge management in higher education, with an emphasis on unintended consequences and future implications"--Provided by publisher.
Includes bibliographical references and index.
ISBN 1-59140-509-2 (hardcover) -- ISBN 1-59140-510-6 (soft cover) -- ISBN 1-59140-511-4 (ebook)
1. Education, Higher--Economic aspects. 2. Knowledge management. 3. Education, Higher--Effect of technological innovations on. I. Metcalfe, Amy, 1967-
LC67.6.K57 2006
338.4'3378--dc22

2005020184

British Cataloguing in Publication Data
A Cataloguing in Publication record for this book is available from the British Library.

All work contributed to this book is new, previously-unpublished material. Each chapter is assigned to at least 2-3 expert reviewers and is subject to a blind, peer review by these reviewers. The views expressed in this book are those of the authors, but not necessarily of the publisher.

Knowledge Management and Higher Education:

A Critical Analysis

Table of Contents

Section IV: Case Studies

Section V: Resources

Preface

Knowledge Management and Higher Education

Although the use of knowledge management (KM) principles in the business sector has been the focus of many books, seminars, and professional development workshops, the application of KM in higher education has been heretofore only partially examined. This book addresses the social aspects of KM that are largely ignored in the literature. Using various social science perspectives, the authors provide critical analyses of KM in higher education, with an emphasis on unintended consequences and future implications. The objectives of this book are to examine the strengths and weaknesses of KM, and to provide examples of the social effects of the implementation of KM in the field of higher education. Many of the conclusions drawn from the research presented in this volume will be of interest to not only those concerned with the future of higher education, but also to professionals who work in other highly-institutionalized and information-intensive fields, such as health care, government, and private business.

Organization of the Book

Knowledge Management and Higher Education: A Critical Analysis has been organized into three sections. Section I is titled, "The Application of Knowledge Management in Higher Education" and explores both the conceptual and practical issues of KM within postsecondary settings. In the first chapter, titled, "The Political Economy of Knowledge Management in Higher

Education," I discuss several theoretical constructs that can aid in understanding the adaptation and application of knowledge management techniques in higher education settings. These theories allow us to consider dimensions of power and influence within the workplace, which can become embedded within technological structures.

In Chapter II, Lisa Petrides and Lilly Nguyen introduce the promises and potential pitfalls of KM in "Knowledge Management Trends: Challenges and Opportunities for Education Institutions." Utilizing their extensive background in consulting for educational institutions, Petrides and Nguyen guide us through the ways in which KM must be adapted from the business culture to best suit an academic implementation. In particular, they find that higher education institutions can benefit from understanding that KM is more than just data management; it is a cycle that includes data, information, knowledge, and most importantly, action.

To complement the information learned from Petrides and Nguyen, John Milam presents a systems approach of academic knowledge in "Ontologies in Higher Education." Dr. Milam provides us with an understanding of the higher education sector from a structural perspective by discussing the various classification schemas and taxonomies used to distinguish academic institutions and their components. The chapter also provides useful guidelines for developing academic ontologies, an overview of software that is currently being used in this capacity, and a discussion of future trends in the classification of higher education institutions, processes and outputs.

Section II, "Administrative Issues and Knowledge Management" contains three chapters that discuss the socio-technical concerns of information management in higher education. In Chapter IV, my co-authors (George McClellan, Gary Cruz, and Richard Wagoner) and I present a forecast of the future of higher education in "Toward Technological Bloat and Academic Technocracy: The Information Age and Higher Education." We draw upon economic and social theories to explain the rise in technocratic leadership in academic organizations and to predict the role of these leaders in the future. We intend the chapter to be thought-provoking and cautionary in that we point out that an increase in IT managerial positions and investments in the technological infrastructure necessary to accommodate KM strategies are not without cost, both organizationally and financially.

Building upon the ideas expressed in the previous chapter, Richard Wagoner presents an example of KM implementation in Chapter V, "We've Got a Job to Do—Eventually: A Study of Knowledge Management Fatigue Syndrome." Dr. Wagoner presents compelling reasons why technological solutions are not always easily implemented within a higher education setting. Using interview data and other qualitative methods, he explores the efficacy of a new enterprise computer system from the point-of-view of the academic staff members who are the primary users. He finds that the concept of "knowledge management fatigue syndrome" aids in the understanding of how a campus-wide IT overhaul can stall in mid-implementation and result in both infrastructural and organizational adaptations to the technological needs of the system.

As knowledge management has been closely tied to the institutional research function of higher education, José Luis Santos' chapter titled, "Institutional Research (IR) Meets Knowledge Management (KM)" is a significant contribution to this volume. In an era of increased attention to accountability measures, institutional research offices are faced with presenting large amounts of data to university constituents. Yet, as Dr. Santos writes, those who are charged with creating and utilizing institutional databases are often not fully aware of the part they play in the creation of "knowledge" rather than the mere reporting of "information." This chapter provides a clear example of how knowledge and information differ, and how academic managers can fail to understand these dissimilarities.

Section III of this volume is titled, "The Knowledge Management of Teaching and Learning," and contains two chapters. Chapter VII, "Revealing Unseen Organizations in Higher Education: A Study Framework and Application Example," by Lucie Sommer, describes MIT's Open Courseware Project and the Open Knowledge Initiative from a structural perspective. In this chapter, Sommer places MIT's course management system within a social context, reframing the technology within a reflexive and communicative social environment. She concludes that in the process of creating online digital environments, higher education institutions may be (unknowingly) creating a new form of educational organization. The revelation of a paradox is a key contribution of her work to the field of KM as Sommers recognizes that a process of knowledge management can lead to an unknown and misunderstood progression of organizational reorganization.

Finally, Veronica Diaz and Patricia McGee have contributed Chapter VIII, which is titled, "Distributed Learning Objects: An Open Knowledge Management Model." The authors use their expertise in instructional technology to guide us through the various ways in which learning objects are stored and classified for retrieval. The chapter contains a sophisticated understanding of how the products and processes of learning are influenced by both an open knowledge system and thc market-driven knowledge economy. This chapter is significant in that multiple schemas for classification still exist, and various paradigms for ownership, sharing, and distribution are still possible.

The final section of the book, Section IV, contains six case studies on the topic of information management in higher education. The case studies were chosen for their applicability to a knowledge management framework and for their utility in describing the myriad of social forces at work in educational organizations. This section includes the following case studies: "Policy Processes for Technological Change" by Richard Smith, Brian Lewis, and Christine Massey; "Enterprise System Development in Higher Education" by Bongsug Chae and Marshall Scott Poole; "Higher Education Culture and the Diffusion of Technology in Classroom Instruction" by Kandis Smith; "Wiring Watkins University: Does IT Really Matter?" by Andy Borchers; "Challenges of Complex Information Technology Projects: The MAC Initiative" by Teta Stamati, Panagiotis Kanellis, and Drakoulis Martakos; and "A Case of an IT-Enabled Organizational Change Intervention: The Missing Pieces" by Bing Wang and David Paper. At the end of the case studies is a set of discussion questions and notes for instructors. These teaching materials may be used in conjunction with the case studies or the chapters in this volume and may be useful in a variety of classroom settings.

Additional resources for scholars and practitioners are included at the end of this volume. Appendix A includes resources for further exploration, including online clearinghouses for information on KM and higher education. Appendix B contains a bibliography of KM literature and related topics that the authors and I have complied. Furthermore, Appendix C contains a glossary of terms related to the field of knowledge management. We hope you find this section useful in your exploration of KM in the higher education sector.

Acknowledgments

The editor would like to acknowledge the help of all of those involved in the process of producing this volume. Without their help, this project could not have been completed.

First, I would like to thank Dr. Gary Rhoades and Dr. Jennifer Croissant of the University of Arizona for allowing me to participate in a seminar they co-taught for the Center for the Study of Higher Education in the spring of 2003 on the topic of knowledge management in higher education. The class readings and discussion focused on the intersections between the social dimensions of information technology, the social construction of technology, and the sociology of professions. It was in this seminar that I developed the prospectus for this book.

Second, I want to thank the authors who contributed to this volume. As the social-constructivist approach we have taken here is somewhat new in the field of knowledge management, I appreciate their innovative thoughts and ability to pursue a topic beyond the present scope of the literature. Also, several of the authors also served as reviewers, for which I am very grateful.

Special thanks also to the staff at Idea Group Inc. In particular, I would like to thank Managing Director Jan Travers and Development Editor Michele Rossi for their encouragement and interest in this topic. In addition, I am in debt to the kindness and guidance fo Kristin Roth, Development Editor, who has helped me shape this volume into its present state. I am also appreciative of the work and dedication of Mehdi Khosrow-Pour who has provided the field of knowledge management with an important set of publications and resources.

Amy Scott Metcalfe, PhD

The University of British Columbia, Canada

June 2005

Section I

The Application of Knowledge Management in Higher Education

Chapter I

The Political Economy of Knowledge Management in Higher Education

Amy Scott Metcalfe
The University of British Columbia, Canada

Abstract

In this chapter, I discuss the economic and political implications of knowledge management in higher education. First, I examine the linkages between KM and capitalism, with the help of theoretical frameworks that connect increasing managerialism in higher education with the promises of profit-making in the New (Knowledge) Economy. Next, I discuss the politics of information and the ways in which knowledge is stratified in postsecondary institutions. Third, the social dynamics of information and communications technologies (ICT) are explored in the context of higher education institutions. These perspectives provide a counter-balance to the decidedly functionalist views of much of the knowledge management literature. The intent of the chapter is to provide a foundation for the rest of the volume and the more specific studies of KM in higher education to follow.

Introduction

As the external environment increased pressure upon institutions of higher education to become more productive and business-like, it is not surprising that business management techniques are promoted as the best vehicles for change (Ewell, 1999). In the Information Age, the management techniques that have been the most popular in the private sector pertain to e-business, the art of combining the marketplace with high technology and opportunities provided by the Internet. E-business initiatives are also becoming common in higher education, with Web-based portals linking academic units to shared databases and common business rules (Katz et al., 2000). Distance education courses are hosted on the World Wide Web, and "e-learning" has become standard jargon in the field. Academic managers have embraced information technology since the age of the mainframe computer, which has resulted in the development of techno-centric institutional infrastructures, electronically-driver business cores, and wired classrooms in colleges and universities throughout the industrialized world.

Ushered into academe on the heels of information technology and institutional restructuring, knowledge management promises to lead to better decision-making capabilities, improve academic services, and reduce costs (Kidwell, Vander Linde, & Johnson, 2001). KM is often loosely defined, but its central purpose is the action of "transforming information and intellectual assets into enduring value" (Kidwell et al., 2001, p. 3). Founded on the notion that "intellectual capital" is a hidden asset of many businesses, KM seeks to bring this essential knowledge to light in order to make organizations more competitive. In the arena of higher education, KM is being touted as a method that will increase institutional innovation (Lyman, 2000). Getz, Siegfried, and Anderson have stated that, "higher education occupies a strategic role in productivity growth, not only because it is an industry itself, but also because it is a source of new ideas and trains the managers that affect productivity throughout the economy" (Getz, Siegfried, & Anderson, 1997, p. 605). It is in this context that

KM proponents have noted that the absence of KM principles in higher education is a striking oversight (Serban & Luan, 2002).

Colleges and universities are obvious sites to explore the implementation of knowledge management (KM) principles in the public sector, given the historic connections between academe and the production of knowledge. While the creation and dissemination of knowledge has long been the social role of colleges and universities, recent neoliberal shifts in the political climate have led to legislative and private sector demands for evidence of a return on investment for public expenditures to higher education. As state support for postsecondary education dwindles, more attention is paid to "productivity" measures and ways in which institutions are maximizing public and private investments. Institutional research offices have been at the core of the data collection efforts. An increase in the use of information technology has provided more opportunities to measure and codify the production capacities of higher education institutions, from the learning mission to research output. Data points such as graduation rates, expenditures per student, faculty/student ratios, the cost to raise a dollar, grant revenues received, patents granted, and other factoids are collected, contextualized, and distributed by academic institutions to their public and private constituents. Thus, the information gathered and evaluated is used to determine financial aid formulas, institutional rankings, state appropriations, and other important "knowledge-based" decisions that affect higher education.

Recently the principles of KM have been applied to academic settings to help in these efforts. As an outgrowth of the data-gathering opportunities afforded by the widespread adoption of information technology (IT), KM is wedded to the technological infrastructures of modern organizations. Therefore, issues of access to and control over IT systems and the social power differential between those who are the "monitored", those who are the "users", and those who are the "managers" of technology are inherent to KM implementation, regardless of the size and type of organization where it occurs. Academic labor and its products have been traditionally shaped by professional norms and peer-review, but a shift toward technocratic decision-making in an environment marked by academic capitalism (Slaughter & Leslie, 1997; Slaughter & Rhoades, 2004) has permitted new value systems to prevail. In such an organizational climate, the intellectual capital that was previously considered a public good is now a "knowledge asset" that has the potential to increase institutional legitimacy and to provide new revenue streams. Knowledge management, as it has been defined and shaped by the private sector, is thus being employed in the public sphere in order to "capture" these assets and codify them into tangible objects with market value. However, academic managers who employ KM techniques do not have to adopt business values that promote the commoditization of knowledge for profit. This book offers an alternative expression of ideas and case study evidence to encourage a more thorough exploration of the uses of KM in higher education.

In this chapter, I discuss the economic, political, and social implications of knowledge management in higher education. First, I examine the linkages between KM and capitalism, with the help of theoretical frameworks that connect increasing managerialism in higher education with the promises of profit-making in the New (Knowledge) Economy. Next, I discuss the politics of information and the ways in which knowledge is stratified in postsecondary institutions. Third, the social dynamics of information and communications technologies (ICT) are explored in the context of higher education institutions. These perspectives (economic, political, and social) provide a counter-balance to the decidedly functionalist views of much of the knowledge management literature. The intent of the chapter is to provide a foundation for the rest of the volume and the more specific studies of KM in higher education to follow.

The Economics of Knowledge Management

The ability to produce and consume information and knowledge products situates the field of knowledge management in a capitalist cycle, and therefore dimensions of power and inequality are inherent in the application of this (or any) managerial schema. From an economic standpoint, information and knowledge are commodities, either exchanged for free in the gift economy market (Lessig, 2001) or for a price in the consumer market. Thus, even when KM is used in non-profit settings, the *ability* to profit from the capture and diffusion of information and knowledge is embedded in the best-practices and technical infrastructures that were created for the business context. Further, as colleges and universities move closer to private-sector behaviors and values as described by acadmic capitalism theory (Slaughter & Leslie, 1997; Slaughter & Rhoades, 2004), opportunities for the influx of business strategies into higher education institutions increase. For these reasons, we must begin to understand how market principles affect the implementation of knowledge management in the public arena. In addition, I will introduce the theory or academic capitalism, describe the increase in managerialsim in academe, and explore the ways in which higher education institutions are intertwined with digital capitalism.

Academic Capitalism

Academic capitalism is a term used by Slaughter and Leslie (1997) to describe the market-like behaviors of higher education organizations. They noted that the production of human capital is one of the more important functions of higher education in modern society. They stated that:

Universities are the repositories of much of the most scarce and valuable human capital that nations possess, capital that is valuable because it is essential to the development of the high technology and technoscience necessary for competing successfully in the global economy. The human capital possessed by universities, of course, is vested in their academic staffs. Thus the specific commodity is academic *capital, which is not more than the particular human capital possessed by academics. This final step in the logic is to say that when faculty implement their academic capital through engagement in production, they are engaging in* academic capitalism. *Their scarce and specialized knowledge and skills are being applied to productive work that yields a benefit to the individual academic, to the public university they serve, to the corporations with which they work, and to the larger society. It is indeed academic capitalism that is involved, both technically and practically.* (pp. 10-11)

Central to their analysis was the use of resource dependency theory, as outlined by Pfeffer and Salancik (1978). Resource dependency theory describes the ways in which organizations become dependent upon other organizations through resource allocation. Pfeffer and Salancik list three factors used to determine the extent of dependence: the importance of the resource and its criticality to organizational survival, organizational discretion over the allocation of the resources in question, and the presence or absence of alternative resources (Pfeffer & Salancik, 1978, pp. 45-46). Slaughter and Leslie noted that "national and state/provincial restriction of discretionary resources created increased resource dependence at the institutional level, causing institutions and professors to look to alternative revenue sources to maintain institutional income" (Slaughter & Leslie, 1997, p. 64). While resource dependence largely defines organizational behavior as reactive to external forces, it has also been applied to help understand intraorganizational power relationships (Salancik & Pfeffer, 1974).

The theory of academic capitalism was further developed by Slaughter and Rhoades (2004), who posited that the shift toward market-like behaviors in academe is an outgrowth of the New Economy. Slaughter and Rhoades noted the linkages created among individuals working in academic settings and in industry, realizing that these relationships are far more complex and mutually supportive than resource dependency is able to describe. They conceptualized that:

> *The theory of academic capitalism focuses on networks—new circuits of knowledge, interstitial organizational emergence, networks that intermediate between public and private sectors, extended managerial capacity—that link institutions as well as faculty, administrators, academic professionals and students to the new economy. Together these mechanisms and behaviors constitute an academic capitalist knowledge/learning regime.* (p. 15)

Interestingly, the interpersonal and interorganizational networks noted by Slaughter and Rhoades are enhanced by information and communications technologies. These ICT networks, which form the basis for the academic capitalist knowledge/learning regime, are sources of data for knowledge management. When the human capital of faculty, administrators, academic professionals, or students is transferred to a digital environment, it can be measured and commodified by the organization through the use of KM principles in order to achieve competitive advantage and increased revenue at the institutional level.

Academic Managerialism

While academic capitalism theory provides a lens through which to understand the changing relationship between academe and the marketplace, other perspectives can be utilized to better comprehend the shifts in the internal division of labor within higher education institutions. The changes brought about by the New Economy affect more than the production process, according to Castells. He stated:

> *...the economy is informational, not just information-based, because the cultural-institutional attributes of the whole social system must be included in the diffusion and implementation of the new technological paradigm, as the industrial economy was not merely based on the use of new sources of energy for manufacturing but on the emergence of an industrial culture, characterized by a new social and technical division of labor.* (Castells, 2000, p. 100)

In the academic arena, the new social and technical division of labor described by Castells can be seen most readily in the instructional function, where information and communications technologies have had a profound impact on the cycle of production. This new social and technical division of academic labor is described by Rhoades (1998). He utilizes "enskilling" and "deskilling" labor theories to comment on the changing roles of faculty in relation to the instructional function of higher education. As the instructional paradigm has changed due to the use of ICTs in teaching and the massification of postsecondary education, the role of faculty is in flux. Faculty may either be retrained to utilize instructional technologies or be side-lined by technical experts who can perform the function for them. The decision to "opt out" of using instructional technologies poses career risks for faculty, especially those who are untenured and those who teach large undergraduate courses. Rhoades posited that when faculty shift their teaching to a digital environment they are subjected to increased managerial control and loss of autonomy. He stated that, "new technologies can pose a threat to that freedom, enabling detailed monitoring and/or surveillance of workers' activities" (Rhoades, 1998, p. 199).

Indeed, the instructional purview of faculty is undermined by the increase in the numbers of "managerial professionals," described by Rhoades and Sporn as "neither professors nor administrators," but individuals with "professional associations, conferences, journals and bodies of knowledge that inform their practice" (Rhoades & Sporn, 2002, p. 16). Rhoades and Sporn commented on the impact of managerial professionals on the instructional function of higher education by stating that, "most [universities] now have teaching centres and professional development centres staffed by full-time managerial professionals who directly and indirectly impact instructional delivery—for example, encouraging the use of instructional technology in classrooms" (Rhoades & Sporn, 2002, p. 16). The increase of managerial professionals creates a "matrix mode of production," meaning that the division of labor within academe is more distributed among various employment categories (Rhoades & Sporn, 2002). In other words, whereas the instructional function was previously performed by the lone faculty member with perhaps the aid of graduate teaching assistants, laboratory technicians, and secretaries, today faculty share the instructional function with instructional designers, multi-media specialists, courseware support analysts, library information specialists, and classroom technicians.

Although KM is seen as a rational (impartial) approach to asset valuation and strategic planning, it is critical for academic employees to recognize the ways in which professional self-preservation might affect the adoption and implementation of KM in the postsecondary environment. Knowledge management intersects this new production cycle often at the level of the managerial professional or upper-level administrator. As "management" is at the core of KM, it follows that those who manage will be the first to consider the use of KM in their workplaces, and the "problem-definition" phase of KM will be informed by their perspectives. Yet it is important for academic managers to fully comprehend the changes that have occurred in higher education with regard to the division of labor and production functions. For example, if one of the goals of KM is to optimize the quality/cost ratio, the increased expense of additional administrators and managerial professionals must be taken into account (Leslie & Rhoades, 1995). The cost of additional academic staff is particularly significant with regard to the instructional function, where expenditures for the technologies themselves are not likely to be fully recovered through increases in efficiency or by the implementation of new fees. Therefore, instructional expenditures per student must include the associated costs of instructional support staff and the technological infrastructure, not just faculty/student ratios.

Digital Capitalism

Digital capitalism frames the growth of the IT sector as an extension of the previous industrial economic cycle, with concessions to the thought that an observed "amplification" of capitalism might be a signal of the New Economy (or at least, *a* new economy). In *Digital Capitalism: Networking the Global Market System* (1999), Dan Schiller described the neoliberal transformation of electronic networks into a profit-generating system, where communications and data processing would eventually be deregulated in the United States. From military use to a federally funded inter-university research tool, what would become the Internet developed as a shared network using open-source software (Hafner, 1996). As the use of networks grew in U.S. business and finance, investment in computer equipment outpaced all other forms of capital from the late 1970s through the 1990s (Schiller, 1999). Schiller stated that "information technology investment, finally, and network applications in particular, comprised the pivot of a restructuring of big capital—both industrial and financial" (p. 17). The commercialization of the Internet led to a new production cycle, centered on the need for hardware and software to serve the growing number of (primarily American) business clients seeking to perform network transactions.

Although research universities were central to the early stages of the Internet, the role of such institutions since the 1970s is not fully explained by Schiller. Higher education's ties to digital capitalism are discussed in three ways in his book: the commoditization of education (through distance learning and electronic courseware), as a site of consumption of information technology, and as a partner with industry in research alliances. Schiller described the role of universities in research centers with strong ties to business, but only mentioned the use of information technology or production of software at these facilities in passing (Schiller, 1999, p. 164). Although listed by name as corporations with a large impact on worldwide markets for information technology throughout the book, Schiller provided just one sentence to say that "Netscape, Sun Microsystems, and Cisco comprise three leading Internet companies that were each direct spin-offs from academe" (p. 162). Instead of focusing on the development of information technologies on college campuses, Schiller centered on the consumption of technology in higher education, noting the speed at which schools were outfitted with high-speed networks, computers, and high-tech classrooms (p. 190). Yet, Schiller mentioned the for-profit provision of educational services through distance education and courseware production as a contribution to knowledge capital (pp. 185-202). Absent from his discussion of digital capitalism in academe is the growth of revenue-generating courseware and other instructional materials in the public education system, which Melissa Anderson describes as a form of "instructional capitalism" (Anderson, 2001). Further, it must be understood that information technology companies are active in the higher education sector and are becoming closely aligned with the business core of academic services (Metcalfe, 2004).

Thus, colleges and universities are closely tied to both production and consumption through their utilization and creation of information technology products. The framework of digital capitalism, also explored by McChesney, Wood, and Foster (1998), reminds us that the ubiquity of IT in our modern lives rivals that of ever-present capitalism. Not since the creation of the plastics industry have we been so transformed by a particular corporate sector, and just as we rarely object to the use of extruded petroleum byproducts in our lives these days, we rarely mind the ways in which IT has become a fixture of our work and leisure hours. Indeed it could be said that higher education is an environment that is at the forefront of the digital age, and that our campuses are places where it is difficult to labor or learn without high-technology. We might be lured, however, into the belief that academe is a hallowed grove more informed by the agrarian age than a post-industrial one, especially if we find ourselves in liberal arts institutions. Yet, Castells pointed us to the crux of working in a knowledge factory in a knowledge age when he stated that "in the new, informational mode of development the source of productivity lies in the technology of knowledge generation, information processing, and symbol communication" (Castells, 2000, p. 17). He further clarified this notion by stating that "what is specific to the informational mode of development is the action of knowledge upon knowledge itself as the main source of productivity" (Castells, 2000, p. 17).

The Politics of Knowledge Management

Although computer systems may seem inherently apolitical, the opposite is true as the digital environment is able to be shaped by nearly any political system or method of control (Loader, 1997). While most peope understand that organizations are rife with internecine struggles, few comprehend how these "turf battles" affect the informational culture and IT landscape. While power and control are at the heart of much of organizational strife, these battles may become most evident in political discussions of jurisdiction and territory. In this section, I discuss the connections between knowledge management and notions of digital democracy and the changes that globalization brings to the electronic environment in academe.

Digital Democracy

Since its introduction to society at large, networked computing has been considered in political terms. Jordan (2001) described early computer culture as anarchist and libertarian, citing organizations such as the Electronic Frontier Foundation and the Center for Democracy and Technology as influential in the formation of basic political values of the Internet and computing (see also Borsook, 2000). Jordan also noted the dominance of Anglo-American norms in cyberspace, including language preference (English) and the desire for self-governance. Other early proponents of the Internet imagined it to be an "electronic agora" (Rheingold, 1993), referencing the notions of egalitarianism and democracy thought to exist in ancient Greek marketplaces. This perspective saw the ancient agora as a place where free exchange of ideas and goods took place, and where equality was common. However, in the same manner that Jeffersonian Neoclassicists championed the characteristics of Greek society that best suited them (such as political representation solely for landowning male gentry), while ignoring considerable social injustices (slavery and the disenfranchisement of women, to name two examples), the application of false notions of ancient "democracy" to the Internet and computing environments only served to obfuscate the existence of digital power and inequality.

In fact, rather than having its roots in democratic ideals, the term "cyberspace" derives from another classical reference, the Greek word *kubernetes*, meaning helmsman or governor. Thus, at its very core, the digital environment is framed by administrative issues and governance structures (hence the job title "systems administrator"). Knowledge management, then, from a political perspective is as much about jurisdiction as it is about jurisprudence. This is readily understood when one considers the power of information and misinformation within a polarized or politicized organizational environment. Information technology networks are not just conduits for the flow of binary bits and bytes; computer systems are pathways between knowledge *territories* (Herbert, 2000).

In higher education institutions, this can be seen in the networked domains of separate colleges and departments, each with their own servers. Thus it can be said that higher education institutions exhibit characteristics of both provincial and federal systems of control. The languange of computing reinforces these territories by using words like "domain" to describe areas of administrative control. Knowledge management efforts rarely acknowledge these multi-layered organizational jurisdictions in a way that satisfies both the proponents of decentralization and the champions of central managerialism.

Campus environments can be both decentralized in their computing networks as well as bound together by a single "enterprise" system that serves as the business core of the organization. These campus-wide systems are today more often than not commercial products, sold to institutions by companies such as Sungard SCT, Datatel, and Campus Management. The enterprise software allows for integration of various campus units, such as student admissions, course registration, financial aid, and business services. In many cases, these units previously had their own computing systems and only minimal data sharing with other academic departments. As these units are linked by shared enterprise software and common datasets, information administration becomes more centralized. In circumstances where such campus-wide software is purchased, some degree of control over academic information management is ceded to the private sector. In fact, there are campuses where IT management is performed by employees of the vendors of enterprise software, with these "Outsourced CIOs" sitting on the president's cabinet (Metcalfe, 2004). The mix of public and private managers in these situations complicates the flow of information in higher education organizations, as work-processes themselves are seen as proprietary information and therefore subject to classification as "trade secrets" rather than open systems where anyone in the organization can track the flow of information from individual to individual.

Globalization

The term "globalization" is difficult to define, and even more difficult to determine where and if it exists. However complicated it may be to describe, most scholars agree that a restructuring is occurring on a global scale, affecting capital systems and social structures. In higher education, evidence of these changes are seen in the migration patterns of students and faculty, the development of cross-national education programs such as distance learning initiatives, and increasing internationalization of colleges and universities. Vaira (2004) noted the shifts in postsecondary education by stating:

> *...higher education is witnessing a process of deep institutional change that involves the deinstitutionalization of its rooted policy and values frameworks and the parallel institutionalization of new ones. These processes entail more or less strong resistances, conflicts, [and] tensions but also efforts to conciliate, adapt, translate, assemble the new with the*

old, the national features of higher education system with the new globalizing pressures, the single institutions structural and cultural features with the new imperatives and demands. (p. 485)

The institutionalization of new policy and values frameworks, as informed by a globalized economic, social, and political reality, may be seen in the information systems of modern campuses. For knowledge management practitioners, it is important to note that as higher education is becoming more tied to global markets, the value of knowledge assets will be increasingly determined on a global stage. For example, if a university has an International Memorandum of Agreement with another university in a different country, intellectual capital built between the partners could be considered a shared commodity with different value for each contributing agency. What might have the most value to one of the partners might have the least value to the other partner, but the value is still there to be understood and recognized by both. This will be most important in terms of intellectual property policies and copyright laws, which may differ from institution to institution, country to country.

Furthermore, globalization affects the learning environment of higher education in such a way that KM practices should consider the various cultural and language systems embedded within information technology, especially courseware. In a multi-ethnic, multi-lingual learning environment, what values are conveyed by the course management systems given that many have been created in North America (e.g., WebCT and Blackboard)? Are there cultural forms of expression that cannot be conveyed online? Does this have a negative impact on teaching and learning? Perhaps most importantly, does the exportation of courseware reinforce economic, social, and political structures? For example, if Mexican higher education institutions purchase courseware developed in Canada or the United States, does this perpetuate the political and economic dominance that has already made North America an unbalanced trade region? What are the effects of the commercialization of academic IT on national identity? What forces prevent Mexican institutions from developing their own courseware, in Spanish? As globalization continues to become evident in higher education, questions such as these should guide information technology managers in the academic setting.

The Sociology of Knowledge Management

The field of knowledge management can benefit from sociological perspectives for several reasons. First, the social study of science, including computer science, has led to a rich body of literature detailing the ways in which patterns of communication and interpersonal relations affect organizational systems. The scholarship, often under the heading of society, technology and society (STS) studies, provides much food for thought for those who attempt to shape "irrational" organizations through seemingly "rational" means. Also, sociological perspectives are important to knowledge management as it is people who are the most important assets of an organization. Understanding the motivations and influences of individual actors is critical to successful KM implementation. In addition, it is important for KM practitioners to understand that technology is not "neutral;" that it is instead created from a particular world-view, and as such performs as a proxy for specific individuals within an organization. In this section I briefly describe the social construction of technology.

Social Construction of Technology

The term "technological determinism" can be defined as the impact of technology on society and the way in which social processes and progress are fixed by the development of particular technological innovations (see Winner, 1977, 2001). While it is not impossible to imagine a world without computers, for example, it is difficult to conceptualize what our contemporary lives would be like without such a technological development. Yet it is more challenging to parse out how computers have determined particular social structures, functions or layers of social contact that would not exist without them. Ultimately, it is first a human that sets the technological "wheel" in motion, and the consequences of that action are either beneficial or harmful to society at large (Tenner, 1996).

A conceptual framework for research on the relationship between technology and society was presented by Pinch and Bijker in a chapter titled, "The Social Construction of Facts and Artifacts: Or How The Sociology of Science and The Sociology of Technology Might Benefit Each Other" (1987). They discussed the empirical approach to the social construction of technology (SCOT) as a three-stage process. First, they stated that the "interpretive flexibility" of the technology or technological artifact must be acknowledged. They elaborated by saying that, "By this we mean not only that there is flexibility in how people think of or interpret artifacts but also that there is flexibility in how artifacts are *designed*" (p. 40). In other words, technological artifacts are shaped by the inventor as much as they are shaped by the subsequent users. Second, they discuss a period of "stabilization and closure" that occurs with the development of technologies, where the artifact in question has "solved" a particular problem or the problem for which the artifact was originally intended is no longer relevant. This stage is an interesting one in that it highlights the ways that technology is used and repurposed by relevant social groups, rather than just the outcomes that were intended by the developer. Their final stage of analysis involves the "wider context" and how a particular technological innovation has affected the "sociopolitical milieu" (p. 46). This stage involves the development of values and social meanings around objects and their function. While this particular research method has its critics (see Klein and Kleinman, 2002), it nonetheless is an important process from which to consider the mutual shaping of technological artifacts and social systems.

For the field of KM, the research techniques outlined by Pinch and Bijker can be useful ways to understand how information and communications technologies are both created and utilized in an organizational setting. Pertinent questions can be asked by following the SCOT approach, including "What is the problem that is to be solved," and "Who is involved in the process of developing the system (the relevant social groups) to solve this problem?" Furthermore, the SCOT approach acknowledges that there are many possible solutions to any given problem, and the final product will be constructed by the "technological frames" or viewpoints and value-systems held by the developers.

Complimentary approaches to understanding the impact of technological innovations on society include Thomas's "power-process" model. In *What Machines Can't Do: Politics and Technology in the Industrial Enterprise* (1994), Thomas discussed his "power-process" model, which offers a new perspective on the forces behind the development and implementation of new technologies. Thomas argued that too often the study of technology focuses only on the implementation stage of technological change, and infrequently considers the social and political factors present within an organization that affect the choices made during the entire process. Thomas identifies three stages of change: (1) the identification of the problem that requires attention and the proposal for technological change, (2) the selection between presented technological alternatives, and (3) the implementation of the chosen innovation. Thomas also presented a set of methodological guidelines to use while studying the process of technological change. He promotes taking account of the organizational and decision-making history, paying greater attention to how dissimilar logics are coupled (e.g., technological determinism and social change theory), focusing on the process of choice, and assessing the role of power and worldview of the decision-makers and other organizational members.

Like the SCOT approach, the power-process model contextualized technological change within a social or organizational environment. It recognizes that many individuals are involved in the development of technological solutions, and also highlights the consequences of leaving key players out of the development process. A central element of the model that is critical for those who want to utilize KM techniques is the understanding of the role of power and authority within an organization. Who makes the final decisions in an organization is often more important than the many hours of preparation and planning that might occur around technological change.

Finally, it must be understood that the technology itself bears the imprint of the values and attitudes of its designers. This is made very clear in Forsythe's research as presented in her article, "New Bottles, Old Wine: Hidden Cultural Assumptions in a Computerized Explanation System for Migraine Sufferers" (1996). Forsythe describes the development and implementation of a digital solution to the problem of the tedium of taking patient histories during a doctor's visit in a medical office. Due to the exclusion of migraine sufferers from the design phase, the computerized system that was finally developed was "designed to persuade the patients that the physician's diagnosis of their headaches is correct" rather than truly discover the root causes of the patients' headaches (p. 566). Forsythe found the development of the system as an example of a "technological imperative." She stated that:

practitioners in medical informatics take for granted the benefits of automation, including computerizing the doctor-patient communication that might otherwise take place face to face. In medical informatics, intelligent systems technology is treated as a solution in search of a problem. (p. 570)

Forsythe's work reminds us that "innovation" is often in the eye of the beholder. For KM practitioners, it is important to recognize that personal zeal or affinity for a technological solution may not be in the best interest of the community that the solution is intended to serve.

Conclusion

In the Information Age, technological infrastructure is an instrument of power, "whether transparent or opaque." Star (1995, 1999) noted that "the ecology of the distributed high-tech workplace, home, or school is profoundly impacted by the relatively unstudied infrastructure that permeates all its functions" (p. 379). As such it is important for us to recognize the economic, political, and social motivations behind the development of technological "solutions" in organizational settings. In higher education in particular, the knowledge-intensive environment would seem especially ready for the variety of changes that can be brought by way of information technologies, but the "technological imperative" must not sway developers and users of these systems. The "build it and they will come" approach may result in costly development of an underutilized system if in fact the people involved in the implementation are not keen on the project or its intended effects.

Thus, the use of knowledge management principles should proceed only with the careful examination of the economic, political, and social implications of knowledge codification in higher education. Aspects of market-value, political power, and social stratification will impact the development of any technological solution. To counteract the potentially negative effects of technological change in higher education, critical questions must be asked. We must ask why the products of higher education are to be evaluated relative to market value rather than the social good. We should ask who will gain access to our common and individual intellectual property. Furthermore, we should insist that we are made aware of the ways in which our work will be monitored and by whom. Finally, we need to know exactly who will reap the reward when our knowledge is "captured."

References

Anderson, M. S. (2001). The complex relations between the academy and industry: Views from the literature. *Journal of Higher Education, 72*(2), 226-246.

Bijker, W., Pinch, T., & Hughes, T. (Eds.) (1989). *The social construction of technological systems.* Cambridge, MA: MIT Press.

Borsook, P. (2000). *Cyberselfish: A critical romp through the terribly libertarian culture of high-tech.* New York: PublicAffairs Press.

Castells, M. (2000). *The rise of the network society* (2nd edition). Oxford: Blackwell Publishers.

Ewell, P. T. (1999). Imitation as art: Borrowed management techniques in higher education. *Change, 31*(6), 10-15.

Forsythe, D. E. (1996). New bottles, old wine: Hidden cultural assumptions in a computerized explanation system for migraine sufferers. *Medical Anthropology Quarterly, 10*(4), 551-574.

Getz, M., Siegfried, J. J., & Anderson, K. H. (1997). Adoption of innovations in higher education. *Quarterly Review of Economics and Finance, 37*(3), 605-631.

Hafner, K. (1996). *Where wizards stay up late: The origins of the Internet.* New York: Simon and Schuster.

Herbert, S. (2000). Zoning cyberspace. *Studies in Law, Politics, and Society, 20*, 101-123.

Jordan, T. (2001). *Cyberpower: The culture and politics of cyberspace and the Internet.* New York: Routledge.

Katz, R. N. & Oblinger, D. G. (Eds.) (2000). *The "E" is for everything: E-commerce, e-Business, and e-Learning in the future of higher education.* San Francisco: Jossey Bass.

Kettinger, W. J. (1990). The decentralization of academic computing: Defining future roles. *CAUSE/EFFECT, 13*(3).

Kidwell, J. J., Vander Linde, K. M., & Johnson, S. (2001). Applying corporate knowledge management practices in higher education. In G. Bernbom (Ed.), *Information alchemy: The art and science of knowledge management* (pp.1-24). San Francisco: Jossey-Bass.

Klein, H. K. & Kleinman, D. L. (2002). The social construction of technology: Structural considerations. *Science, Technology, & Human Values, 27*(1), 28-52.

Leslie, L. L. & Rhoades, G. (1995). Rising administrative costs: On seeking explanations. *The Journal of Higher Education, 66*(2), 41-61.

Lessig, L. (2001). *The future of ideas: The fate of the commons in a connected world.* New York: Random House.

Loader, B. (Ed.) (1997). *The governance of cyberspace: Politics, technology and global restructuring.* New York: Routledge.

Lyman, P. (2001). Knowledge discovery in a networked world. In G. Bernbom (Ed.), *Information alchemy: The art and science of knowledge management* (pp.1-24). San Francisco: Jossey-Bass.

McChesney, R. W., Wood, E. M., & Foster, J. B. (1998). *Capitalism and the Information Age: The political economy of the global communication revolution.* New York: Monthly Review Press.

Metcalfe, A. S. (2004). *Intermediating associations and the university-industry relationship.* Unpublished doctoral dissertation, Center for the Study of Higher Education, The University of Arizona.

Pfeffer, J. & Salancik, G. R. (1978/2003). *The external control of organizations: A resource dependence perspective.* Stanford, CA: Stanford University Press (original work published 1978).

Pinch, T. & Bijker, W. (1987). The social construction of facts and artifacts: Or how the sociology of science and the sociology of technology might benefit each other. In W. Bijker, T. Hughes, & T. Pinch (Eds.), *The social construction of technological systems: New direction in the sociology and history of technology* (pp. 17-50). Cambridge, MA: MIT Press.

Reingold, H. (1993). *The virtual community: Homesteading on the electronic frontier.* Reading, MA: Addison-Wesley.

Rhoades, G. (1998). *Managed professionals: Unionized faculty and restructuring academic labor.* Albany: State University of New York Press.

Rhoades, G. & Sporn, B. (2002). New models of management and shifiting modes and costs of production: Europe and the United States. *Tertiary Education and Management, 8*, 3-28.

Salancik, G. R. & Pfeffer, J. (1974). The bases and use of power in organizational decision making: The case of a university. *Administrative Science Quarterly, 19*(4), 453-473.

Schiller, D. (1999). *Digital capitalism: Networking the global market system.* Cambridge, MA: MIT Press.

Serban, A. M. & Luan, J. (Eds.) (2002). *Knowledge management: Building a competitive advantage in higher education. New Directions for Institutional Research, No. 113.* San Francisco: Jossey-Bass.

Slaugher, S. & Leslie, L. (1997). *Academic capitalism: Politics, policies, and the entrepreneurial university.* Baltimore: Johns Hopkins Press.

Slaughter, S. & Rhoades, G. (2004). *Academic capitalism in the new economy: Markets, state, and higher education.* Baltimore: Johns Hopkins Press.

Star, S. L. (1995). *The cultures of computing.* Cambridge: Blackwell Publishers.

Star, S. L. (1999). The ethnography of infrastructure. *American Behavioral Scientist, 43*(3), 337-391.

Tenner, E. (1996). *Why things bite back: Technology and the revenge of unintended consequences.* New York: Alfred A. Knopf.

Thomas, R. J. (1994). *What machines can't do: Politics and technology in the industrial enterprise.* Berkeley: University of California Press.

Vaira, M. (2004). Globalization and higher education organizational change: A framework for analysis. *Higher Education, 48*(4), 483-510.

Winner, L. (1977). *Autonomous technology: Technics-out-of-control as a theme in political thought.* Cambridge, MA: MIT Press.

Winner, L. (2001). Where technological determinism went. In S. H. Cutcliffe & C. Mitcham (Eds.), *Visions of STS: Counterpoints in science, technology and society studies* (pp. 11-17). Albany: State University of New York Press.

Chapter II

Knowledge Management Trends: Challenges and Opportunities for Educational Institutions

Lisa A. Petrides
Institute for the Study of
Knowledge Management in Education, USA

Lilly Nguyen
Institute for the Study of
Knowledge Management in Education, USA

Abstract

While the pressure of public accountability has placed increasing pressure on higher education institutions to provide information regarding critical outcomes, this chapter describes how knowledge management (KM) can be used by educational institutions to gain a more comprehensive, integrative, and reflexive understanding of the impact of information on their organizations. The practice of KM, initially derived from theory and practice in the business sector, has typically been used to address isolated data and information transfer, rather than actual systemwide change. However, higher education institutions should not simply appropriate KM strategies and practices as they have appeared in the business sector. Instead, higher education institutions should use KM to focus on long-term, organization-wide strategies.

Introduction

Knowledge management (KM) can be used by educational institutions to gain a more comprehensive, integrative, and reflexive understanding of the impact of information on their organizations. Specifically, the practice of KM, initially derived from theory and practice in the business sector as described in the previous chapter, provides a framework to illuminate and address organizational obstacles around issues of information use and access (Davenport, 1997; Friedman & Hoffman, 2001). Yet introducing the concept of KM into the educational arena from the business sector has been a slow and often underutilized process. This is partially due to the fact that KM is a multi-layered and systems-oriented process that requires organizations to rethink what they do and how they do it (Brown & Duguid, 2000; Senge, 1990). Additionally, educational institutions are traditionally hierarchical with silo-like functions, making cross-functional initiatives difficult to implement (Friedman & Hoffman, 2001; Petrides, McClelland, & Nodine, 2004).

However, educational institutions can perhaps learn from KM efforts in the business sector, in terms of the limitations and drawbacks associated with KM. In fact, there are several compelling reasons why educational institutions have not, and perhaps should not, simply re-appropriate KM, as popularized by the business sector, into their own organizations. For example, in the business sector, there has been an appeal to focus on information technology and systems as solutions to problems of knowledge transfer and knowledge sharing (Hovland, 2003; Huysman & de Wit, 2004). Coupled with a profit motive, KM as it exists in the business sector is often limited in its ability to create far-reaching organizational change (Hammer, Leonard, & Davenport 2004). Furthermore, recent trends in the field also fail to fully distinguish between data, information, and knowledge (Huysman & de Wit, 2002). Consequently, organizations merely address singular and isolated data and information transfer, rather than actual systemwide and organization-wide change.

These particular limitations are especially salient now as higher-education institutions face an increasing number of challenges that have forced them to rethink how they are accountable to external demands, as well as how to improve internal accountability. Rather than focus on micro-level information-sharing activities, implementing KM strategies and practices requires these educational institutions to examine the larger context of information sharing within the organization, specifically how their people, processes, and technology function within it. As such, neither data-sharing activities nor technological implementation should be viewed as the ultimate objective and final stage of a KM strategy. Instead, KM practices necessitate strategies that build upon current practice, leading to more comprehensive and organization-wide changes in knowledge practices and actions.

How then can educational institutions translate isolated sharing activities into long-term learning? This chapter illustrates how KM strategies and practices enable higher-education institutions to distinguish between data, information, knowledge, and action and how this iterative cycle can help organizations assess their available resources—that is, their people and processes along with their technology. In turn, this chapter demonstrates how KM can help educational institutions place themselves on the path toward continuous learning and organizational reflexivity.

Concepts and Theories

An overview of KM practices in the business sector demonstrates an overwhelming focus on simplified solutions, specific applications, and singular information-transfer activities. Recent accounts suggest that KM has seen limited impacts in the private sector due to overemphasis on technological hardware and software (Hammer et al., 2004; Hovland, 2003; Huysman & de Wit, 2004). This may be due in part to the fact that it is often easier to persuade organizations to acquire new technology tools than to modify or redesign existing organizational processes (Coate, 1996).

However, these particular approaches to KM are less likely to embrace a systematic approach to how organizations function. By focusing too narrowly on isolated information-sharing activities, organizations are prematurely confined and prevented from engaging in a more integrative approach to KM. These information-sharing activities, which some might argue are wrongly classified as KM, may include electronic search and retrieval, document management, and data warehousing systems. These examples demonstrate important yet isolated occurrences of information activities and practices. However, these practices are often implemented disassociated from a larger organization-wide strategy. Secondly, and perhaps more importantly, the interpretation of these as KM does not acknowledge a vital distinction between information and knowledge. It is this delineation that pinpoints the incremental process behind the implementation of KM strategies and practices: Information is data with contextual meaning, data that has been categorized, or subjected to a process of sense-making and interpretation. Knowledge is information that is put into action through the process of problem-solving, decision-making, feedback processes, and so on (Davenport, 1997).

Therefore, developing policies and processes that fundamentally support and organizationally align information-sharing activities to each other is one of the first steps an organization must take to embrace and develop successful KM strategies. Often, an organization will try, yet fail, to implement an entire host of activities related to data collection and information access, only to find that the necessary organizational conduits for information sharing and new knowledge creation are not in place. How an organization shares information, along with the incentives and rewards to do so, and a culture that supports information-based decision-making are all key components that need to be in place before KM can be successfully implemented.

People, Processes, and Technology

KM strategies and practices come to embody the interactions between people, processes, and technology. These three—people, processes, and technology—all function as an integral part of the ongoing dynamics as organizations struggle to meet their information needs. First, it is people, not systems or technology, who "know." Thus, it is people who manage the policies, priorities, and processes that support the use of data, information, and knowledge. KM strategies and practices seek to engage different groups of people across various levels of an organization in the process of collective sense-making and decision-making. Whether these groups are formal or informal, a KM strategy includes supporting individuals in coming together to share information to address their collective needs.

Likewise, self-evident processes or embedded, day-to-day work practices can greatly affect the exchange and sharing of information within any organization. For example, it may be common practice within an organization for decision-making authority to be exercised only at the most senior level. These kinds of decision-making processes can create barriers to ownership, in which individuals are not provided with the appropriate incentives to make their own decisions and changes, let alone use data and share information. By uncovering these processes, KM strategies and practices can help identify knowledge gaps, and thus enable people to obtain the information they need and encourage them to share it with others, sometimes creating new knowledge and improved decisions. In highlighting patterns of information use that might not be evident otherwise, KM practices encourage a certain level of organizational reflexivity, which allows organizations to better understand themselves, in turn leading to more informed decision-making.

Rather than situating technology as the focal point, KM practices approach technology as an essential resource that is necessary for changes in organizational process to occur, but not sufficient. Recent trends in KM may grant technology disproportionate authority in how organizations share information. However, technology and information systems are neither the driver of information sharing, nor are they tangential to the process. Instead, technology is of equal importance in its ability to impact how information flows throughout an organization. Therefore, KM is the combination of people, processes, and technology that come together to promote a robust system of information sharing, while guiding organizations toward ongoing reflexivity and learning.

In summary, recent KM trends in the business sector often do not explicitly address all of the organizational resources necessary to implement KM, namely, the people and processes as well as the technology. To some, KM is used as a phrase to describe the technology that is used to manage an organization's data, such as data on monthly sales figures or a database of successful sales strategies. However, the way that these information systems are used is fully contingent on the strategies and policies employed by the organization, and does not constitute KM on its own. It is not uncommon to hear a claim that a vendor has developed "knowledge management software," rather than "developing software that could be used to help an organization implement KM strategies and practices." Although this distinction may appear to split semantical hairs, we argue that these types of technology present only one part of a larger whole within organizations, but they often do not address the necessary steps to become an organization that uses information and knowledge to develop continuous learning throughout.

Data–Information–Knowledge–Action

KM strategies and practices are predicated on the distinction between information and knowledge. Other research in KM makes this distinction to highlight that information undergoes a series of processes that transform it into knowledge as it flows and is exchanged among individuals within an organization (Davenport & Prusack, 1997; Drucker, 1998; Wilson, 2002). To further refine this notion, we assert that information and knowledge need to be further delineated. As such, we propose four stages that comprise the KM cycle: data, information, knowledge, and action. Data are the facts and quantitative measures that are available within any organization. When groups or individuals take data and contribute their own interpretation and categorization, data can be transformed into information. In turn, knowledge is the resulting understanding that allows people to share and use this information that is now available to them. Once this knowledge is applied to make specific decisions or address problems, it is transformed into an action. Each component of the cycle builds upon the preceding element, feeding back and connecting actions and decisions and new learning, which eventually translates back to new questions that are informed by data once again.

There is a certain set of activities and practices that typically takes place in each part of the cycle, where each component builds upon the one before it, making it an iterative process of change or improvement. Data activities in the KM cycle can include accessing data by departmental request, or retrieving data directly from information systems and placing them within personalized spreadsheets. Information activities may include analyzing data to find patterns, problems, and discrepancies, or aggregating and disaggregating data, writing reports, or discussing findings from the data with colleagues. Knowledge activities entail formal and informal discussion and collaboration to address issues and problems in the context of the data and information. It is important to note that the knowledge stage of the KM cycle encompasses a process of collective sense-making, which includes ongoing discussion, collaboration, and feedback, thus shifting individual data and information practices into the organizational environment. The last stage of the cycle is then implementation of changes and action that result from the iterative process.

Therefore, organizations that simply engage in the collection and distribution of data are engaged in data management activities only. However, knowledge management is more than the mere aggregation of data management practices. KM practices include the management of the infrastructure that supports the data–information–knowledge–action cycle, as well as the implementation of the process. In these examples, we see then that KM activities and practices bring together all four components of the cycle: data, as well as information, knowledge, and action. In turn, KM strategies embrace practices at every stage of this cycle, and integrate the people, processes, and technology within the organization. It is important to note that each stage of the KM cycle is not

Figure 1. The data-information-knowledge-action cycle

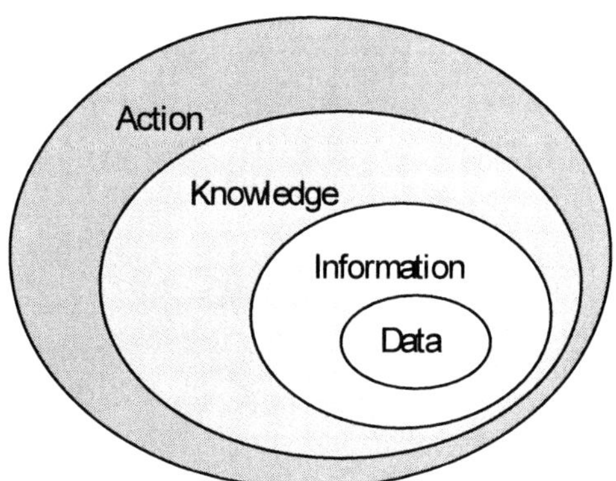

mutually exclusive. An organization that fully adopts KM strategies and practices also demonstrates activities within each component of the KM cycle simultaneously. Engaging in the knowledge stage of the KM cycle also includes individuals engaging in data and information activities. In fact, KM practices necessitate that individuals simultaneously engage all three stages of practice, data, information, and knowledge as they implement changes and action (see Figure 1).

Thus, the KM cycle demonstrates the dynamic qualities of KM strategies and practices. Their simultaneous, ongoing, and cyclical nature further highlights the necessary feedback and iterations that serve as the foundations for ongoing reflexivity and learning. As such, KM practices demonstrate how knowledge is most valuable not when stored in static repositories, but when exchanged across groups of people, used and applied to inform actions and change. KM strategies and practices can help organizations better identify their information-sharing and knowledge-generating activities, which, in turn, can help organizations capitalize on the iterative nature of knowledge-sharing activities.

Current Challenges for KM in Higher Education

Increasing pressures and demands for data on student success have translated into an increased call for reliable information regarding critical outcomes in higher education. Due to rising public accountability pressures and strains on fiscal resources, many legislators have begun to demand information that can be directly linked to academic outcomes. As a result, these institutions are faced with requirements to provide accurate data and information around a growing number of issues and outcomes. In order to do so, the institutions are now re-evaluating their own knowledge strategies and practices.

However, these processes of re-evaluation have proven to be challenging. To begin with, the information technology infrastructure at many higher-education institutions is problematic. Rather than having one robust and integrated system, educational institutions more often maintain several information systems that support various functions throughout the organization, some of which are antiquated legacy systems. In addition to this fragmented information technology infrastructure, there are often inconsistent priorities around data collection, which can result in inaccessible or unreliable data. These characteristics translate into disparate data silos throughout the organization, redundant data gathering, and information hoarding, the cost of which is an impaired ability to sustain knowledge development, growth, and effective decision-making (Petrides et al., 2004). In an increasingly performance-driven climate, this only exacerbates these already problematic and costly practices.

Furthermore, cultural issues associated with information hoarding and overall disincentives for sharing and cross-functional cooperation can undermine KM implementation strategies in educational institutions. In a climate of accountability, data and information can appear threatening as well as politically charged, particularly when programs or other initiatives are under fiscal strain. Nevertheless, educational institutions can minimize these potentially negative consequences by developing KM strategies under a set of policies that explicitly encourage change and progress rather than penalize mistakes. A culture that is intolerant of mistakes can severely impede KM initiatives (Davenport & Prusack, 1997). The psychological instability that can arise is a very real challenge that can curtail any change initiative. As such, when implementing a KM strategy, educational institutions are better served by fostering an environment that reduces the sense of fear and retribution that individuals within the organization may face, for example, as they uncover data and information that may support unpopular opinions.

KM practices also require long-term strategies and commitments in order to fully realize their benefits. While educational institutions have tentatively begun to incorporate KM strategies, they will benefit from gaining a better understanding of the current limitations of these recent approaches to KM in the business sector, such as the narrow focus on seemingly easier-to-address solutions—for example, creating a data warehouse from which to extract student data. In microscopically fixating on specific information solutions, many current trends in KM do not help these institutions build the capacity to sustain long-term organization-wide change, but instead limit the potential that information and knowledge sharing can have.

While KM researchers may recognize the importance of distinguishing between data, information, and knowledge, KM practitioners in the private sector have not necessarily taken into account these distinctions. In this particular conception of KM, knowledge is then simply used as an overarching term for all three—data, information, and knowledge. Subsequently, many of the products, repositories, and exchange activities that are currently termed KM prove to merely support data and information, rather than actual knowledge. Doing so runs the risk of prematurely curtailing the necessary feedback mechanisms for continuous organizational learning.

However, it becomes much more difficult to address systemic barriers to knowledge sharing. The desire to find narrow and short-reaching solutions is often rooted in a compartmentalized understanding of the nature of organizational barriers to information sharing, even though these problems are more than technological. These problems include people's prevailing attitudes, beliefs around knowledge sharing, and systematic and structural disincentives to share and exchange. For example, the politics of information are often heavily embedded in organizational culture and structure, which complicates efforts to change processes that could be used to potentially support and drive knowledge sharing and creation. Recent evolutions of KM do not necessarily take into account the organizational cultures and structures that serve as barriers to data sharing, information sharing, and eventually knowledge sharing. Furthermore, these recent developments in KM fail to acknowledge the evolving and iterative qualities of knowledge. Knowledge is only useful when it is shared, transmitted, or acted on in some capacity. During these exchanges, knowledge undergoes an ongoing and continual cycle of change from data, information, knowledge, and action. However, these distinctions are lost as KM practitioners attempt to find solitary solutions to problems of data and information.

If these attempts at KM remain truncated and narrowly focused on simplified solutions, specific applications, and singular knowledge-transfer activities, these tools can only marginally improve an organization's use of information and knowledge and do not address the deep-rooted processes and strategies necessary to overcome these barriers. Information technologies and applications only incrementally improve an organization's ability to facilitate data sharing and information exchange. As such, these approaches demonstrate a bounded set of limitations that ultimately prevent organizations from overcoming their current obstacles and diminish their ability to build a self-sustaining and long-term organization-wide system, thus undermining the very benefits KM practices have to offer.

Therefore, we suggest that educational institutions should not simply appropriate KM strategies from the business sector and apply them to their organizations. If KM is being implemented poorly, does that mean it should be done away with completely? Or does it hold its own as a concept worth striving for? The current limitations and drawbacks of KM in the private sector should serve as a warning for educational institutions. These organizations should be careful not to prematurely fragment their KM practices and focus on narrow applications and solutions. Instead, higher-education institutions stand to benefit from an approach that incorporates a more long-term and inclusive strategy to their knowledge activities. As such, improved methods of data and information sharing need to be coupled with embedded and long-term KM strategies in order to address the organization-wide factors that can either impede or promote an ongoing culture of research, reflexivity, and long-term organizational learning. If the evolutionary qualities of knowledge management—as it evolves from data, information, and knowledge—cross through multiple groups of people within an organization, as well as traverse the three key organizational resources available—that is, people, processes, and technology—then the dynamic process that guides successful KM strategies and practices is more readily supported and maintained.

Opportunities for KM in Education

Educational institutions demonstrate a great need for improved knowledge-based systems. We already find that there are many formal and informal administrative processes, information-sharing patterns, work incentives, information silos, and other work practices that have flourished over time, yet these can also critically impede organizational and systematic information flow and knowledge exchange. KM strategies and practices can begin to integrate these disjointed systems. For example, the use of information maps and audits can initially be used to obtain a bird's-eye view of the current processes and practices, and their corresponding strengths and weaknesses. This type of initial diagnosis proves to be important for implementing KM in order to identify the most appropriate entry point for change. The cyclical quality of KM encourages organizations to take an honest and reflexive stance on what is already going on in their organization. KM requires that educational institutions candidly address their current patterns and processes, and only from this position begin to capitalize on the opportunities that KM strategies and practices can offer. This process of organizational re-evaluation and reflexivity proves to be the most difficult challenge for educational institutions. At the same time, the process offers the ideal opportunity for these institutions to integrate KM to promote sustainable learning within their organizations in order to meet these external demands as well as improve organization-wide effectiveness.

Higher-education institutions can begin to translate these strategies into action by identifying their information shortages and needs, including finding out where people are already requesting more data and information. These institutions can also start by identifying groups of people who already maintain synergistic relationships of collaboration and sharing within the institution. In fact, educational settings already demonstrate many information-sharing activities in effect, such as existing formal or informal communities of practice. However, to sustain ongoing inquiry and continuous learning, educational institutions need to strategize as to how they will systemically embed these activities and practices within the very fabric of the organization. Taken individually, information-sharing activities can be used toward incremental improvement; however, when KM is adopted and executed as an organization-wide strategy, improved methods of data and information sharing can be used to continually promote the development of KM-based practices. This can help educational institutions become more informed in their decision-making as a whole. All of this helps to lay the foundation for a robust culture of inquiry and reflexivity, thus establishing the mechanisms for sustainable, long-term organizational learning.

Perhaps more importantly, student access and success are the likely benefactors of these KM practices. KM practices can promote organizational reflexivity in such a way that educational institutions better understand their own weaknesses and strengths, and can then allocate their resources to where they are most needed. As demands for accountability rise, educational institutions need to become much more adept at assessing students' needs along with their own institutional capabilities. KM practices can help bring these two together, that is, aligning institutional capabilities and resources to better address students' needs and thus student success. Subsequently, educational institutions that engage in KM practices for continuous learning at the organizational level also engage in promoting continuous learning for their students.

Opportunities for Continuous Learning

In conclusion, to fully realize the potential of KM, educational institutions will need to change the focus of KM from isolated knowledge-sharing activities to long-term, organization-wide strategies. Thus, KM practices can help educational institutions meet their goal of improved decision-making to advance student learning, allowing these institutions to begin to identify the value of programs and services that contribute to student access and success. This requires not only addressing information policies, but also taking a closer look at the institution's own processes and current practices to stimulate ongoing and constructive data use. Therefore, KM practices can be used to help educational institutions develop a sense of reflexivity across all levels of the organization, thereby providing these institutions with the means for a sustainable culture of inquiry and continuous learning.

References

Brown, J.S. & Duguid, P. (2000). Balancing act: How to capture knowledge without killing it. *Harvard Business Review*, *78*(5), 3-7.

Coate, L.E. (1996). Beyond re-engineering: Changing the organizational paradigm. In A. Kendrick (Ed.), *Organizational paradigm shifts* (pp. 1-18). Washington, DC: National Association of College and University Business Officers (NACUBO).

Davenport, T.H. (1997). *Information ecology: Mastering the information and knowledge environment*. New York: Oxford University Press.

Davenport, T.H. & Prusack, L. (1997). *Working knowledge: How organizations manage what they know*. Cambridge, MA: Harvard Business School Press.

Drucker, P. (1998). The knowledge-creating company. In Drucker, P. et al. (Eds.), *Harvard Business Review on knowledge management* (pp. 1-19). Cambridge, MA: Harvard Business School Press.

Friedman, D. & Hoffman, P. (2001). The politics of information. *Change, 33*(2), 50-57.

Hammer, M., Leonard, D., & Davenport, T. (2004). Why don't we know more about knowledge? *MIT Sloan Management Review, 45*(4), 14-18.

Hovland, I. (2003). Knowledge management and organisational learning, an international development perspective: An annotated bibliography, Working Paper 224. Retrieved October 7, 2004, from Overseas Development Institute (ODI) Web site: *http://www.odi.org.uk/rapid/Publications/Documents/WP224.pdf*

Huysman, M. & de Wit, D. (2004). Practices of managing knowledge sharing: Towards a second wave of knowledge management. *Knowledge Process Management, 11*(2), 81-92.

Petrides, L.A., McClelland, S.I., & Nodine, T.R. (2004). Costs and benefits of the workaround: Inventive solution of costly alternative. *The International Journal of Educational Management, 18*(2), 100-108.

Senge, P.M. (1990). *The fifth discipline: The art and practice of the learning organization*. New York: Currency.

Wilson, T.D. (2002). The nonsense of knowledge management. *Information Research, 18*(1), Paper 144. Retrieved October 7, 2004, from *http://InformationR.net/ir/8-1/paper144.html*

Chapter III

Ontologies in Higher Education

John Milam
HigherEd.org, Inc., USA

Abstract

This chapter provides an introduction to the use of ontologies and taxonomies in higher education. After a brief introduction to the nature of ontology, examples of ontology in higher education are reviewed. Issues in creating taxonomies, including their incorporation into search engines and concept maps, are then discussed. Software solutions for developing and utilizing taxonomies are presented next, along with problems and issues for implementation. Finally, future trends in the development of KM strategies for ontology are discussed.

Introduction

Knowledge Management (KM) is based in large part on systems that help users focus their attention on key information that is relevant, timely, and available on-demand. The preparation of this information requires processes for knowledge acquisition, engineering, and representation because "knowledge and expertise are embedded within otherwise diverse and scattered information sources" (Convera, 2004a, p.1).

Necessary to KM strategies is the act of "imposing a structure on the knowledge acquired in order to manage it effectively" (Benjamins et al., 1999, p. 1). This is because most information is unstructured, doesn't fit easily into database models, and is at best "difficult to manage." "Leveraging unstructured information is a chronic challenge for companies competing in today's economy," explains Venkata (2002, p. S12). Ontologies or taxonomies which categorize information represent "the most promising approach to solving the growing problem of information overload" (Inxight, 2003, p. 2).

In her discussion of taxonomies in the marketplace, Gumport explains that "Higher education often sees itself as an enterprise so unabashedly complex that it can't be sorted, classified, or pigeonholed" (1997, p. 23). There is, however, a long history of grand classification schemes in higher education, including those of the National Center for Higher Education Management Systems (NCHEMS), the U.S. Department of Education, the National Science Foundation (NSF), and The Carnegie Foundation for the Advancement of Teaching.

This chapter provides an introduction to the use of ontologies and taxonomies in higher education. After a brief introduction to the nature of ontology, examples of ontology in higher education are reviewed. Issues in creating taxonomies, including their incorporation into search engines and concept maps, are then discussed. Software solutions for developing and utilizing taxonomies are presented next, along with problems and issues for implementation. Finally, future trends in the development of KM strategies for ontology are discussed.

The Nature of Ontology

An ontology is defined by Noy and McGuinness (2000, p. 1) as "a common vocabulary for researchers who need to share information in a domain. It includes machine-interpretable definitions of basic concepts in the domain and relations among them." The domain is the subject area and ontologies are, basically, systems of categories (Sowa, 2004a). While there is an obvious philosophical underpinning to the nature of knowing, "the subject of ontology is the study of categories of things" and the product of such as study is called an ontology (Sowa, 2004b).

Sowa (2004a) discusses how ontologies contain boxes within boxes of categories, word senses, terms, directories, numbers, and character strings. "All of these lists, hierarchies, and networks are tightly interconnected collections of signs. But the primary connections are not in the bits and bytes that encode the signs, but in the minds of the people who interpret them. The goal of various metadata proposals is to make these mental connections explicit by tagging the data with more signs" (Sowa, 2004a, p. 1).

Even storytelling, a technique valued in KM for codifying tacit knowledge, is subject to taxonomies. Peter Orton of IBM is quoted by Reamy (2002) stating that "One of the most important yet least appreciated facts about story is that perceivers tend to remember a story in terms of categories of information states as propositions, interpretations and summaries rather than remember the way the story is actually presented or its surface features" (Reamy, 2002, p. 1).

Ontologies and taxonomies help to: (1) share a common understanding of information; (2) reuse knowledge; (3) make assumptions about knowledge more explicit; (4) separate domain and operational knowledge; and (5) analyze domain knowledge (Noy & McGuinness, 2000). "Ontologies can be used as an instrument to make knowledge assets intelligently accessible to people in organizations" (Benjamins et al., 1999, p. 1). Ontologies are, however, expensive to develop and can be difficult to change once they are in place.

Due to their complexity and the need for their evolution within a community of scholars and practitioners, ontologies are "still far from being a commodity" (Angele & Sure, 2001). Ontologies are present in the category systems of Web sites such as Yahoo, Amazon, and Google (Benjamins et al., 1998; Leake et al., 2003; Noy & McGuinness, 2000).

Many disciplines have developed ontologies with standardized vocabularies, including medicine and the pharmaceutical industry. There is a taxonomy of non-profit, organizational entities for the Internal Revenue Service (NCCS, 2004). There are several taxonomies of businesses, including the North American Industry Classification System (NAICS), which was "developed jointly by the U.S., Canada, and Mexico to provide new comparability in statistics about business activity across North America" (U.S. Census Bureau, 2004, p. 1). A new North American Product Classification System (NAPCS) is also being developed and will focus first on service industries, with manufacturing products to be added in the future.

A standard ontology for news articles called the Applied Semantics' News Series is widely used, based on the International Press Telecommunications Council subject codes (Lamont, 2003). The Library of Congress and Dewey Decimal System classification schemes for bibliographic records are a taxonomy and coding system, as is the ERIC Thesaurus of Descriptors used to document educational materials.

Examples of Ontologies in Higher Education

There are a variety of applications for higher education for ontologies. These include:

- The marketplace of institutions
- Academic disciplines
- The documentation of data
- Metadata about learning management systems (LMS)
- The nature of the higher education enterprise
- Online resources, such as links and training materials

The Marketplace of Institutions

Designed to identify categories of colleges and universities, the Carnegie Classification of Institutions of Higher Education is the most widely recognized effort to document the higher education marketplace. First developed in 1971, The Carnegie Foundation for the Advancement of Teaching's classification scheme identifies categories that are "homogenous with respect to the functions of the institutions and characteristics of students and faculty members" (Shulman, 2001, p. vii). Classification reports have been published five times between 1971 and 2001 and a new structure and methodology will be released in 2005. This new edition will "provide a sophisticated, adaptive set of tools that allows users to cluster institutions in different ways" with users being given different "lenses through which to examine and analyze institution mission and other important differences among institutions" (p. viii).

Similar in stature if not in acceptance is the U.S. News and World Report's college rankings effort. Begun in 1983, the U.S. News rankings have evolved from being purely reputational in nature, driven by surveys of college presidents, to include elaborate formula with many complex variables. The tier structure and types of schools represent a category system and taxonomy comparable to the Carnegie classification. While there is great controversy about the methodology and results, U.S. News and other college admissions publishers such as the College Board and Peterson's have "become part of an integral movement—one that aims to provide the public with ever improving information about higher education" (Kleiner, 2004, p. 74).

Gumport (1997) and the National Center for Postsecondary Improvement (NCPI) have recognized that there is a "market for postsecondary education that can be readily described, even quantified" (Gumport, 1997, p. 23). However, "one design would not fit all." The NCPI research project found that "traditional categories for aggregating groups of institutions (size, Carnegie Classification, control) were unable to explain the real differences in student outcomes observed in key national data sets documenting educational attainment and labor market outcomes" (p. 24). As a result of this effort, a new taxonomy for the marketplace was created and "the idea and structure of the taxonomy resonated intuitively" with institutional leaders (Anonymous, 2001, p. 53).

Yet, as Grasel (1999) explains in *The reality of brands: Toward an ontology of marketing*, "The ontology of marketing, particularly the question of what products and brands are, is still largely unexplored" (p. 1). This is especially true in higher education.

Academic Disciplines

Disciplinary taxonomies have been in place for many years. From a national standpoint, these can be traced to efforts by the U.S. Department of Education's National Center for Education Statistics and the National Science Foundation's division of Science Resources Statistics. Student enrollment, degrees conferred, and research expenditure data by institution are collected at the discipline level by one or both agencies. A variety of sample survey data about students, graduates, faculty, and employees (especially science and engineering) are also collected from individual respondents, including information about field of study and field of occupation.

The NCES disciplinary data were originally collected using four-digit HEGIS (Higher Education General Information Survey) codes, part of the HEGIS data collection system used between 1966 and 1985. "These codes were updated into six-digit CIP codes" in 1985, with a "taxonomic coding scheme for secondary and postsecondary instructional programs" (NCES, 2004a, p. 1). CIP codes are "intended to facilitate the organization, collection, and reporting of program data using classifications that capture the majority of reportable data. The CIP is the accepted federal government statistical standard on instructional program classifications and is used in a variety of education information surveys and databases" (NCES, 2004a, p. 1).

NSF incorporates a three-digit classification scheme in its institutional surveys, one with a finer level of detail than previously offered by CIP codes for science and engineering disciplines, especially medicine. A slightly different three-digit scheme is used for the interagency-funded Survey of Earned Doctorates. NSF also provides a two-digit list of CASPAR discipline codes to which other disciplinary taxonomies may be rolled up for aggregate data. These are available as part of its WebCASPAR online data tool. NSF incorporates several crosswalks between different disciplinary taxonomies, including CIP, HEGIS, and occupation codes, in WebCASPAR.

Many other efforts to map the academic disciplines have been created and are in use today, including those of the National Research Council, the Council of Graduate Schools, Peterson's, the College and University Personnel Association, and other organizations, agencies, and associations. Whether collecting data on enrollment, degrees, faculty, salaries, research expenditures, or equipment, each of these must include some form of disciplinary taxonomy. For their internal use, most colleges and universities map their departments to the reporting requirements of NCES using CIP codes. States regulate the approval of majors and programs with degree inventories that typically combine CIP code and award level.

Despite these many efforts, it requires extreme care to maintain the currency of these taxonomies. The nature of disciplinary work is becoming more fragmented and compartmentalized into specialized academic niches and fields of research. In order to understand supply and demand issues and the emergence of new knowledge and research, there must be a concerted dialogue about these taxonomies. Much of their evolution is due to mandated reporting requirements which, while sufficient for many purposes, fail to address cutting edge changes because they are often too gross in their level of detail. It is then up to disciplinary bodies to track the nature of their professions through refining data collections over time. Fortunately, Web survey software is now more widely available and the result is that it is less expensive for disciplinary associations to conduct this needed work in this disciplinary ontology of higher education.

Documentation of Data

In their efforts to promote best practices to improve data collection and reporting, several national organizations have developed standard taxonomies for higher education data. The National Center for Higher Education Management Systems (NCHEMS) has incorporated disciplinary and department data in its vision of resource allocation models since the 1970s, promoting the use of crosswalks between human resource, student, course, and finance data through organizational mapping. It is impossible to conduct complex cost of instruction models without disciplinary taxonomies and departmental crosswalks and NCHEMS has spearheaded this effort for 30 years.

Crystal and Jones (1985) expanded the early NCHEMS work to focus on accreditation, with their monograph *A common language for postsecondary accreditation: Categories and definitions for data collection*. One of the early NCHEMS products was its NCHEMS Data Element Dictionary (Thomas, 1971). A new version of *Data definitions for colleges and universities* was released in a joint effort of NCHEMS and the Consortium for Higher Education Software Services (CHESS). CHESS was designed to foster agreement on terminology and definitions, standardize definitions, and help structure information architecture for an institution. It was released on CD-Rom in Microsoft Access.

CHESS includes several components: data definitions, MetaData Administrator software to maintain institutional files, and the CHESS taxonomy. The taxonomy was first published in 1994 as the CHESS Taxonomy of Administrative Activities for Colleges and Universities and was updated with the second edition released in 2004. It provides "a comprehensive annotated list of academic and administrative activities at a typical college or university. It also provides a detailed guide for categorizing and describing the operations of colleges and universities and the activities that relate to information technology support" (Thomas, 2004, p. 2). There are five levels of hierarchy in the taxonomy, starting with major functional area.

Another national effort to promote effective data practices is that of the National Postsecondary Education Cooperative (NPEC). NPEC was authorized by Congress in 1994 to promote the quality, comparability, and utility of postsecondary data and information that support policy development at the federal, state, and institution levels. NPEC receives funding from NCES and as part of its focus on "Quality Data Practices" has undertaken a variety of taxonomy-related projects. These include the work of an NPEC working group on "Best Practices for Data Collectors and Data Providers" that asked "What can be done to better coordinate data definitions and surveys on a national basis to achieve greater comparability and relieve institutional data burden?" (NPEC, 1999). Other related NPEC projects include an "Examination of the Data Requirements of the Workforce Investment Act and the Perkins Act of 1998," a study of "Technology and Its Ramifications for Data Systems," and an analysis of "Unit Record Versus Aggregate Data: Perspectives on Postsecondary Education Data Collection, Retention, and Release."

Another long-term effort of NPEC is the ANSWERS (Accessing National Surveys with Electronic Research Sources) Web site, which includes a variety of online tools to help different types of users or audiences find the data and developer resources they need. At the heart of ANSWERS is a matrix of data dictionary information about almost 25,000 variables from over 110 datasets. Each of these data elements is content analyzed and coded using the unique ANSWERS taxonomy that was developed especially for this purpose, with over 340 subject/topic combinations. ANSWERS is no longer available online as part of the NPEC Web site, but is maintained by the developer at http://highered.org/answers.

Without a tool of this type, it is impossible to keep up with the availability of complex population and survey data about postsecondary education. ANSWERS also includes references to key citations about developing surveys and using national datasets. It includes a question bank of questions used in sample surveys of faculty and students and a definition bank of standard glossary terms and definitions. Hard-to-find information about surveys is also included, with information such as average response rates and handling of missing data. With a combination of search and category-driven tools, ANSWERS is an important ontology resource for higher education.

Learning Management Systems (LMS)

Recognizing that information about learning must be shared between different computer systems, various groups have developed metadata standards about learning management systems (LMS). In the U.S., the National Learning Information Infrastructure and other standards boards are promoting standards for learning courseware. In Europe, ARIADNE and ELENA are examples of applications that support the exchange of knowledge resources.

An early EDUCAUSE article from 1997 spells out the vision and promise for metadata:

The primary purpose of metadata is to provide more helpful information about a work than can be obtained by inspecting the contents of the work, e.g., a Web page may be designed to teach mathematics skills to a third grade audience, but the terms "third grade" and "mathematics" may not appear in any of the text of the Web page. Therefore, traditional Web search engines, which often utilize full-text search indexes, would not return the page if "third grade and mathematics" were used as the search criteria. Standards for metadata allow information and materials to be easily and consistently located. Unfortunately, where metadata solutions exist today, they are not consistent and are often proprietary. This has created an administrative nightmare for organizations that own or manage large collections of Web-based materials. It is these administrative challenges and the potential benefits to users that are driving the Internet industry to solve this metadata problem. The NLII IMS is building upon the industry's technology efforts by defining the necessary metadata elements to support widespread reuse, discovery and sharing of learning materials via the Internet. (Griffin & Wason, 1997, p. 1)

Since 1997, the National Learning Information Infrastructure (NLII) project has made great progress in defining standards for metadata for instructional management systems (IMS). The NLII Annual Review for 2003 documents the current key themes, among them learning materials, software, and service markets; learning objects; and specifications/standards development (NLII, 2004). Metadata standards have now been developed and disseminated and are being implemented widely by developers and institutional IT staff for documenting courseware and learning objects.

New types of peer-to-peer (P2P) software such as Edutella use the Universal Brokerage Platform to share learning objects across Web servers. All of these developments are taking place because an infinitely growing array of learning objects are becoming available in all media types and modes of delivery. Organizational users will not be able to take advantage of them, however, unless there is a common taxonomy for documenting their availability.

Learning Object Metadata (LOM) are used to define a "Base schema that defines a hierarchy of data elements for learning objects metadata" (Ogbuji, 2003, p. 1). These metadata schema must incorporate many types and categories of information, including:

- **General information**
- **Lifecycle:** "features related to the history and current state of this learning object and those who have affected this learning object during its evolution"
- **Meta-Metadata:** "information about the metadata instance itself"
- **Technical:** technical requirements and characteristics
- **Educational:** "educational and pedagogic characteristics"
- **Rights:** "intellectual property rights and conditions of use"
- **Relation:** "features that define the relationship between the learning object and other related learning objects"
- **Annotation:** "comments on the educational use of the learning object," including "when and by whom the comments were created"
- **Classification:** "describes this learning object in relation to a particular classification system" (Ogbuji, 2003, p. 1).

Wiley (2000) presents a taxonomy to "differentiate possible types of learning objects available for use in instructional design." The "taxonomy's characteristics' values (such as high, medium, and low) are purposefully fuzzy, as the taxonomy is meant to facilitate inter-object comparison, and not to provide independent metrics for classifying learning objects out of context" (Wiley, 2000, p. 22).

Learning objects or knowledge chunks represent the most efficient focus of technology in teaching. By focusing on serving and finding learning objects, faculty no longer have to fight for scarce resources. The first steps have been taken with the development of standards for learning object metadata and instructional management systems. Now steps are being taken to build new types of learning object repositories. These require complex taxonomies and new types of search engines which combine the best features of searching and classification.

The Higher Education Enterprise

Halstead's (1979) *Higher Education Planning: A Bibliographic Handbook* was published in the era when higher education administration was first becoming a professionalized field of study. This document, along with *Higher Education: A Bibliographic Handbook Volume II* (Halstead, 1981), helped to establish and map the knowledge base of the higher education enterprise, from admissions to space management to student affairs.

Twenty-five years later, the enterprise of higher education is being mapped in new ways, with great interest in virtual colleges and universities (VCUs). Epper and Garn (2004) cite the work of Wolf and Johnstone, whose "taxonomy classifies VCUs along a dimension of collaboration ranging from independence to highly distributed collaboration" (p. 34).

The CHESS taxonomy documents the myriad departments and organizational units which exist in typical institutions. From financial information systems which must include a chart of accounts that is mapped into departments and units, to course and student data with alpha codes used to describe majors and academic departments, numerous taxonomies are implemented throughout the higher education enterprise.

The U.S. Department of Education's HEGIS surveys of financial data were the first attempt to categorize types of expenditures and revenues into an agreed-upon taxonomy. The newest IPEDS data categorize finance data in different ways, depending upon the implementation of new required forms from the Financial Accounting Standards Board (FASB) and the Governmental Accounting Standards Board (GASB). Unfortunately, as stated by the NCES documentation for the IPEDS Finance survey, "As data users attempt to compare institutions that cross accounting models, it becomes difficult to put them on the same scale. Some accounting differences cannot be adjusted for, but an understanding of them may help" (NCES, 2004b, p. 1).

The National Association of College Auxiliary Services (NACAS) developed its own taxonomy several years ago. The NACAS Data Bank includes almost

100 "operational categories of auxiliary services" ranging from amusement games to laundry to security.

Online Resources

KM initiatives in higher education cover a breadth and depth of online applications, including portals, intranets, data warehouses, data mining, environmental scanning, document management systems, digital dashboards, content management systems, customer relations management, and e-learning resources (Knowledge Integrity, 2000; Nylund, 2000; Survey Tracks, 2001). All of these systems require developers to make assumptions about how resources will be presented to the user. Some applications are customized and presented based on data from user-compiled profiles. Others are based on the audience, such as portals with categories of links geared to new students, parents, alumni, and the media.

As online resources are created and integrated into existing applications for admissions, registration, online courseware, and faculty advising, they all need to be categorized. Content management systems are used behind-the-scenes to manage the thousands of Web pages and database structures necessary for a complex university or college setting. These systems must have a sophisticated and dynamic taxonomy. While much of the portal and administrative information system software delivers a foundation for these categories and ontology, they are only a starting point. For as the emergence of Google and the new breed of search algorithms points out, search techniques only go so far to providing relevant resources. Subject matter experts and others must be used to create taxonomies for the Web that make sense within the context of higher education and within the unique institutional setting. It is critical that developers recognize and document their assumptions about taxonomies when implementing portals, intranets, and even basic Web sites for a department or unit. Simple questions such as: "How are you going to categorize new information on the site?" can be very difficult to answer.

Issues in Creating Taxonomies

Search Retrieval and Content Management

Bernbom writes that KM involves the "discovery and capture of knowledge, the filtering and arrangement of this knowledge, and the value derived from sharing and using this knowledge throughout the organization" (2001, p. xiv). While KM proponents share this goal, organizations are still overwhelmed by the need to "rapidly analyze and classify unstructured information." This is the result of many forces, including staff retirements and turnover, budget cutbacks, an unqualified labor pool, lack of skills and/or training, and changing mission. However, problems of staffing and the continuity of knowledge within an organization become exacerbated because explicit information is often not readily available and is maintained out of context.

Recognizing that there is "too much information out of context," it is difficult to "discern high-quality, relevant information from hearsay, inaccurate, unqualified, or outdated information" (Delphi Group, 2003, p. 2). It is also difficult to capture and communicate tacit information. At the heart of documenting knowledge assets is the work of content management. Content and process are "inextricably linked" and many KM proponents believe that "Content Management is all that matters" (Moore, 2003, p. S2). Whether stored in file cabinets, electronic filing systems, document management systems, intranets, portals, or KM repositories, the critical issue is finding and using content.

Both search engines and ontologies have undergone a significant evolution in the past few years as users became inundated with millions of Web sites on the World Wide Web and expectations for relevant search results have grown with tools such as Google. With "exponential growth in the amount of data available across the globe," search engines "return such large numbers of irrelevant results that frustration persistently triumphs" (Inxight, 2003, p. 3).

Major problems with search engines involve: (1) making results relevant; (2) ensuring secure and efficient collection of a breadth of data; (3) allowing various language methods for imputing information; and (4) the ability to scale a search product to very large indexes and volumes of queries (Andrews, 2003). Taxonomies are "often used in tandem with search and retrieval tools... However, unlike search technology alone, taxonomies reveal the overall structure of a knowledgebase in a hierarchy that is visible to the user" (Lamont, 2003, p. 1).

Creating Ontologies

There are two activities involved in creating ontologies: coding new documents into a beginning taxonomy and modifying the taxonomy to handle new types of information. These usually occur "through a combination of automation and human intervention. Classification techniques include keywords, statistical analyses that look for patterns of words, and use of a semantic network or ontology that analyzes words for the meaning in context" (Lamont, 2003, p. 2). Verity and other search engine tools incorporate auto-classification to generate rules for categories using sample documents. Ontologies have been a central discussion of the artificial intelligence community (Kalfoglou, 2002).

Noy and McGuinness (2000) explain that: "The ontology should not contain all the possible information about the domain: you do not need to specialize (or generalize) more than you need for your application (at most one extra level each way)" (p. 19). The authors break ontologies into information about classes, subclasses, slots, and instances. Most ontology discussion focuses on classes, which "describe concepts in the domain" or subject area.

For example, a class of wine represents all wines. Specific wines are instances of this class. The Bordeaux wine in the glass in front of you while you read this document is an instance of the class of Bordeaux wines. A class can have subclasses that represent concepts that are more specific than the superclass. For example, we can divide the class of all wines into sparking and non-sparkling wines. Slots describe properties of classes and instances: Chateau Lafitte Rothschild Pauillac wine has a full body; it is produced by the Chateau Lafite Rothschild winery. We have two slots describing the wine in this example: the slot body with the value full and the slot maker with the value Chateau Lafite Rothschild winery. At the class level, we can say that instances of the class wine will have slots describing their flavor, body, sugar level, the maker of the wine, and so on. (Noy & McGuinness, 2000, p. 3)

The steps to developing an ontology therefore include: defining classes, arranging the class into subclasses within a hierarchy, defining slots and the possible value labels for them, and documenting specific instances using the slot value labels (Noy & McGuinness, 2000).

Numerous efforts are underway to develop a standard ontology for application on the Internet. The Suggested Upper Merged Ontology (SUMO) exists to help in building ontologies and includes over 1,000 concepts that are "interconnected into [a] semantic network" with over 4,000 axioms (Ahrens & Huang, 2003; Niles & Pease, 2001; Sevcenko, 2003). An online tool called the SUMO Browser is available to help users navigate and use the SUMO.

Software Solutions

Due to the complex nature of knowledge, ontologies can be constructed almost infinitely. Therefore, "ontology harvesting must identify ontologies that are desirable to share, worth converting, and usable by others" (Kalfoglou, 2002, p. 54).

An interview with Dialog's architect of content management, Steve Samler, reports that: "Our key issues are keeping the taxonomy current and presenting information the way the user wants to see it... Part of our value-added in filtering stories is the judgment of our subject matter experts" (Lamont, 2003, p. 4). Subject matter experts (SME) need to be closely involved in creating taxonomies and concept maps, according to Venkata (2002). Experts "play an active role in the knowledge capture process," explain Leake et al (2003).

Some software tools such as Convera's Retrievalware are able to develop a taxonomy dynamically. This "combines searching with classification to produce dynamic classification" (Lamont, 2003). The Convera product literature states that "users can launch and automatically classify the results based on pre-defined or dynamically generated classifications. The underlying taxonomies can consist of Convera's pre-packaged industry taxonomies, customer defined taxonomies or custom taxonomies" (Convera, 2004, p. 4). The benefit of this process is that "rather than being forced to fit searches within the constraints of inflexible categories, users can create their own information categories based on the context of their search at the moment" (Convera, 2004, p. 5). The query results are presented as a hierarchy of classification folders.

Retrievalware software also offers searching by concept, pattern, and Boolean strings (and/or/not). The concept search "does what we naturally do in conversation with each other—account for the individual differences in the way we express similar ideas." The pattern search uses a "sophisticated vote and rate scheme that considers a number of different features of the pattern instead of just character pairs." The Boolean search incorporates "advanced linguistic analysis to ensure high precision and recall" (Convera, 2004, p. 3).

Other software such as The Texis Categorizer "assigns documents to the categories in a taxonomy and automatically attaches subject codes and other metadata after being trained on sample documents." There needs to be a "close and interactive relationship between categorization and search" (Lamont, 2003, p. 6).

The importance of pattern and concept mapping is illustrated in an example about effective electronic communications compliance in financial services. Compliance personnel need to "proactively identify patterns of suspicious activity. For example the phrases 'IPO' and 'preferred customer' appearing within separate but related documents may have little apparent connection to one another" (Delphi Group, 2002, p. 3). It is their proximity and relationship in the same document which help compliance staff find the next Martha Stewart policy breach.

This linguistic approach to mining the results of searches is part of a larger effort to create a "real Semantic Web" (Kasteren, 2003). The Inxight SmartDiscovery software tool is based on work done at Xerox and "automates the creation of structure on otherwise unstructured data sources by leveraging more than 20 years of research in natural language processing and data visualization techniques" (Inxight, 2004, p. 2).

Problems and Issues in Maintaining Taxonomies

The greatest problem encountered with these automated processes is that taxonomies must be dynamic and changing. Venkata (2002) describes how developers must refine and enhance taxonomies by:

- Adding new topics to capture changing relationships between informational resources being classified, reflecting new subject domains that the taxonomy must accommodate;
- Optimizing the taxonomy structure to more accurately reflect both the informational content as well as organizational requirements;
- Deleting and/or aggregating topics that are no longer of value;

- Increasing topic coherency and optimizing statistical training sets to maintain or enhance classification accuracy as content changes over time (Venkata, 2002, p. S13).

Angele and Sure (2001) evaluate the limitations of software tools for ontology and document the many problems they must overcome. These include:

- Language conformity, with standardized syntax
- Consistency with respect to semantics
- Interoperability for exchanging ontologies between tools
- Turn around ability, so that users see it consistently over time
- Performance through benchmark tests
- Requirements for memory allocation in hardware to perform according to benchmarks
- Scalability to more complex and larger taxonomies
- Ease of integration into frameworks of other tools
- Connectivity to other tools.

Benjamins et al. (1998, 1999) document similar problems. These include technological risks, including tool support, maintenance, and scaling up; and social and organizational risks, including the need for a minimum number of participants in creating a taxonomy, the climate of competitive mentality, and incentive systems. Collaborative thinking about ontology needs to be free of a competitive environment, according to the authors. An incentive system is necessary because "Given the high workload of today's employees, it may be easily felt that contributing to a knowledge management effort is a waste of time, or at least does not have priority" (Benjamins et al., 1998, p. 17).

There are many more issues to consider in constructing ontologies and the reader is referred to the Web site of Sowa (2004), who discusses many issues, including:

- The relationships of process types
- Distinctions in roles and relations
- Causality

- Agents
- Thematic roles
- Alignment of concepts, relations, and commonalities between ontologies
- Properties, features, and attributes to differentiate categories
- Hierarchy
- Identity conditions.

Concept Maps

Papadopoullos (2003) discusses how "The relations between terms help to describe the conceptual interactions between words or expressions and thus will directly impact precision and recall" (p. 9). There are five types of term relationships: (1) part-whole, such as bumper and automobile; (2) collocation, occurring frequently in a sentence; (3) paradigmatic relations such as sun and solar; (4) synonymic; and (5) antonymic. "The principal challenge lies in assessing the effect of these relationships on information retrieval results" (Papadopoulos, 2003, p. 9).

Milam et al. (2000) and Carnot et al. (2003) describe the use of concept maps in educational software applications. Milam et al. explains that:

Even with clear assumptions and good qualitative research methodology, there are a myriad of ways to create a single type of map of the same content. It is important to either involve a group of scholars in developing a map and/or to recognize that the resulting map is simply a pattern for documenting the links between complex ideas. The groupware features for the collaborative creation of concept maps have great potential for developing these consensual maps and need to be explored further within an education context. (Milam, et al, 2000, p. 63)

Benjamins et al. (1998) explain how ontologies can be represented visually through software such as Ontobroker, which displays a hyperbolic query interface. Clicking on the main node takes the user to related classes. "Ontology browsing" involves a visual representation of a taxonomy, based on the principles of hyperbolic geometry. "This visualization technique allows a quick navigation to classes far away from the center as well as a closer examination of classes and their vicinity. Classes can be dragged around while the size of the visualization nodes changes corresponding to their location, that is, the more centric the bigger they appear" (Benjamins et al., 1999, p. 7).

Leake, et al (2003) explain that concept maps are similar to "vector-space models" in the way that knowledge is represented. Some systems are weighted, with higher weights given to top keywords. These systems can "consider the number of outgoing and incoming links to a concept node, strengthening the weights of keywords in nodes for concepts with many connections to other concepts in the map" (p. 5). In generating and suggesting new concepts using data mining techniques, the CMapTools software lets users "control how far the retrieval algorithm descends in the hierarchy tree to search for related concept maps…" (p. 5). A "keyword correlation metric" is used that measures the distance between concepts on a map. These and other automatic categorization techniques help present relevant topics to the user. There are limits to the results, however, and other scholars have created software such as EXTENDER (Extensive Topic Extender from New Data Exploring Relationships) that "identifies and suggests novel topics" (Leake et al., 2003).

Specific Issues in Taxonomies for Higher Education

In practice, the development of taxonomies for higher education is a much more imprecise process than is suggested by the previous discussion of dynamic classification software and semantics for the Web. The following section addresses very specific issues in taxonomies related to the author's experience with portals, campus-wide information systems, cataloging Internet resources, disciplinary taxonomies, and using national datasets.

Portal developers, whether open source or vendor-driven, have not evolved elaborate and complex categories for providing links to Web resources. The department, college, and university staff who build Web sites often do not understand the principles of content management. Many of these sites are not database-driven, which provides a mechanism for standardization. This work is done piece-meal, in a haphazard fashion using student workers, and without much foresight about managing site content and appearance over time. The Web site taxonomy, if there is one, is changed only when there is a site makeover, and often this process is compressed into a timeframe that leaves little time for reflection and analysis of site navigation problems, much less user input.

Almost all colleges and universities have a Web presence. This is different from portals geared to different sets of user needs and applications and from Intranets with administrative information systems for operations. Campus-Wide Information Systems (CWIS) are the most visible symbol of an institution on the Internet and must represent many perspectives. There are inherent categories of content for a CWIS, from special audience pages to lists of academic departments to topical information such as directions, admissions, and student services. In the author's experience, the choice of categories is often a political process, geared not so much to usability and the needs of a majority of users as to the images and perception which the institution wants to promote as its public "face." In Milam's study of the "politics of Web sites," the conclusion emerged that CWIS are a form of sense-making, focused more on aspirational ideas than reality (Milam, 1998).

Another taxonomy developed by the author is the Web site Internet Resources for Institutional Research, which has been maintained since 1995 and includes thousands of links in numerous categories. When begun, there were few efforts to catalog the Web by subject area and there were few links related to higher education, so the job was relatively easy. With a growing number of links, it became necessary to implement a rudimentary cataloging system. Hundreds of links were grouped by subject on single page. With interest in listservs, institutional fact books, and institutional research office Web sites, special pages were added and kept up separately. By 1997, an Access database was developed and ColdFusion software was used in a menu structure to document and serve over 100 pages by topic. Any link could be coded with multiple topics. Attempts were made to share the upkeep process with other volunteers, but the decision rules for coding and editing links were not made explicit. At some point, certain categories were hot, such as Web database information; while others were little used. The site and work benefited when the ERIC Clearinghouse for Higher Education began linking to specific pages within the site.

The Internet Resources Web site should have deleted unnecessary categories and continued to evolve new ones, but the process was time-consuming. Briefly, the site was turned over to part-time staff of the Association for Institutional Research to maintain, but this was never fully implemented and the expectations of the author were not communicated clearly. The site is still maintained and new links are added and bad links removed. The evolution of the taxonomy is stalled due to the amount of effort needed to maintain it correctly. This requires the author's or other's subject matter expertise and a degree of discernment about relevance and interest to users. Any link changes or additions provided by users are made quickly, but the vision for Internet resources has not been modified since the late 1990s. While it is highly used by institutional researchers and some faculty who teach higher education administration, it badly needs a makeover.

The work of NCHEMS, NCES, and NSF provides needed standards for data collection that implement de facto taxonomies. However, these are typically five or more years out of date, owing to the development and approval processes involved. They are more often a map of where higher education has been, not where it is going. The recent release of the CIP Code 2000 disciplinary taxonomy is a case in point. By the time the 2000 CIP Codes were developed, reviewed, made available for comment, finalized, approved, and implemented into the software architecture of collections of student and degree data, they were already obsolete. There were thousands of changes, however, between CIP 1990 and CIP 2000 and the upgrade involved a massive effort. It is important to recognize the development of complex taxonomies as an evolutionary process.

In developing the taxonomy of subject and topic codes used for the NPEC ANSWERS project, the author found himself immersed in ontology issues. Relying on the principles of naturalistic inquiry, polychotomous coding categories were developed. These were not mutually exclusive, but allowed for multiple, redundant coding of variables into different combinations of subject and topic. It was recognized that hierarchical models make inherent value judgments about the best way to describe a piece of data. Therefore, every effort was made to categorize variables in as many ways as possible. The most difficult part of this work was the re-work needed after a new coding category was added. This required that all previous variables be analyzed to see whether they could also be coded under the new category. This is a routine part of content analysis, the constant comparative method, and ethnography. Special software was developed to import, export, pre-select, and anticipate coding categories based on previous variables.

Recently, approximately 5,000 variables from NCES sample surveys were added to the ANSWERS matrix. The cost and time involved in hand-coding each variable were tremendous. However, another taxonomy was already in place from other Data Analysis System (DAS) software which made these same variables available. Multiple attempts were made to crosswalk the ANSWERS and DAS taxonomies. While this worked for some variables, many others had to be recoded. All attempts to automate the process were inadequate, though they represented a valid starting point. The difficulty of modifying taxonomies and building relationships between taxonomies was made clear. This is another reason why great care must be taken to construct categories. Numerous subject matter experts were used during the creation of the ANSWERS taxonomy, due to the help of NPEC Working Group members, and this is essential for ontology.

In using national datasets such as IPEDS and the Survey of Earned Doctorates, researchers are reluctant to compromise on the level of detail they desire. For example, in developing a study of faculty supply and demand, the author brought together datasets about students, degrees, faculty, and employees to estimate how many doctoral recipients were interested in entering academe by discipline and how many entry level faculty positions were available to them. Data on retirements, rank mobility, and other factors were also included. Each dataset that contributed to the model had its own level of disciplinary taxonomy. But in building crosswalks between all of the different datasets, it was only possible to rely on either two-digit CASPAR or two-digit CIP Codes. Much meaningful data are lost this way. Only a relatively small number of two-digit U.S. Census occupation codes are provided to document postsecondary faculty employment. This meant that after many hundreds of hours spent learning about and implementing complex disciplinary taxonomies, data could be analyzed at only a superficial and gross level. It was impossible to create the model with comparable disciplinary taxonomies in each dataset.

Similarly, the author recently worked with a consulting firm and national association to help them use IPEDS data. The researchers wanted to provide historical trends of IPEDS financial data. The initial data suggested many unpredicted anomalies and outliers. What they researchers did not know was that the data categories themselves had underlying taxonomy issues. These included the changing nature of the data collection, which involved a move from paper to the Web; implementation of new forms based on different accounting standards; cutbacks in the NCES budget for IPEDS for a specific year which resulted in decreased collection and editing of some data; and decisions made not to release a certain year of data in final format because it could not pass adjudication requirements. The categories and types of data over time appeared to be comparable. Only a sophisticated user of IPEDS trend data would be aware of these concerns.

Future Trends

This is an unprecedented era of what Gandel, Katz, and Metros (2004) call "Information Abundance" for higher education. This requires new ways of thinking about "boundless information" and how institutional repositories can be rebuilt "from the bottom up." Meta-tools for capturing metadata, especially ontologies, are badly needed.

In building taxonomies, it is critical that developers not try and reinvent the wheel. They need to understand existing efforts, where they succeed and where they are less useful than expected. Since ontologies are not yet a commodity and since they cost so much to develop, these efforts at KM must be valued. An organizational culture must be prized in which KM is rewarded, especially those hidden and less glitzy projects such as building a taxonomy.

In order for taxonomies to be fluid and changing to meet many different sets of needs, developers must incorporate the principles of dynamic classification. Exciting new software such as Convera and Inxight is now available to combine the best of taxonomies and search engines.

Developers need to incorporate concept maps, pattern recognition, Boolean logic, and subject matter experts. They need to understand the natural problems which occur in creating and interfacing between ontologies. While the CHESS/NCHEMS taxonomy of data structures is very impressive and the metadata efforts promoted by NLII for IMS are essential and remain at the forefront of current thinking about learning and technology, these are very expensive to develop and maintain. These initiatives need to continue to evolve and require a substantive commitment of resources and vision.

While sometimes deemed too costly, ontology is shown in this chapter to be central to KM strategies in higher education for capturing and utilizing knowledge assets. The case still needs to be made for the return on investment (ROI) of KM for higher education. This is very critical for content management through taxonomies. Work on ontologies must be given the resources and attention it deserves if content management is going to succeed in helping institutions handle the onslaught of information which is overload existing systems and personnel. The loss of critical knowledge assets with employee turnover and retirement must be stemmed through capturing and leveraging knowledge. This is only possible through the use of dynamic classification.

The development of ontologies for higher education is still a nascent field. There is much exciting, groundbreaking research to be done. It is important that institutional leaders and policymakers recognize the value that ontology holds for future work in KM and make the necessary investments now. This starts with a shared vision of what ontology offers to higher education and how taxonomies are interwoven throughout administrative information systems and all Web-based learning applications.

References

Ahrens, K., Chung S.F., & Huang, C. (2003). Conceptual metaphors: Ontology-based representation and corporate driven mapping principles. In *Proceedings of the ACL workshop on the lexicon and figurative language*. Retrieved October 26, 2004, from *http://acl.ldc.upenn.edu/acl2003/lexfig/pdf/Ahrens.pdf*

Andrews, W. (2003). Visionaries invade the 2003 search engine magic quadrant. *Gartner research.* Retrieved November 7, 2004, from *http://www3.gartner.com/mq/asset_50500.jsp*

Angele, J. & Sure, Y. (2001). Whitepaper: Evaluation of ontology-based tools. Workshop presentation at the *13th International Conference on Knowledge Engineering and Knowledge Management*. Retrieved October 26, 2004, from *http://www.aifb.uni-karlsruhe.de/WBS/ysu/publications/eon2002_whitepaper.pdf*

Anonymous (2001). Resurveying the terrain: Refining the taxonomy for the postsecondary market. *Change*, *33*(2), 53.

Benjamins, V.R., et al. (1998). Knowledge management through ontologies. *Proceedings of the 2nd international conference on practical aspects of knowledge management.* Retrieved October 26, 2004, from *http://citeseer.ist.psu.edu/benjamins98knowledge.html*

Benjamins, V.R., et al. (1999). $(KA)^2$: Building ontologies for the Internet: A mid term report. Retrieved October 26, 2004, from *http://citeseer.ist.psu.edu/276747.html*

Bernbom, G. (Ed.) (2001). *Information alchemy: The art and science of knowledge management. EDUCAUSE leadership series #3.* San Francisco: Jossey-Bass.

Carnot, M.J., et al. (2003). A summary of literature pertaining to the use of concept mapping techniques and technologies for education and performance support. Technical report submitted to the chief of naval education and training, Pensacola, FL. Retrieved October 26, 2004, from *http://www.ihmc.us/users/acanas/Publications/ConceptMapLitReview/IHMC%20Literature%20Review%20on%20Concept%20Mapping.pdf*

Convera (2004a). Mission-critical search & categorization for the enterprise. Retrieved October 26, 2004, from *http://www.ihssolutions.com/canada/documentation_library/index.cfm*

Convera (2004b). RetrievalWare's advanced categorization and dynamic classification. Retrieved October 26, 2004, from *http://www.convera.com/Products/rw_categorization.asp*

Crystal, M.E. & Jones, D.P. (1985). *A common language for postsecondary accreditation: Categories and definitions for data collection.* Boulder, CO: National Center for Higher Education Management Systems.

Delphi Group (2002). *Enabling electronic communications compliance. Snapshot.* Boston: Delphi Group.

Delphi Group (2003). *Maximizing organizational 'know how' in government entities. Snapshot.* Boston: Delphi Group.

Epper, R.M. & Garn, M. (2004). Virtual universities real possibilities. *EDUCAUSE Review, 39*(2).

Gandel, P.B., Katz, R.N., & Metros, S.E. (2004). The weariness of the flesh: Reflections on the life of the mind in an era of abundance. *EDUCAUSE Review, 39*(2), 40-51.

Grasel, W. (1999). The reality of brands: Toward an ontology of marketing. *American Journal of Economics and Sociology, 58.* Retrieved October 26, 2004, from *http://ontology.buffalo.edu/brands.html*

Griffin, S. & Wason, T. (1997). The year of metadata. *Educom Review, 32*(6). Retrieved October 26, 2004, from *http://www.educause.edu/LibraryDetailPage/666&ID=ERM9763*

Gumport, P.J. (1997). In search of strategic perspective: A tool for mapping the market in postsecondary education. *Change,* November/December.

Halstead, D.K. (1979). *Higher education planning: A bibliographic handbook.* Washington, DC: U.S. Department of Education, National Institute of Education.

Halstead, D.K. (1981). *Higher education: A bibliographic handbook volume II.*. Washington, DC: U.S. Department of Education, National Institute of Education.

Inxight. (2003). *Inxight SmartDiscovery: Discover the true value of information.* Sunnyvale, CA: Inxight Software, Inc. Retrieved October 26, 2004, from *http://www.inxight.com/products/smartdiscovery/*

Kalfoglou, Y. (2002). Maintaining ontologies with organisational memories. Retrieved October 26, 2004, from *http://www.ecs.soton. ac.uk/ ~yk1/kalfoglou-kluwerKMOMbook.pdf*

Kasteren, J. van (2003). Semantic web should be based on well-founded ontologies: An interview with Nicola Guarino. *DigiCULT: Towards a semantic Web for heritage resources, Thematic Issue 3,* May.

Kleiner, C. (2004). Decades of rankings. *America's best colleges 2004 edition.* Washington, DC: U.S. News and World Report.

Knowledge Integrity, Inc. (2000). Collecting quality customer data. *Knowledge Management*, *3*(2), 78-80. Retrieved October 26, 2004, from *http://www.destinationcrm.com/km/dcrm_km_article. asp?id=226*

Lamont, J. (2003). Dynamic taxonomies: Keeping up with changing content. *KM World, 12*(5). Retrieved October 26, 2004, from *http://www.km world.com/publications/magazine/index.cfm?action= readart icle &Article_ID=1508&Publication_ID=90*

Leake, D.B., et al. (2003). Aiding knowledge capture by searching for extensions of knowledge models. *Proceedings of the International Conference on Knowledge Capture*. Retrieved October 26, 2004, from *http://portal.acm.org/citation.cfm?id= 9456 55&dl=AC M& coll=GUIDE*

Milam, J.H. (1998). The politics of web sites. Panel presentation at the *Annual Forum of the Association for Institutional Research*, Minneapolis, MN.

Milam, J.H., et al. (2000). Concept maps for web-based applications: ERIC technical report. Retrieved October 26, 2004, from *http:// highered.org/docs/milam-conceptmaps.PDF*

Moore, A. (2003). The next big thing… again. *KM World* supplement, April. Retrieved October 26, 2004, from *http://www.kmworld.com/ publications/whitepapers/ECM03/moore.pdf*

National Center for Charitable Statistics (NCCS) (2004). *National taxonomy of exempt entities – Core codes.* Retrieved October 26, 2004, from *http://nccs2.urban.org/ntee-cc/irs_code.htm*

National Center for Educational Statistics (NCES) (2004a). *IPEDS glossary.* Retrieved October 26, 2004, from *http://nces.ed.gov/ipeds/glossary/*

National Center for Educational Statistics (NCES) (2004b). *IPEDS finance data FASB and GASB – What's the difference?* Retrieved October 26, 2004, from *http://nces.ed.gov/ipeds/web2000/gasbfasb.asp*

National Center for Postsecondary Improvement (NCPI) (1998). The user-friendly terrain: Defining the market taxonomy for two-year institutions. *Change,* January/February.

National Learning Infrastructure Initiative (NLII) (2004). *2003 NLII annual review.* Washington, DC: National Learning Infrastructure Initiative. Retrieved October 26, 2004, from *http://www.educause.edu/nlii/*

National Postsecondary Education Cooperative (NPEC) (1999). *Best practices for data collectors and data providers.* Washington, DC: National Postsecondary Education Cooperative. Retrieved October 26, 2004, from *http://nces.ed.gov/pubsearch/pubsinfo.asp?pubid=1999191*

Niles, I. & Pease, A. (2001). Towards a standard upper ontology. Paper presented at *FOIS Conference,* October.

Noy, N.F. & McGuinness, D.L. (2000). Ontology development 101: A guide to creating your first ontology, Stanford Knowledge Systems Laboratory Technical Report KSL-01-05 and Stanford Medical Informatics Technical Report SMI-2001-0880, March 2001. Retrieved October 26, 2004, from *http://www.ksl.stanford.edu/people/dlm/papers/ontology-tutorial-noy-mcguinness-abstract.html*

Nylund, A.L. (2000). Finding patterns in a deluge of data. *Knowledge Management, 3*(2), 69-71. Retrieved October 26, 2004, from *http://www.destinationcrm.com/km/dcrm_km_ article.asp? id=189*

Ogbuji, U. (2003). XML knowledge management flourishes in learning technology initiatives. Retrieved October 26, 2004, from *http://www-106.ibm.com/developerworks/xml/library/x-think21.html*

Papadopoullos, A. (2003). *Meaningful search: Why PET scanners are not about cats & dogs.* Carlsbad, CA: Convera.

Reamy, T. (2002). Imparting knowledge through storytelling, Part 2. *KMWorld, 11*(7). Retrieved October 26, 2004, from *http://www.kmworld.com/publications/magazine/index.cfm?action= readart icle&Ar ticl e_I D=1328&Publication_ID=74*

Sevcenko, M. (2003). Online presentation of an upper ontology. *Proceedings of Znalosti 2003*, Ostrava, Czech Republic, February 19-21. Retrieved October 26, 2004, from *http://ontology.teknowledge. com/Sevcenko.pdf*

Shulman, L.S. (2001). *The Carnegie Classification of institutions of higher education.* Menlo Park, CA: The Carnegie Foundation for the Advancement of Teaching.

Sowa, J.F. (2004a). *Ontology.* Retrieved October 26, 2004, from *http://www.jfsowa.com/ontology/*

Sowa, J.F. (2004b). *Ontology, metadata, and semiotics.* Retrieved October 26, 2004, from *http://users.bestweb.net/~sowa/peirce/ontometa.htm*

Thomas, C.R. (1971). *NCHEMS data element dictionary.* Boulder, CO: National Center for Higher Education Management Systems.

Thomas, C.R. (2004). *CHESS data definitions* (2nd ed.). Boulder, CO: National Center for Higher Education Management Systems.

U.S. Census Bureau. (2004). *North American Industry Classification System (NAICS).* Retrieved October 26, 2004, from *http://www.census.gov/epcd/www/naics.html*

Venkata, R. (2002). Taxonomies, categorization, and organizational agility. *KM World* supplement. October. Retrieved October 26, 2004, from *http://www.kmworld.com/publications/whitepapers/KM2/venk ata.pdf*

Wiley, D.A. (2000). *Connecting learning objects to instructional design theory: A definition, a metaphor, and a taxonomy.* Retrieved October 26, 2004, from *http://www.reusability.org/read/chapters/wiley.doc*

Section II

Administrative Issues and Knowledge Management

Chapter IV

Toward Technological Bloat and Academic Technocracy: The Information Age and Higher Education

George S. McClellan, Dickinson State University, USA

Gary A. Cruz, The University of Arizona, USA

Amy Scott Metcalfe, The University of British Columbia, Canada

Richard L. Wagoner, The University of Arizona, USA

Abstract

While the strategic goals of Knowledge Management might seem new to the academy, higher education has been central to the growing Knowledge Economy and the Information Age for some time. As electronic communications and information systems have been widely adopted in colleges and universities, little scholarship has reflected upon the organizational and social changes that these technologies bring to the academic workplace. This chapter provides the theoretical groundwork for understanding three key transformations in higher education: the digital restructuring of academic labor; the use of technology as basis for efficiency arguments; and the unintended consequences of IT accretion, which we call "technological bloat." As a consequence of these transformations, a new organizational structure may be emerging in higher education.

Introduction

The 1990s and the early 21st century have seen the rise of a new capitalist production cycle called the New Economy (Carnoy, Castells, Cohen, & Cardoso, 1993). The New Economy is a product of the Information Age, a period marked by rapid ascendance of the importance of knowledge and access to information (Rifkin, 2000). This chapter explores the impact of one aspect of the Information Age: the increased use of computers and computer-mediated communication in higher education institutions.

The exploration begins with a discussion of the increasing pressures experienced by higher education in the Information Age and then moves to a description of the ways in which the conceptual framework known as *academic capitalism* can be useful for understanding the context within which higher education is acting and reacting to change. Next, the theory of *technocracy* is identified, discussed, and related to higher education and the use of information technology. The chapter then turns to a discussion of the implementation and efficacy of information technology in higher education, specifically in the field of student affairs. The discussion addresses the extent to which expressed budgetary and service goals are met by the implementation of new technologies and the potential for *technological bloat* as an unintended outcome. The chapter concludes with the suggestion that the predominant organizational structure of higher education may be shifting to that of an academic technocracy as a result of the impact of higher education's focus on computing and computer-mediated communication. Suggestions for future research are also offered.

Conceptual Frameworks

Concepts of the marketplace are useful lenses through which to study the economically charged environment in which higher education operates. Academic capitalism is used in this chapter as a conceptual lens to view the use of IT in higher education. In addition, the concept of technocracy is explored to better understand the stratified nature of employment within high-tech organizations, and how this might impact decision-making in higher education institutions.

Academic Capitalism

Academic capitalism, the encroachment of the profit motive into the academy, has been studied by a number of scholars (Breneman, 1993; Etzkowitz, 1983, 1989; Fairweather, 1988; Gumport & Pusser, 1995; Massy & Zemsky, 1990; Rhoades, 1997), but it finds its richest description in the work of Slaughter and Leslie (1997) and more recently Slaughter and Rhoades (2004). The authors discuss academic capitalism as institutional and professional market or market-like efforts to secure external funds for higher education. Slaughter and Leslie (1997) argued that with the rise of globalization, the state has decreased its share of funding to higher education in the form of block grants, but has increased support of research and innovation that is tied to economic development and competitiveness. In other words, state expenditures have become more focused on regional and national returns-on-investment rather than on overall social returns from higher education. While state support as a percentage of higher education budgets has decreased, demand for education, especially education and training tied directly to business and industry, has dramatically increased. Society sees higher education as the means for training the future workforce, making it an integral part of economic growth. Further, higher education institutions have become important sites of innovation and technological development, with an increasing ability to seek markets for their products due to a changing legislative landscape that favors university-industry relations. Yet, expansion of the mission of higher education has stretched institutional budgets beyond the breaking point. Colleges and universities have turned to private sector funding and cost-saving measures to continue the development of diversified services while sustaining their original focus on undergraduate education. Breneman (1993) argued that this entrepreneurial condition is not temporary, but a new reality to which higher education must permanently adjust.

The conceptual framework of academic capitalism has been recently revisited by Slaughter and Rhoades (2004). While Slaughter and Leslie focused on the entrepreneurial activities of universities in three geographical regions (Australia, United Kingdom, and the United States), Slaughter and Rhoades examined the market-like behaviors of university administrators, faculty, and staff at U.S. institutions. They found that the trend toward seeking outside resources beyond the state is increasing, and entrepreneurial behavior on college campuses is happening to a much larger extent than previously noted. The authors provide several examples of the opportunity-seeking behaviors within academia, challenging the notion that institutions of higher education are merely responding to environmental resource stress.

We find academic capitalism to be a particularly useful theoretical framework for understanding the trend toward the use of information technology in higher education, particularly in the field of student affairs. As public funds are increasingly restricted and applied toward academic endeavors thought to help states and regions become more competitive in a global market, the labor-intensive work of student affairs is often viewed as a loss-producing function that is ancillary to the research mission of colleges and universities. Electronically distributed student services, however, are sold to higher education institutions with the promise that they will allow for more efficient provision of high-quality services to student "clients." As the student-as-consumer model becomes more entrenched in the academic business core, student affairs will likely be evaluated in terms of revenue-generation, cost savings, and customer service goals.

Technocracy

Technocracy is an organizational theory used to explore organizations in the late 20th and early 21st century. The model is generally applied to post-industrial/post-Fordist organizations that rely heavily on technology, especially computerization and other types of high technology, to accomplish their mission. Building on the work of others (Clegg, 1990; Colclough & Tolbert, 1992; Collins, 1979; Heydebrand, 1979, 1983, 1989; Kouzmin, 1980), Burris (1993) developed a detailed description and study of technocracy. Technocracy has a number of distinguishing features. While no organization necessarily embodies all of them, each characteristic is indicative of a technocracy.

First, technocracy polarizes workers into expert and non-expert sectors with clear gender and racial distinctions between them. In the U.S., experts tend to be white and male, non-experts often are non-white and/or female. Experts possess more abstract, diagnostic, and technical skills, which replace more traditional skills. Daday and Burris (2001) suggested that marginalized (non-expert) employees in a technocracy can gain a sense of prestige-by-association through working in teams that mix both experts and non-experts.

Second, technocracies flatten bureaucratic hierarchies (Burris, 1993). The polarization between expert and non-expert personnel and flattening of hierarchies can lead to erosion of internal job ladders. Once a person has assumed a position in a technocracy, there may be little chance of promotion. This condition is further strengthened because technocracies place an increased emphasis on credentialing, which creates advancement and participation barriers for non-certified employees. Such barriers create an atmosphere where technical expertise is the primary source of legitimate authority. Technical expertise at the executive level is seen not only as desirable, but as inevitable because the advanced technological nature of organizations makes the experts the only people capable of making informed and correct decisions.

Third, technocracies have flexible configurations of centralization and decentralization, which generally lead to increased consolidation of the most critical means of control and a corresponding delegation of more superficial organizational tasks. These task segregations are linked to data management and information flows so that centralized systems handle the most critical and controlled organizational operations. In this way organizations are often tied to a central financial system for their accounting procedures, but may be permitted decentralized databases for sub-unit tasks.

Finally, Burris added that technocracies must be viewed as a complex interweaving of technical, social, and political concerns, which leads to one of her strong critiques of other technocratic theorists. Burris (1993) argues that too often technocracy is associated with technological determinism, a theory that assumes technology naturally progresses from one stage to the next causing innovation and change and that technology can always present the one right solution to any challenge. Those who hold this positive notion of technology are the most optimistic about the outcomes of technocracy; for them, it is a panacea, the beginning of an Utopic future where technology shapes society for the better. However, we view technology more as an increasingly powerful tool that can be misused for control and exploitation. From our viewpoint, technology has the potential to increase managerial control, de-skill certain individuals in the labor process, lead to increased worker stress, and contribute to occupational health problems.

Discussion of Issues

How do we assess higher education's efforts to respond to the pressures of academic capitalism and technocracy? We address this question through a discussion of three key issues: the digital restructuring of academic labor; the use of technology as basis for efficiency arguments; and the unintended consequences of IT accretion (which we call technological bloat) and the emergence of "academic technocracy" as a new organizational structure in higher education.

Restructuring Higher Education with Technology

There is a strong connection between labor, capital, and information in the academic workplace. It is for this reason that information technology should be suspect when presented as a labor-saving initiative, as it may in fact be a labor-controlling mechanism. In discussing the Information Age and the new division of labor, Robertson (2000) stated:

> *The emergence of a post-industrial economy in the developed world has been accompanied by dramatic shifts in the division of labour. Whereas the social division of labour was formerly based on the ownership of private property and labour power, the new informational division of labour will be based on ownership of, access to, and the management of information.* (p. 85)

As labor is restructured and controlled through information technology, the increased use of adjunct faculty, decreased control of academe by academics, increased threats to tenure, and reduced academic freedom are likely (Leik, 1998). Concerns about the New Economy's threat to academic freedom and tenure are not overstated. One only has to read the comments of Massy and Zemsky (1995) on the topic of capital-labor ratios to understand what the future may hold if IT is utilized to replace aspects of faculty work:

Finally, technology provides more flexibility than traditional teaching methods once one moves beyond minor changes that can be instituted by individual professors. The "career" of a workstation may be well less than five years, whereas that of a professor often exceeds 30 years. Workstations don't get tenure, and delegations are less likely to wait on the provost when particular equipment items are "laid off." The "retraining" of IT equipment (for example, reprogramming), while not inexpensive, is easier and more predictable than retraining a tenured professor. Within limits, departments will gain a larger zone of flexibility as the capital-labor ratio grows. (p. 7)

Thus it can be said that when the use of IT is viewed from a labor and technocracy perspective, issues relating to the changing nature of work, the nature of technical and non-technical workers, and the emergence of workplace power can be examined.

In higher education, technocratic decision-making can place undue faith in the power of information technology to achieve organizational goals. For example, computers might be utilized to perform tasks previously done by individuals in an effort to save labor costs. Barley (1996b) described this way of changing the work landscape as *substitutional*, in that a technology has become a substitute for human labor. This type of technological change has limited impact, according to Barley, because the substitution happens on a small scale, usually by having a machine perform a routine task without any further implications on the production cycle. It is this sort of change that is being described by IT advocates who call for the restructuring of academic labor through the use of information technologies.

Massy and Zemsky (1995) listed economies of scale as one of the benefits of the introduction of IT to higher education. Citing the need to "do more with less," Massy and Zemsky touted the ability of IT to substitute for some parts of the academic production cycle:

Using IT for "more-with-less" productivity enhancement requires that technology replace some activities now being performed by faculty,

> *teaching assistants, and support personnel. With labor accounting for seventy percent or more of current operating cost, there is simply no other way. Faculty will have to reengineer teaching and learning processes to substitute capital for labor on a selective basis.* (p. 6)

The type of solution they describe is similar to Barley's substitutional technological change, yet Barley warned that sometimes what appears to be substitutional may in fact be *infrastructural*.

Barley (1996b) stated that infrastructural change occurs when the technology has the potential to cause widespread disturbances in the production cycle. He cited the second industrial revolution as an example of a period of infrastrutural change, when electricity and telecommunications were combined with the advent of the internal combustion engine to produce a new wave of manufacturing (p. 24). Yet, Barley noted that some regarded these infrastructural changes as merely substitutional technologies, using the example of people's inability to foresee that the "horseless carriage" would be the advent of a revolutionary international system of automobile-based transportation. As we enter a post-industrial era, the danger to higher education is that information technology might be conceived merely as a substitutional method for increasing productivity and not as a possible infrastructural adaptation that could profoundly affect the nature of academic culture. The risk is that what was once considered a cost-saving measure can actually be a step toward a more expensive organizational paradigm in terms of both the machinery substituted for human labor and the increased personnel necessary to operate the "cost-saving" equipment. For example, a case study at the Pratt Institute illustrated the process of restructuring with new technology as the campus combined the functions of the bursar, registration and financial aid in one system (Karns, 1993). The system was restructured to use enhanced automated technologies, to make the process more user-friendly for the students, and to provide them more control in their transactions. There was, however, no evidence of significant savings of resources, either human or financial. Instead, staff had to be trained and new accountability measures and policies instituted.

Technology and Efficiency in Higher Education

Innovation and increased time-to-market are imperative practices for businesses seeking to be competitive in the Information Age. The need to be competitive, particularly for external recognition and funding, is now acute in the higher education sector as well. Yet, business rules are not always easy to insert into the traditional academic culture of higher education institutions, as noted by Duderstadt (2000):

To meet growing societal demand for higher education at a time when costs are increasing and public support is declining, most institutions have been forced to sharply increase tuition and fees, triggering public concern about the costs and availability of a college education. As a result, most colleges and universities are now looking for ways to control costs and increase productivity, but most are also finding that their current organization and governance makes this very difficult. It seems clear that the higher education enterprise in America must change dramatically if it is to restore a balance between the costs and availability of educational services needed by our society and the resources available to support these services. (p. 3)

There is an underlying assumption in Duderstadt's statement that colleges and universities are failing to meet "production standards" due to an inability to control costs. However, it may be that rising administrative costs have less to do with inefficiency than they do with the growth of the academic support personnel necessary to meet changing institutional goals in an age of mass education (Gumport & Pusser, 1995; Leslie & Rhoades, 1995). We hold that efficiency arguments must be supported by clear data outlining the expenses associated with "cost-saving" measures. In particular, as higher education stakeholders turn to information technology solutions, more needs to be understood about the capital (both human and material) needed to implement these strategies.

There is little evidence in the business literature and none in higher education that there has been a return on investment for information technology (Paulsen, 1997; Strassmann, 1997). In fact, the data suggest that the costs exceed the benefits in most cases (Peebles & Antolvic, 1999; Smallen, 2004). The lack of empirical evidence for cost savings has not prevented speculative discussion regarding the potential for financial gain as the result of technological innovation. Guskin (1994) argues that administrative costs must be reduced through the implementation and use of new technologies with resultant reduction in labor before it will be possible to restructure the faculty so that its energies are directed toward appropriate learning outcomes. El-Khawas (1994) reported that nearly 70 percent of colleges and universities had undertaken some form of administrative reorganization, but substantially fewer were actually reducing staff. Colleges are instead making efforts to increase productivity and develop additional revenue streams (Rhoades, 1995). As Rhoades noted, "Currently, the push is toward brief, efficient encounters that do not engage students or promote relationship" (p. 34). Cohen (1998) observed that this is not a new phenomenon:

The quest for efficiency in instruction has a long history ... These patterns are tried continually. Failure to find the magic bullet that would yield a notable increase in efficiency is attributed variously to professors who stubbornly refuse to work longer hours, uncaring administrators and bean-counters who look only to the bottom line of passing more students through so that tuition and state reimbursements remain high enough to balance the budget, and apathetic students who refuse to apply themselves to their studies. (pp. 366-367)

He continues, "Educators have long sought technology that would enrich the learning environment and reduce students' dependence on the live instructor" (p. 367). Cohen then sited Cuban's (1986) work exploring the efforts that have taken place since the 1920s to incorporate technology in teaching. Cuban concluded that each successive wave of technological pressure came supported by self-motivated claims from interested stakeholders regarding the power of the innovation to impact positively on learning. Initial implementation was followed by academic studies showing more modest gains and by frustrations with the slow place of complete transformation. The administrative response to those frustrations has been to blame faculty who are characterized as resistant to change. Cuban (1986) referred to this recurring pattern as "the exhiliration/scientific-credibility/disappointment/teacher-bashing cycle" (p. 5).

Cohen (1998) stated that the shift toward technology, which has been patterned on a similar earlier shift in business, is unlikely to offer cost savings or to enhance attainment of learning outcomes. Cohen noted that the unrealized expectations of technology within higher education are not unlike those experienced in the business world upon which they were modeled:

> *The quest for saving money through increasing productivity, with technology as the centerpiece, has merged with the desire to make people more responsible for their own education and with the changes in hierarchical systems in the workplace. But technology does not operate itself; instructional programs are not self-generating ... By no measure has information technology resulted in greater instructional productivity. For that matter few industries have enjoyed increased per capita output sufficient to justify the billions spent on it. Nonetheless, higher education has been compelled to install it because it is an essential component of student literacy. The graduates will enter a world where all forms of information technology are basic tools ... The colleges have to install technology and their staff has to use it, even if it adds to the cost of instruction.* (pp. 371-372)

Why has the infusion of computing and computing-networks not helped to reduce administrative costs substantially in higher education? Hilmer and Donaldson (1996) answer that it is because machines and computers can perform mathematical functions and routinized sorting tasks but are incapable of carrying out the more qualitative analytical and interpersonal communication functions of middle- and senior-level management. An area of service where this can be observed is in student affairs administration.

Student affairs is a profession that focuses on a student's personal and psychosocial development by providing those opportunities for them to gain cultural capital through the development of their interpersonal, communicative, leadership and social skills (Wolf-Wendel & Ruel, 1999). Student affairs work requires face-to-face contact with students. While technology can augment this process, to force the technology upon this institutional unit is to force a philosophical change in the mission of the student affairs profession (Moneta, 1997).

Student affairs are not rooted in a one-size-fits-all philosophy (West & Dagigle, 1997). Rather, student services and student affairs are tailored to the individual. West and Dagigle (1997) present a number of reasons to incorporate a technological infrastructure in student services: speed and accuracy, convenience, efficiency, interactivity, and professionalization. The challenge is how to customize the use of technology so as to accommodate the individual student. This would require student service professionals to move from the role of information provider toward that of information facilitator. In other words, it would require them to provide students with the know-how to search for information and be more self-sufficient through the use of technology, a model that is being explored in the student-faculty relationship as well. Furthermore, to be fully effective in the new technological paradigm student affairs professionals must assume the roles of systems architects, educators, learners, and policy makers while forming collaborative links to academic affairs and information technology industries (Ausiello & Wells, 1997). However, it may be that the goals of student affairs are not being incorporated into the information systems as student services professionals are not being fully included in the design process (Barratt, 2001).

Students have become "more informed consumers, demanding a level of university service comparable to that which they receive from other entities in society" (Karns, 1993, p. 27). Students are paying more for their education and there is a greater influx of adult students who are demanding greater service and accountability for the expenses to higher education. Hoover (1997) stated that the student affairs profession faces increasing pressure from administration to provide empirical evidence of the value of face-to-face services and programs versus the value of those same services and programs provided at a distance. Although technologically-delivered student services also entail high costs, it is interesting that it is the efficiency of personal interactions that must be justified rather than the technological expenditures. In an academic climate prone to technocratic decision making, technology often trumps the personal (and the personnel).

Technological Bloat

As noted earlier in this chapter, very little data have been collected to show just how much institutions of higher education spend on information technology (Green & Jenkins, 1998). Decentralization has been targeted as the cause for this lack of information as campus units may find different ways to manage their budgets and make appropriations for new technology expenditures, making it difficult to "find the money" in the institutional accounting structure (Green & Jenkins, 1998). Likewise, in discussing the phenomenon of administrative bloat, Rhoades (1998) observed that empirical information is sorely lacking with respect to administrative costs in higher education. Rhoades noted that administrative costs are frequently hidden because they are distributed throughout departments and centers. The costs of implementing and maintaining the new technology in higher education may be similarly hidden throughout institutional budgets. Newly created positions such as chief information officer (CIO) and vice president for information technology (VP for IT) and the staff formally associated with IT units are readily identifiable. However, these are by no means the only staffing positions associated with supporting the implementation and maintenance of computing and computer-mediated communication. Departmental network administrators and support staff may be overlooked in a simple enumeration of formal IT personnel. Rhoades recommended vertical and horizontal disaggregation as a means to understand the nature and extent of administrative costs, and applying the model to studying the diffusion of costs related to technology in higher education would be useful.

Like other aspects of higher education, technology is labor intensive. Barley (1996a) has described the emergence of technicians as a new class of workers who span the boundaries between emerging technology and older and more established professions. It may well be the case that as colleges and universities increasingly rely on computers and computing networks for administrative and academic purposes that there will be an accretion of technicians throughout their campuses (Bates, 2000).

Conclusion

This chapter uses current higher education literature as well as economic, labor, and organizational theories to suggest that the forces of academic capitalism and technocracy may be in part responsible for the increased use of computing and computer-mediated communication in higher education. Given this perspective, in the course of implementing and maintaining technological innovations, it may be the case that the organizational structure of professional bureaucracy (Mintzberg, 1979) is giving way in higher education to that of *academic technocracy* in which the competing and overlapping interests of the academy and technocracy shape structures, processes, and decisions in higher education.

Further research would be informative in determining whether or not the posited processes and changes are in play in higher education. Possible areas of inquiry and analysis include: complete accounting of expenses for new technology; socio-technical construction of labor as a result of the new technology; explication of the changing definitions of efficiency and quality in light of the new technology; and exploration of the impact of technology on organizational structure and decision-making.

Academicians and practitioners alike must begin to pay closer attention to the significant changes that are at hand in higher education as a result of the increasing role of computing and computer-mediated communication. We agree with Heller (2001) when he stated, "technological innovation and adoption for its own sake will not serve the public interest" (p. 255). Rather, we support evidence- and discovery-based approaches to understanding how information technology can be best utilized to meet the expanding missions of higher education institutions.

References

Ausiello, K. & Wells, B. (1997). Information technology and student affairs: Planning for the twenty-first century. *New Directions for Student Services, 78,* 71-81.

Barley, S.R. (1996a). Technicians in the workplace: Ethnographic evidence for bringing work into organization studies. *Administrative Science Quarterly, 41*(3), 404-441.

Barley, S.R. (1996b). *The new world of work.* London: British-North American Committee.

Barratt, W. (2001). Managing information technology in student affairs: A report on policies, practices, staffing, and technology. Paper presented at the *Annual Conference of the National Association of Student Personnel Administrators,* Seattle, WA, March 17-21.

Bates, A.W. (2000). *Managing technological change: Strategies for college and university leaders.* San Francisco: Jossey-Bass.

Breneman, D.W. (1993). *Higher education: On a collision course with new realities.* Washington, DC: Association of Governing Boards of Universities and Colleges.

Burris, B.H. (1993). *Technocracy at work.* Albany: SUNY Press.

Carnoy, M., Castells, M., Cohen, S.S., & Cardoso, F.H. (1993). *The new global economy in the Information Age: Reflections on our changing world.* University Park: The Pennsylvania State University Press.

Clegg, S.R. (1990). *Modern organizations.* Newbury Park, CA: Sage.

Cohen, A.M. (1998). *The shaping of American higher education: Emergence and growth of the system.* San Francisco: Jossey-Bass.

Colclough, G. & Tolbert, C. M. (1992). *Work in the fast lane: Flexibility, divisions of labor, and inequality in high-tech industries.* Albany, NY: SUNY Press.

Collins, R. (1979). *The credential society.* New York: Academic Press.

Cuban, L. (1986). *Teachers and machines: The classroom use of technology since 1920.* New York: Teachers College, Columbia University.

Daday, G. & Burris, B. (2001). Technocratic teamwork: Mitigating polarization and cultural marginalization in an engineering firm. *The Transformation of Work, 10,* 241-262.

Duderstadt, J.J. (2000). Can colleges and universities survive in the information age? In R.N. Katz and Associates (Eds.), *Dancing with the devil: Information technology and the new competition in higher education* (pp. 1-25). San Francisco: Jossey-Bass.

El-Khawas, E. (1994). Campus trends 1994: A time of redirection. *Higher Education Panel Report, no. 84*. Washington, DC: American Council on Education.

Etzkowitz, H. (1983). Entrepreneurial scientists and entrepreneurial universities in American academic science. *Minerva, 21*, 198-233.

Etzkowitz, H. (1989). Entrepreneurial science in the academy: A case of the transformation of norms. *Social Problems, 36,* 14-29.

Fairweather, J.S. (1988). *Entrepreneurship and higher education.* Washington, DC: Association for the Study of Higher Education.

Green, K. & Jenkins, R. (1998). IT financial planning 101: Developing an institutional strategy for financing technology. *NACUBO Business Officer,* March.

Gumport, P.J. & Pusser, B. (1995). A case of bureaucratic accretion: Context and consequences. *The Journal of Higher Education, 66*(5), 493-520.

Guskin, A.E. (1994). Reducing student costs and enhancing student learning, part I: Restructuring the administration. *Change, 26*(4), 23-29.

Heller, D.E. (Ed.) (2001). *The states and public higher education policy: Affordability, access, and accountability*. Baltimore: Johns Hopkins University Press.

Heydebrand, W. (1979). The technocratic administration of justice. *Research in Law and Society, 2*, 29-64.

Heydebrand, W. (1983). Technocratic corporatism: Toward a theory of occupational and organizational transformation. In R. Hall & R. Quinn (Eds.), *Organizational theory and public policy* (pp. 93-114). Beverly Hills, CA: Sage.

Heydebrand, W. (1989). New organizational forms. *Work and Occupations, 16*(3), 323-357.

Hilmer, F.G. & Donaldson, L. (1996). *Management redeemed: Debunking the fads that undermine corporate performance*. New York: The Free Press.

Hoover, R.E. (1997). The role of student affairs at metropolitan universities. *New Directions for Student Services, 79,* 15-25.

Karns, J. (1993). Redesigning student services. *Planning for Higher Education, 21*(3), 27-33.

Kouzmin, A. (1980). Control in organizational analysis: The lost politics. In D. Dunkerly & G. Salaman (Eds.), *The international yearbook of organization studies* (pp. 56-89). Boston: Routledge and Kegan Paul.

Leik, R. (1998). There's far more than tenure on the butcher block. *Sociological Perspectives, 41*(4), 745-755.

Leslie, L.L. & Rhoades, G. (1995). Rising administrative costs: Seeking explanations. *The Journal of Higher Education, 66*(2), 187-212.

Massy, W.F. & Zemsky, R. (1990). *The dynamics of academic productivity*. Denver: State Higher Education Officers.

Massy, W.F. & Zemsky, R. (1995). *Using information technology to enhance academic productivity*. White paper, EDUCAUSE National Learning Infrastructure Initiative.

Mintzberg, H. (1979). *The structuring of organizations*. Engelwood Cliffs, NJ: Prentice Hall.

Moneta, L. (1997). The integration of technology with the management of student services. *New Directions for Student Services, 78,* 5-16.

Oettinger, A.G. (1969). *Run, computer, run: The mythology of educational innovation.* Cambridge, MA: Harvard University Press.

Paulsen, E. (1997). What does support really cost? *Support Management*, May/June, 14-22.

Peebles, C.S. & Antolovic, L. (1999). Cost (and quality and value) of information technology support in large research universities. *Educom Review*, *34*(5).

Rhoades, G. (1995). Rising stratified administrative costs: Student services' place. In D. Woodard (Ed.), Budgeting as a tool for policy in student affairs. *New Directions for Student Services, 70*. San Francisco: Jossey-Bass.

Rhoades, G. (1997). *Managed professionals: Unionized faculty and restructuring academic labor.* Albany: State University of New York Press.

Rhoades, G. (1998). Reviewing and rethinking administrative costs. In J.C. Smart (Ed.), *Higher education: Handbook of theory and research, volume XIII.* New York: Agathon Press.

Rifkin, J. (2000). *The age of access: The new culture of hypercapitalism, where all of life is a paid-for experience.* New York: J.P. Tarcher/ Putnam.

Slaughter, S. & Leslie, L.L. (1997). *Academic capitalism: Politics, policies, and the entrepreneurial university.* Baltimore: The Johns Hopkins University Press.

Slaughter, S. & Rhoades, G. (2004). *Academic capitalism and the New Economy.* Baltimore: Johns Hopkins University Press.

Smallen, D. (2004). Benchmarks: Helping your president understand IT investments. Presentation at the *EDUCAUSE Annual Conference*, October, Denver, CO.

Strassmann, P.A. (1997). *The squandered computer: Evaluating the business alignment of information technologies.* New Canaan, CT: Information Economics Press.

West, T.W. & Dagigle, S.L. (1997). The 4-D world of higher education: A new context for student support services. *NACADA Journal, 17*(2), 13-22.

Wolf-Wendel, L.E. & Ruel, M. (1999). Developing the whole student: The collegiate ideal. *New Directions for Higher Education, 105,* 35-45.

Chapter V

We've Got a Job to Do – Eventually:

A Study of Knowledge Management Fatigue Syndrome

Richard L. Wagoner
The University of Arizona, USA

Abstract

The implementation of knowledge management systems at universities can be tremendously costly in terms of both human and capital resources. One reason for this cost is the extended time period, generally measured in years, not months, over which they are implemented. This qualitative study presents data on the implementation of one such project at a Research I university in the southwestern United States. The analysis focuses on the concept of knowledge management fatigue syndrome and the increase of technological bloat and academic technocracy as a result of the project.

Introduction

Unforeseen costs and consequences of knowledge management projects at universities frequently are cited in the press. For example, the California State University system began a $400 million overhaul of its administrative information system in 1998. By 2003, there were many questions about the appropriateness and efficiency of the system, and it was clear that it has caused numerous unintended consequences to numerous administrative functions from accounting to student advising (Olsen, 2003). Similarly, an unforeseen problem with a management software upgrade at the University of Florida led to a delay in the processing of paychecks of more than 400 hundred graduate teaching assistants for nearly a month (Carnevale, 2004). These are just two examples of the problems universities face when implementing knowledge management systems. Given such problems, one wonders why a university would choose to implement these large-scale "enterprise" systems and what that process entails. This study illuminates one such implementation demonstrating knowledge management fatigue syndrome (Hakken, 2003). Further, the case study shows how knowledge management implementation can lead to technological bloat and academic technocracy (see Chapter IV).

This chapter is concerned with how such a long term project has affected the units of the university that have been directly involved in the first rounds of implementation, how users have responded to the system, and how the overall structure of units have changed. I will explore these questions by presenting data from e-mails, informal interviews and participant observation in one of the units that have been directly involved with the first round of the system's implementation. Before presenting data, I will discuss the conceptual framework that guided my inquiry.

Conceptual Framework

Many organizations, including universities, in the 1990s chose to use knowledge management systems to improve the efficiency and service quality of their operations. As indicated in Chapter IV, these intended gains in efficiency and quality have remained elusive at best. Why, then, have organizations continued to pursue such goals? The concept of an academic technocracy presented is central to my analysis. In the previous chapter, my colleagues and I discuss three consequences of higher education institutions' efforts to respond to the pressures of academic capitalism and technocracy: the digital restructuring of academic labor, the unproven efficiency argument of academic technology, and the emergence of "technological bloat." Each of these phenomena may be giving rise to an "academic technocracy." In part, this chapter will present data that helps to support these hypotheses, but, more importantly, the chapter will incorporate Hakken's (2003) idea of "knowledge management fatigue syndrome" as an explanation of how an institution-wide knowledge management implementation project could continue for more than a decade.

More than 10 years ago a Research I university in the southwest (Southwest University) proclaimed in a strategic planning document for information technology that it would "leap forward utilizing information technology to fulfill the University's goal of becoming the best land grant institution in the country." Certainly, the goals of this project were grand. While it is not necessarily shocking to see a university desiring to improve its status in the U.S. higher education system, the study university does demonstrate a new dimension in how it intends to create this increased prestige. "Southwest University" intended that an information technology system would create the change needed to achieve the goal. Initially, the implementation process was intended to take only two years; today, after more than a decade, the project has yet to be fully realized. As discussed above, Southwest University envisioned a knowledge management system that would allow students and staff alike the ability to access essential data at any time, from any place. This access, of course, would be attainable because of the Internet and other advanced information technology. Hakken (2003) suggests that the early to mid 1990s was the prime time for such assertions because at that time knowledge management was the "killer application" that would justify the massive organizational investment in automated information technologies: "It [knowledge management] fed (and fed off) the media hype about the 'knowledge society'" (p. 55). In the early 1990s, it was reasonable to assume that a university attempting to improve its ranking would look to an all-encompassing, integrated knowledge management system to achieve its goals, as was the case for Southwest University. Hakken (2003) adds that as a result of the rhetoric of the information society, the New Economy, and globalization, "it was not difficult to convince the typical manager that highly touted information technology, as it got more complex, would provide an infrastructure for 'sharing the knowledge' among distributed staff" (p. 65).

Given the initial enthusiasm and high expectations that a new knowledge management system would solve all of the university's data access, manipulation, storage, and, particularly, integration problems, it is surprising that Southwest did not complete the project reasonably close to its initial two-year timeline. It can be argued, however, that the failure to complete the project in a timely manner was the result of knowledge management fatigue syndrome (Hakken, 2003). As conceptualized by Hakken, knowledge management fatigue syndrome results when enthusiasm for knowledge management solutions evaporates, projects are stalled, and discussion about them is stifled. Hakken offers five technical and conceptual explanations for the emergence of knowledge management fatigue syndrome in organizations: (a) the short shelf life of automated information technology slogans; (b) the overselling of products in a crowded marketplace; (c) continuing technical difficulties in using Web-based interfaces to merge complex information databases; (d) the inappropriateness of IT products designed for one purpose being sold for another; and, (e) the failure of many KM projects to take sufficient account for the social. Generally, technical explanations tend to be more apparent from outside an organization, while the conceptual explanation is more easily viewed from inside an organization.

Hakken's first technical explanation evokes Birnbaum's (2000) concept of management fads in higher education, where higher education institutions adopt popular management trends from the private sector before they have been proven effective. According to Birnbaum, by the time higher education organizations have adopted such practices, private businesses already have moved on to a new strategy because the initial one has lost its luster. In combining these two ideas, the first technical explanation for knowledge management fatigue syndrome would be understood as short-term information technology fads. Hakken (2003) explains that although knowledge itself still might be important to organizations, the term "knowledge management" can cease to have any importance and is, therefore, no longer "fashionable."

Over-competitiveness in a potentially lucrative market defines Hakken's (2003) technical explanation for knowledge management fatigue syndrome. That is, technology firms in their desire to capture market share with the appearance of "cutting edge" technology would simply repackage data and information networking products—without substantive modifications—as "knowledge management" products. Knowledge management in name only, these products were not designed to "address the problems of creating the trust, commitment, and community-life feel of teams/thick knowledge networking, on greater, more complex scales" (p. 65). Once again, this technical explanation for knowledge management fatigue syndrome is also related to Birnbaum's (2000) conception of higher education management fads. Too often higher education organizations seek easy answers in a new management style or system for what is a complex human issue. In the case of knowledge management, this second explanation illuminates the problem that information technology is unable to offer an easy solution to complex problems involving both data and human responses to it and to each other through it. Hakken (2003) suggests that too often inappropriate products were sold as knowledge management solutions.

The third technical explanation is mirrored in the dot com bust at the turn of the century. Initially, the Internet (and networking itself) was championed as the new, efficient model for all businesses and organizations. Unfortunately, that promise was found to be lacking in many instances. One such problem was the relative inability of Web-based products to always integrate large and complex sets of data; let alone doing it instantaneously from remote locations. Each of these three technical explanations, then, gives rise to the fourth. No technology—hardware or software—can be a panacea, the correct and efficient answer to all problems.

Hakken (2003) also offers one overarching conceptual explanation for knowledge management fatigue syndrome: "the failure of many KM projects to take sufficient account for the social" (p. 66). This conceptual explanation is closely related to the second technical explanation. Not only a means to integrating vast amounts of data into useful knowledge, knowledge management systems also need to integrate and coordinate various units in an organization, units which are often territorial about the data they control and the power and leverage such data grants them. To function properly, a knowledge management system must foster a real sense of cooperation and teamwork among units that may have no history of such interactions. This human function is much more complex than even the technical challenges facing knowledge management systems. Through both technical and conceptual frames, Hakken (2003) offers a means to examine the implementation of a fully integrated student information system at Southwestern University.

Data and Methods

This study was a qualitative analysis of the experiences of one student services unit at a southwest university as it worked to implement a new student information software during the 2003/2004 school year. Data for the study included: informal interviews, participant observation, and most importantly for this chapter, analysis of two forms of documents—e-mail communications and historical documents concerning the development of the student information system—based on Hakken's (2003) explanations for knowledge management fatigue syndrome. Initially, I collected unit e-mails regarding the implementation process for a sixth month period, January 2004 – June 2004. After the data were collected, I coded them by Hakken's five explanations—technical and conceptual. I then analyzed the coded e-mail data to look for additional themes based on the challenges presented and discussed in the e-mails (Miles & Huberman, 1984). The informal interviews and my own observation during this period offered a means of triangulation for the e-mail data analysis. That is, the interviews and observations allowed a means of comparison to findings from the document analysis, which increases the validity and reliability of the findings (Creswell, 1994; Marshall & Rossman, 1989; Merriam, 1988) either by confirming patterns found in the document data or presenting contradictions to it.

Analysis

Introduction

Before presenting findings from the study, I will briefly discuss the history of the implementation of the new student information system at "Southwest University." From its inception more than a decade ago, the student information system at Southwest University was intended to be Web-based and available to students, faculty, administration, and any other interested parties. This "anytime, anyplace" access was emphasized as one way that the university could improve its prestige. The new system would integrate data and reporting from all of the university's major academic and administrative units, including student financial aid, student billing, admissions and recruiting, curriculum and registration, and a student Web system.

The student information system project began in the spring of 1994 with the formation of a team to create an information planning study. This initial phase of the project moved quickly, with a report focused on strategic directions for the year 2000 completed by fall of the same year. That fall, a planning team was created to refine the recommendations made in the original strategic directions document. By March of 1996, the planning team had completed more intensive research into the technological needs and aspirations at Southwest. The result of this research phase was to support all of the major recommendations of the original strategic planning document and to suggest that the "initial reengineering" project begin immediately.

Based on evidence found in historical documents, it is unclear what happened with the project between 1996 and 1999. Whatever the cause, there was little action taken during this three-year period. During that period, a request for proposals (RFP) for the new student information software was issued. The RFP stipulated that the module for student prospecting and admissions should be in use by May 1999, with all system components implemented by December 2000. Other than this RFP and its suggested project timeline, there is little evidence of other activity during this period. What is clear is that this timeline was never close to being met.

The university had signed agreements with three corporate partners by March 2000, including a contract with the software company that had won the bid from the RFP. These partnerships were discussed in a March 2000 press release that also claimed that initial testing for the system would begin in July of that year, with complete implementation in three years (spring of 2003). A project newsletter from February 2001 indicated that the spring 2003 timeline was still on target while offering a revision of the project history by indicating that the project had achieved what had seemed impossible "two years ago." This accomplishment was simply completing the initial testing of the system which was still two years from scheduled implementation. The newsletter makes no reference to the RFP which called for full implementation by December of the previous year, let alone the original plan from 1994.

As of the summer of 2004, the project had finally implemented the first of its major modules, but it had not yet completed full implementation. While it may be reasonable to assume that full implementation should be achieved by 2005, that date would be two years after the spring of 2000 projection, five years after the RFP projection, and 11 years after the original strategic plan. The rest of this section seeks to illuminate how this process has taken so long.

Technical Explanantions

In this study, I found ample evidence in both the historical documents about the project and in the e-mails concerned with its implementation of knowledge management fatigue syndrome (Hakken, 2003) and how it indicates increased technological bloat and academic technocracy.

The historical documents associated with the development of the student information system were of particular importance for finding evidence for Hakken's (2003) first technical explanation. In documents from 1994-2000 the need for students, faculty, and staff to access information "at any time and from any place" is repeated in all documents. This 24 hour-a-day, 365 day-a-year need for access to information was one of the mantras of 1990s technology enthusiasts. Certainly it would have been used as a major selling point and justification for any information technology project from the time. Beyond this any time, any place access for those associated with the university, the system was also frequently described as a means to share and capture data with "business partners, high schools, community colleges, the state, and the world." A concern with sharing and capturing data with business partners and, particularly, the world also echo the slogans of the New Economy. Finally, these early project documents also promised "information services [that] are automated, knowledge-based, and easily adapted to changing campus and external requirements." Again, the language of the need for constant adaptation of the New Economy is a central premise of the original project documents. From the beginning of the project, then, it is obvious information technology slogans (fads) were influential in the development of the new student information system project.

The historical documents also show a desire on the part of the university to foster partnerships with major technology corporations, including both hardware and software manufacturers. Specifically, the university created a hardware partnership with a major computer manufacturer and operation software corporation that made changing hardware and software platforms virtually impossible because of the nature of the agreements. It is important to note that neither of these companies was known in any way as leaders in the higher education administrative technology systems market; however, they did offer considerable in-kind donations to the university project, allowing the university to decrease its initial capital investment, while allowing the products of both companies to become entrenched in the system. The other major partnership was with the software company that would provide the actual information system software. While this company had worked with several major research universities, it was relatively small and from the beginning of the project it was clear that its software modules would need tremendous customization to fit the university's needs. All three of the partnerships were critical in the initial development of the student information system project at Southwestern University. But, as predicted by Hakken (2003), none of these partners actually had experience with meeting the exact needs of the university. By partnering with these firms, the university put itself in a position to be constrained by the technical limitations of the partners and to be left without viable alternatives when problems arose because of the nature of these exclusive partnerships.

While historical documents were important in establishing the relevance of the first two technical explanations, the experience of student services system analysts and staff members as documented by e-mail communications demonstrate the importance of the third technical explanation (Hakken, 2003). At the most basic level, the continuing technical difficulties in using Web-based interfaces to merge complex information bases is witnessed by the fact that since 2001 there have been three updates to the system minimum requirements for computer hardware and operation system software needed to use the student information system program. In other words, even at this basic level, the technical requirements for the program remain a moving target, demanding continual investments in technology infrastructure for the university. Related to these basic hardware and software changes, in July 2004 the student information system software, which had yet to go live in all units of the university, itself was upgraded. That is, the student information system, although it was not yet in campus-wide use, was already experiencing upgraded versions.

Beyond these continual changes in infrastructure, there were three general problems during the opening months of 2004 that demonstrate the challenges of using a complex Web-based system. Data has been lost, there have been problems with properly synchronizing data from units and central computing, and there was a potential data security problem. While there were only two instances mentioned in e-mails during the first half of 2004, student data was lost in the information system for unknown reasons. The second incidence left "no audit trail at all." Clearly, lost data, especially when there is no indication why it was lost, is a critical problem in such an information system. While not as critical as lost data, improperly synchronized data files were much more frequent than lost data. According to one e-mail, the system was "experiencing an inordinate number of file synchronization errors." With both data loss and data synchronization problems, data-entry and data-processing staff members were required to retrace steps taken with lost or improperly synchronized files and report to two different system analysts, one for the unit itself and one for the central information technology unit. It would take analysts from both units to correct these problems. Finally, because of the net-based nature of the system, users were instructed to "dump their browser cache (including offline content)" because of a "potential" security "issue." Each of these examples amply demonstrates the challenges of using a Web-based interface to manage complex data files among various organizational units and the labor intensive solutions required to remedy such problems.

The fourth technical explanation for knowledge management fatigue syndrome is closely related to the first three: it is particularly challenging for an organization to easily and successfully implement a new knowledge management system when the system was not originally designed for that purpose. The experience of Southwestern University clearly demonstrates this point. In the historical documents, the student information system was described as a product that already had been developed and implemented at several other higher education institutions and would only need to be customized to fit the university's needs. By the spring of 2004 the system was described in an e-mail from the student services director as "a software product that has not been used anywhere else in the world." So, what had been billed as an off-the-shelf product needing some minor modifications was later trumpeted as a unique system. In the same e-mail, the director also described the information system as having "a mind of its own."

Conceptual Explanation

The evidence from the section above provides a clear picture that each of Hakken's (2003) four technical explanations for knowledge management fatigue syndrome manifested themselves during the implementation of the student information system at Southwest University. Beyond these four explanations, there is evidence of a conceptual explanation at Southwest as well. The need for input and cooperation from all members of the university community was stressed throughout both the historic documents and unit e-mails. The planning stages of the project were highlighted by numerous university-wide committees that were intended to work cooperatively together to create a description of a single information system that would meet the needs of all units.

These cooperative workgroups themselves would certainly be an example of Birnbaum's (2000) management fads, but more importantly they demonstrate how disparate and sometimes competitive units were expected to define and solve problems together throughout the entire process. The historical documents present technical reasons for why this needed to happen, but there was no suggestion as to how members from these units would be able to work together to accomplish the project's goals. The complex social interactions required of such a process are virtually ignored in the historical documents, leaving one to assume that it was a matter of faith that the promise of an advanced knowledge management system would unite all units of the university with a minimum of problems.

By the spring of 2004, one method of achieving unification became clear. In an e-mail, the director of the department in this study explained to all of its members that the systems personnel from the study's department along with their counterparts in both the financial aid and the curriculum and registration offices were "being merged into one Enrollment Management Information unit. In an effort to improve life for all of the systems people and to improve the service [the student information system] provides to the offices." So, what had originally been envisioned as a means to increased cooperation and information distribution between units finally had become a wholesale reorganization of student services departments at Southwestern University. While all data indicates that this was not an intended result of the new student information system, the system itself had caused the reorganization and redefinition of key student services units.

Ironically, the explanation given for the reorganization of the systems personnel emphasizes the centralized power of experts (as in a technocracy) over the independence and interconnectedness of individual units at the university. In the same e-mail, the unit director explains that "the new unit will expand the resources available to address any one problem in any of the units to a group of 20+ people instead of the limited personnel resources of each unit." Essentially, the use of technology and the information available to each unit would now be controlled by one central group whose individual members would have no direct connection or allegiance to any particular student services unit. It is possible to imagine that without personal ties to the needs of individual units, this new systems unit might be concerned with what it deems best from a technological standpoint without considering the human needs of the various student services units it is intended to serve—a serious sociological consequence of the implementation of the new student information system.

Conclusion

In this study, I was concerned with two central questions. First, can Hakken's (2003) concept of knowledge management fatigue syndrome be used to analyze and understand the implementation of the student information system at Southwest University? And, does the implementation of the system show evidence of technological bloat and academic technocracy? The data from this study clearly present evidence of each of Hakken's (2003) descriptions of knowledge management fatigue syndrome and those descriptions provide a means to interpret the long process of the student information system's implementation. Given this evidence one other question arises: Why continue with the project if there is knowledge management fatigue syndrome? The answer to this question is at once simple and complicated. The university is heavily invested in the technology infrastructure demanded by the project—there are tremendous sunk costs. They cannot simply ignore the project; they must forge ahead. At Southwest University, as at other higher education institutions, there may be fatigue, but such labor and capital intensive projects must be completed. Interestingly, there has been little fanfare about the project during the last two school years. A project that was heralded as a means to achieving prominence for the university is now quietly nearing completion. Although understated, the project's implementation has led to a complex reorganization of several student services units into a single enrollment management systems unit.

The new enrollment management systems unit shows evidence of technological bloat and academic technocracy. This new unit is centered on ever-changing advanced technology, and many of its positions which were originally defined as temporary for the project have become institutionalized—clearly a form of bloat. With this new unit, technocrats have assumed an increasingly important role in student services and administrative strategic planning. This increased prominence of "experts" will increase their influence at Southwest—a precursor of academic technocracy.

It is possible to view this technological bloat and academic technocracy as a consequence of knowledge management fatigue syndrome. Because the project has taken an inordinate amount of time to complete, the resulting fatigue has caused institutional stakeholders to be less concerned about efficiency and long-term consequences of decisions than they are about finding ways to complete the project—at 10 years and counting, it is easy to understand why.

References

Birnbaum, R. (2000). *Management fads in higher education: Where they come from. What they do. Why they fail.* San Francisco: Jossey-Bass.

Carnevale, D. (2004). University of Florida's software upgrade delays payday for teaching assistants. *The Chronicle of Higher Education, October 1,* A35.

Creswell, J.W. (1994). *Research design: Qualitative and quantitative approaches.* Thousand Oaks, CA: Sage.

Hakken, D. (2003). "Knowledge management fatigue syndrome" and the practical importance of the cyberspace knowledge question. In D. Hakken, *The knowledge landscapes of cyberspace* (pp. 55-69). New York: Routledge.

Marshall, C. & Rossman, G.B. (1989). *Designing qualitative research.* Newbury Park, CA: Sage.

Merriam, S.B. (1988). *Case study research in education: A qualitative approach.* San Francisco: Jossey-Bass.

Miles, M.B. & Huberman, A.M. (1984). *Qualitative data analysis: A sourcebook of new methods.* Beverly Hills, CA: Sage.

Olsen, F. (2003). Giant Cal State computing project leaves professors and students asking, why? *The Chronicle of Higher Education, January 17,* A27.

Chapter VI

Institutional Research (IR) Meets Knowledge Management (KM)

José L. Santos
University of California–Los Angeles, USA

Abstract

In this study, a selected university's capacity to provide necessary and meaningful information under a KM framework in order to guide it through its current and new and sweeping initiatives was examined. Specifically, information generated from a university-created Study Committee charged with studying the IR function and key units that perform this function were analyzed. A critical analysis of the committee, its methodological approach to studying the IR function, the IR units, and the findings of the committee was conducted. It was found that KM principles were employed in a limited fashion, and that no knowledge creation was taking place. Another key finding was that the primary focus of the committee and a key unit in the IR function were much more concerned about the decision support systems and their ability to provide good data that, in turn, they believed would lead to excellent decision-making.

Introduction

Universities and colleges across the United States have an inherent desire and need to establish data/information systems in order to support and, purportedly, to optimize decision-making. In a changing higher education marketplace, this could not be any more central to universities' ability to compete and self-direct in ways that afford them comparative advantages in such a competitive marketplace. As a result of increasing competition and the creation of the field of knowledge management (KM) in the early 1990s, universities have moved in a direction that captures the cumulative endowment of knowledge that universities hold. In order to remain competitive and strategically contend with market forces, universities are engaged in this fast-moving field of knowledge management in several areas: human resources, organizational development, change management, information technology, brand and reputation management, performance measurement, and evaluation (Bukowitz & Williams, 1999). As the young and popular field of knowledge management continues to emerge, some universities will succeed in aligning their organizational activities with KM principles while others will not; others will only adopt parts of a KM framework. For example, some universities may only develop a capacity for data/information systems but fail to develop capacities in other critical areas that are necessary to interpret information that is created from such systems. That is, they will spend large sums of money building system-wide database warehouses and investing in the people that support such systems but will fail to invest in a commensurate fashion in the human capital needed to interpret the information generated from these systems in order to advise decision makers. Such is the case of Western University, a research extensive university and the subject of analysis for this chapter.

Literature Review

Knowledge Management (KM), a term and movement that was coined by the corporate world (Serban & Luan, 2002), is a fairly young field, yet it has gained momentum in both the public and private sectors. In fact, it is becoming a standard in universities whereby they can harness their cumulative knowledge in order to make informed decision-making by taking data in its raw form and create knowledge for decision-making consumption. KM principles are usually found in institutional research offices at universities, the function of which are explored in the following review of the literature.

Institutional Research (IR)

According to Saupe (1990), "Institutional research is conducted within an institution of higher education to provide information which supports institutional planning, policy formation and decision making" (p. 211). These activities include strategic planning, academic program reviews, environmental scans, enrollment management, faculty productivity analyses, budget analyses, and others. The IR function is a decision support model that is structured around applied and basic research—an approach that involves evaluation, problem identification, action research, and policy analysis.

Typical questions asked in an applied approach may involve questions such as: (1) How many sections of a specific course should be offered? (2) By what amount should tuition rates be increased to produce a target amount of tuition income? (3) What impact would increasing tuition have on access for low-income students? (4) Is attrition a problem at our institution? (5) Are our faculty salaries competitive with those paid by peer institutions? and (6) Are there statistically significant differences in salary between men and women or non-minorities and minorities?

As an evaluation function IR addresses the following areas: (1) information on cost and productivity that underlie judgments about efficiency; (2) information on other characteristics of programs, units, and outcomes that lead to judgments about effectiveness or quality; and (3) information on program purposes, on programs offered by other institutions, on the labor market and on potential demand that produce judgments about the need for academic programs.

Problem identification may surface when looking at results from routine queries or tabulations. For example, in the course of querying data for a routine retention report it might be found that certain racial/ethnic groups experience lower rates of persistence from year to year and overall retention during a six-year time period. An action research approach in IR, perhaps, holds the greatest promise for addressing complex questions such as this. IR offices are where the researcher and client (anyone in the organization) work closely throughout the problem definition, research design, data collection, analysis, interpretation, and implementation phases of the project. That is, the institutional researchers work with units throughout the organization in a consultative manner.

KM Overview

According to Serban and Luan (2002), "KM is the systematic and organized approach of organizations to manipulate and take advantage of both explicit and tacit knowledge, which in turn leads to the creation of new knowledge" (p. 8). On the one hand, Crowley (2000) argues that explicit knowledge is easily codified and transmittable in systematic language. On the other hand, Kidwell, Vander Linde, and Johnson (2000) suggest that tacit knowledge is personal, context-specific, difficult to articulate, and often poorly documented. However, Firestone and McElroy (2003) suggest that the dichotomy between explicit and tacit knowledge does not go far enough. In fact, he suggests that tacit knowledge can be made explicit. However, this goal is difficult to achieve in complex organizations such as higher education institutions. One of the greatest ironies in higher education is that such organizations' core business is to create, transform, and transmit knowledge, yet, they tend to lack organized knowledge management systems that may allow them to optimize institutional decision-making (Kidwell, Vander Linde, & Johnson, 2000; Laudon & Laudon, 1999).

IR Meets KM

Serban & Luan, (2002) present a careful overview of KM in the context of Institutional Research (IR). IR and strategic planning have multiple functions in colleges and universities. Joe Saupe (1990), perhaps, provides us with one of the best descriptions of the nature of institutional research, of its role in institutional governance and of the contributions it can make to the function of postsecondary institutions. J. Fredericks Volkwein (1999) provides us with a comprehensive volume about institutional research. Andrea M. Serban (2002) contributed to our understanding of IR by providing us with a look at the contemporary IR person in the knowledge management context. These foundations of IR literature reveal that, theoretically, IR should use and integrate knowledge management principles in order to provide key decision-making support. Moreover, in order for the IR person to be successful, this person must

Table 1. Purposes and roles of institutional research

	Purposes and Audiences	
	Formative and Internal (for Improvement)	*Summative and External (for Accountability)*
Organizational Role and Culture		
Administrative and Institutional	To describe the institution *IR as information authority*	To present the best case *IR as spin doctor*
Academic and Professional	To analyze alternatives *IR as policy analyst*	To supply impartial evidence of effectiveness *IR as scholar & researcher*
Knowledge Management	To gather and transform data into information and knowledge; to collaborate in the creation and maintenance of an institutional official repository of data, information, and knowledge (i.e., portals); to facilitate the process of knowledge creation, capturing, and sharing. *IR as knowledge manager*	

Adapted from Serban (2002, p. 106) and Volkwein (1999, p. 17)

successfully navigate institutional database systems while providing analytical products to decision-makers.

According to J. Fredericks Volkwein (1999), the IR profession is described as having four faces, wholly based on the people served and the culture of the organization where IR is being executed. The four faces he described center around the notion that IR serves as information authority, spin doctor, policy analyst, and scholar and researcher. Andrea M. Serban (2002) adds a fifth face of IR: knowledge management. She contends that "in a knowledge management environment, these four facets continue to exist; however, they converge into a broader, more integrated dimension—the fifth face of institutional research—IR as knowledge manager" (Serban, 2002, p. 105) (see Table 1).

This fifth face of IR requires different training than that referred to by Saupe and Volkwein. In fact, knowledge management requires people with interpersonal

Table 2. Benefits and challenges of KM

Benefits	Challenges
Access to and sharing of knowledge	Strategy—developing a clear sense of direction
Customer responsiveness	Tacit knowledge and organizational cultures
Better understanding of the organization and its customers	Skills and expertise—developing highly technical skills
Operational efficiencies and decentralization of functions	Cost—human and financial

skills that can negotiate an organization's culture and still have strong skills in business processes and technology.

IR in a KM framework has its benefits and challenges, and, therefore, it is best to understand them. According to Serban (2002), "there are clear advantages of implementing knowledge management frameworks and processes" (p. 108), which are summarized in Table 2.

The benefits to KM clearly outweigh the challenges associated with employing such principles. For example, if an organization has a need to somehow leverage its endowed knowledge base in order to be competitive in the marketplace, this can be accomplished by providing its users access to institutional information so that knowledge creation can occur, thereby, adding to the effectiveness and efficiencies in decision-making. However, when information asymmetry exists, the rewards to this KM benefit fail to materialize. The main challenge arises when the organizational culture is not responsive to sharing information and to knowledge creation. Arguably, organizational culture can be an impediment instead of an enabler and can lead to a lack of clear institutional sense of purpose and direction. Culture as an impediment can be symptomatic of a much greater problem such as leadership void in IR, the

IR function, and senior management. As an enabler, culture can be the key ingredient in a recipe that gives rise to competitive and innovative behavior in the higher education marketplace.

Methods

The purpose of this study is to examine whether or not KM principles as described in the knowledge management field were evident and employed at Western University. This analysis uniquely explores deeply seeded beliefs about what the three departments that make up the IR function believed were their strengths. The analysis is a case study using various qualitative techniques. This approach adds depth of understanding as to how IR and strategic planning departments make use of or do not employ KM principles. We should be cognizant however, that this approach is not absent of its limitations, but it is a powerful approach to provide a fuller picture of how KM is used in practice.

Western University (a pseudonym) was selected for this study because it demonstrated a need to take raw data and move it efficiently and effectively through a continuum, beginning with raw facts and numbers and ending with decision-making and planning decisions. Having such a seamless process would be vital to the institution's ability to compete effectively in the marketplace. Further, an effective flow of data toward knowledge creation would help the university.

Western is a public research extensive university with an approximate student body enrollment of 37,000. This university was selected because its IR and strategic planning function has undergone a transformation with respect to its organizational hierarchy. Prior to the reorganization, the IR function within the organization was spread across three separate units. That is, the three units that make up the IR function at Western were: (1) decision & planning support; (2) institutional planning & special services; and (3) assessment and enrollment research. The decision support unit reported to a director, who in turn reported to a senior administrator that oversaw resources in the academic affairs area. The planning unit was managed by a coordinator who also reported to the senior administrator in the academic affairs area. The assessment and enrollment research unit reported to a different senior administrator in academic affairs, a vice president for undergraduate education (see Figure 1).

Figure 1. Organizational chart pre-reorganization

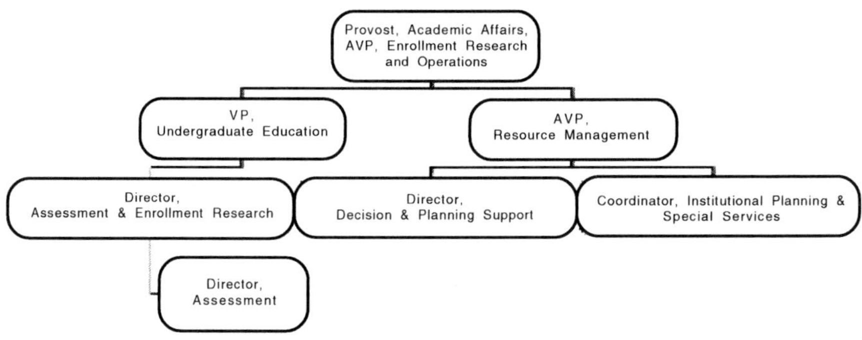

Memoranda and various forms of correspondence from a study committee that was formed to examine the various IR functions and its committee members were analyzed. The author placed himself as a participant observer in some of the data gathering and analysis, providing valuable access to information.

Findings

IR as a Fragmented University Function

In December 2002, a senior and powerful dean at Western sent a letter to the provost expressing concerns about duplication of efforts, resource efficiency, data accuracy, and ambiguity of roles between the decision support, planning, and assessment and enrollment research units. In the dean's letter, strong concerns were expressed about what appeared to be three "organizations doing many of the same things with little coordination."[1] The dean conveyed that "the bottom line that we [the dean speaking on behalf of his college] face at the college level is the lack of accurate information upon which administrators can make informed decisions." Moreover, the dean made a specific recommendation in order to address the concerns expressed by suggesting that the senior administrators who directed these units meet with the academic council in order to address and remedy the dean's concerns. The concerns were never addressed at the venue requested by the dean; however, a team to study these concerns under the backdrop of a new and sweeping university reorganization initiative was formed. This letter would later serve as a significant trigger for the forming of a university-wide study team that came to be known as the "Data, Analysis, and Planning Study Team" (DAPST).

In June 2003, the president of the university and the provost created the new DAPST and charged the newly appointed chief information officer (CIO) to chair the team. According to the chair's invitation letter to prospective DAPST members, "the underlying goal behind this study is to improve the University's ability to bring data and analysis to bear on management decisions." In the same document it was expressed that the "administration is increasingly tied to assessment and projection, both of which are completely dependent on the quality of the data we collect and the analyses we conduct on the data." The chair also found it necessary to illustrate a significant example where IR failure had occurred. The chair stated that the "effort to set future priorities should have involved data-based assessment of academic and support units against a specific set of criteria, and reorganization plans should have been informed by analytic models projecting outcomes and costs for various possible lines of action. The Reorganization Initiative exercises were instead supported largely by such noncomparative narrative records as Academic Program Reviews and constituent testimonials." Clearly, the chair was suggesting that one of the units, if not all, did not successfully coordinate this effort in order to provide the best information possible to inform decision-making for such a high level management initiative.

The DAPST membership was "balanced between academic administration and the various offices that provide support for management through data collection, data warehousing, data analysis, or report generation."[2] Although the DAPST membership did, in fact, comprise a decent balance of academic administrators and various offices of special interest, the attendance of the membership quickly and sharply decreased to just those offices that had a vested interest in the outcome of the "findings" as it pertained to their organizational units.

The Proceedings

At its inception, the chair of the DAPST conveyed a message to its membership that the team would address issues that hindered Western University's ability to respond to sweeping institutional initiatives. It appeared that the problem identification rested in the notion that there was a broken IR function—a function that was unable to mine data elements, resulting in a lack of knowledge creation for tactical and strategic decision-making. The findings from the proceedings and behavior inferred from various membership correspondences suggest that some members agreed with the perceived problem definition and wanted to effectively address it while others dug in, circled the IR wagons and went to great lengths to preserve the status quo.

Digging In

Examining public electronic e-mails, facsimiles, and other documents such as correspondence between the DAPST membership itself, between membership and the chair, and the like suggests that there was a clear struggle among the members who believed that creating data through an existing decision support system known as the Integrated Information Warehouse (IIW) is knowledge creation whereas others believed that such processes are a good starting point for knowledge creation by fully integrating the analysis of such data.

The IIW is a data warehouse that contains Western University's related historical, census, and start-of-business-current-week data, and it is maintained by the decision and planning support department's servers from which internal and external reports can be generated. Census data comes from snapshots taken of operational data at the same time each year. Historical and Census data are used for viewing trends and the state of the institution at the same time each year. The Census data are taken from Western's University Information System (UIS). The UIS is a university-wide data warehouse with start-of-business-current-day data from Western's financial, personnel, space, sponsored project, student, and other operational systems. The UIS is maintained by Western University's computing center that reports to the CIO.

Before the first meeting of the DAPST, there were questions from the three units being examined. For example, the senior executive who oversaw the decision support unit and the planning unit suggested that the provost was interested in hiring an external consultant to review the roles of the three units, a suggestion that was at odds with the articulated function of DAPST. In fact, language was used that appeared to undermine the DAPST chair, the charge of the study team, and the team's eventual findings. When employees of those units raised questions, the executive withdrew from the desire to hire an outside consultant.

The question remains as to what problem this executive and/or the provost was trying to address that was either different from or similar to that of DAPST. Moreover, it is possible that this interest had nothing to do with knowledge management and how to effectively deliver quality information and quality analysis of the information. Rather it can be construed as an exercise to signal to staff in the decision support and planning departments that this executive retained control of these two units and the likely outcome of any reviewing committee.

A member of the decision support unit and a member of the DAPST raised questions and introduced information that might have been helpful to the direction of the study team. This person suggested that to effectively address IR needs there needed to be a focus on "what we should be doing." Moreover, through an electronic correspondence with the chair, this member asked the chair if the team could benefit from viewing the IR function through a systems and integrated approach. This person believed that "the lack of understanding, coordination, and cooperation on data, analysis, and planning from a systems view is a key piece of the puzzle on our suboptimal performance in these critical areas. Can we gain from taking a systems view and creating integrated, holistic, data, analysis, and planning function for our institution?" This was a powerful set of statements not only because the chair responded favorably to the suggestion but also because the DAPST had not previously considered an institutional information systems paradigm.

The decision support unit director highlighted his unit's most significant accomplishment—the Integrated Information Warehouse (IIW). The goals listed by this unit are consistent with KM principles as the unit sought to provide timely and accurate information and tried to be the central repository of institutional data for decision-making. This unit saw itself as playing a role in university "perception management." That is, the unit engaged in the IR role Volkwein (1999) called "spin doctor." Also, this unit, through its direction, seemed to focus much of its energies on data inputting, data editing for the sake of accuracy, and internal and external reporting. It expended its resources around the IIW, as the IIW was the perceived data creation generator and the means for better decision-making. The assumption was that the IIW, with its five gigabytes (GB) plus of data added annually, would somehow yield better decision-making. That is, great data equals great decision-making. The projected public discourse that the director of this unit propagated for DAPST can be summarized in three areas: goals, functions, and systematic information (see Table 3). However, in actuality, the unit diverged from its publicly stated

Table 3. Decision support goals, functions and systematic information

Goals	Functions	Systematic Information
Provide accessible information Provide accurate, timely, and comprehensive information for varied users Help the University understand and interpret its environment, self, and options on critical information	Collect missing information Address key university questions Improve perceptions of the university—"perception management" Provide valid and external reports	IIW—10 plus years of consistent data; 36 GB, add 5 GB more a year Clean, code, and compile system data for ease of use Census and other standard information for most university-wide, non-accounting reporting Flexible web answers to campus questions—X pages a year

rhetoric in a number of significant ways. For example, although the unit expressed the goal to "help the university understand and interpret its environment, self, and options on critical information," no evidence is found that administrators with decision-making authority on critical issues used any information from the IIW that strengthened their decision-making ability. As a result, the fact that this unit had been relatively absent in its provision of key university information also suggests that it had failed in one of its major functions of "address[ing] key university questions." The question does remain as to why this unit was not approached on key university questions on something as central as the university-wide reorganization plan that took place before the formation of DAPST.

Another example rests in the assertion that this unit through its IIW provides "flexible Web answers to campus questions…" This is referring to its ability to provide Web portals for various users (i.e., administrators, university community, and external community). The unit provided Web portals and for the most part one could retrieve information quickly. However, power users found it impossible to access the source codes. That is, in most cases a power user at Western was using Oracle-based SQL or a relational database application such as ACCESS or BrioQuery. These users tried to access the data through

Table 4. The domain of analysis, planning, and assessment

Data Collection	Data Administration/ Management	Reporting/Basic Data	Analysis/ Planning	Assessment/ Evaluation
Admissions	Loading Databases (university database, integrated information warehouse[IIW] maintained by the decision support unit)	IPEDS	Enrollment	General Education Program
Curriculum & Registration	Edit Checks	Governing Board	Budget/Costs	Academic Programs
Financial Aid	Database Maintenance	State Planning Office	Faculty/Staff	Student Development
Bursar	Hardware/ Software	State Legislative Budget Committee	Space	Teaching Evaluation
College & Academic Departments	Documentation	AAUDE	Capital Projects	General Program Evaluation
HR	Software Training	Campus (APRs, Deans, Departments)	IT	Personnel Evaluation
Budget Office	Training on use of data	Ad hoc service requests	College & Academic Departments	Accountability for Governing Board & Accreditation Board
VP Research	Integration w/Subordinate and Shadow Systems	Fact Book/ websites	University Planning Advisory Group Support	Test Scoring & Analysis
Facilities Mgmt	Web (IIW) queries	Public Records	Operating Plan for State Legislative Budget Committee	N/A

the Web portal, the IIW returned data in HTML format and downloadable EXCEL files, but the user was unable to identify the tables and table elements that were used. In other words, one would have to call the unit to request the source code in SQL. For an administrator, this may not be as important but for a support systems analyst that is supporting an administrator at the college level this is extremely important because, in most cases, the source code needs to be modified to fit the specific use.

So how did the assessment and enrollment research unit engage in pubic discourse and assert its projected domain of expertise? The director of the assessment and enrollment research put together a list of activities that were being performed on campus, attempting to make a clear demarcation of some of the questions that were going to be addressed by the DAPST. It was a list of different IR activities that were being performed throughout Western but made no attempt to affix any units to the activities. More importantly, this list took the form of a process-related exercise rather than an outcomes approach that would suggest a rational assignment of activities within domains and the units that would carry out such activities. Moreover, with respect to the assessment and enrollment research unit, examination of this list suggests that this director was not going to overtly project the unit's role within the IR function. Instead, it appears that this director placed the enrollment activity in his purview, in the analysis/planning domain. This is important because it suggests that this director appears to have valued this domain or may have had some reason to believe that administrators valued this domain for knowledge creation and enhanced decision-making. The list of activities is summarized in Table 4.

By the time the planning unit made its case, it had become clear that the discussions in the study team were about data, quality, and the ability to inform decision-making—and, not much about using or not using KM principles in the IR function. The planning department introduced a list of activities that it felt were in its domain and in the course of generating the list aggressively projected the capacity for certain domains. This unit went to great lengths to suggest that in addition to coordinating a university strategic plan, it performed activities designed to inform management. In other words, the unit, through its coordinator, tried to convey that it was central to management decision-making and, thereby, they created knowledge pursuant to KM principles.

In actuality, this unit indicated that it provided certain types of products, but these were not delivered. For example, this unit indicated that it provided quantitative and qualitative analysis. When the products that have been created by this unit were examined no products would fit those criteria. Instead, the five-year strategic plan, summaries of colleges' annual reports, and other similar products were created without any qualitative and/or quantitative techniques. This unit also listed a "departmental profile" as a key accomplishment. Indeed, this product was used for key decision-making as it contained information valuable to the discussion of departmental eliminations and/or mergers. However, it is important to note that this departmental profile is the same report that attracted criticism from and was referred to by the influential dean that triggered the formation of the DAPST in the first place. The dean had indicated that the departmental profile was flawed. The activities of the planning unit can be summarized in Table 5 in the following way by their respective general function.

The findings suggest that the vested units were signaling within the organization how they wanted to be perceived, and what capacities they believed they possessed. This institutional maneuvering resulted in a carefully orchestrated dialogue that would, basically, preserve existing domains and spheres of influence. Interestingly, no final report was generated by the DAPST and none of the committee's findings were disseminated to the university community as promised by the provost and president. Instead, the chair of the DAPST electronically circulated a draft of the final report[3] to its membership soliciting input. The question remains as to why such a high-level review team was charged with studying a generally understood and important function of the university and why the findings were not disseminated as is normally expected

Table 5. Planning activities

Institutional	Planning	Analysis	Ad hoc
Summarize college annual reports Consult & review units' academic program reviews Coordinate accreditation activities & reports	Staff the University Planning Advisory Group Prepare the five-year strategic plan	Quantitative/ qualitative	Departmental Profile

when a task force study team is assembled at a public university. Perhaps the report regarding the process and products of information management was considered too divisive for general review.

The Elusive Final Report

The draft of the final report revealed some very important social aspects. The report was organized into six key thematic groups: trust, culture, awareness, access, questions, and resources. Culture and awareness are the central themes of interest as these were the two areas where most of the conversations centered; whereas the other four themes were given cursory consideration. In the report much space was dedicated to these themes and not much was given to the delivery of services from an IR function in order to take data, create knowledge, and manage knowledge as Serban (2002) suggests is the fifth face of IR. The culture theme revealed:

The organizational culture does not include consensus on the importance of data or acceptance of shared responsibility for data quality. Complaints about errors in data breed cynicism without feeding back into improved practice. We not only lack shared definitions and standardized metric; we also seem to lack an interest in developing them.

Even when discussing culture it appeared that the focus immediately gravitated toward inputs in knowledge creation—data and data quality. The awareness theme revealed:

Data providers must be aware of the data needs of the colleges, and the colleges must be aware of what is available—what data sources, what tools, and what expertise. Everyone must understand what numbers in datasets mean and how they are meant to be used. We need heightened awareness of the "unintended consequences" of measurement and a more thoughtful approach to choice of metrics.

The report focused on one aspect of the battery of skill sets required of a modern day institutional researcher—advanced technical skills centered on data, data definitions, and a heightened awareness in decision rules when querying datasets. Unfortunately, this theme overlooks the other important prerequisite skills required of today's institutional researcher—institutional consultant, policy analyst, and knowledge contributor and creator.

Noticeably absent from the report was any analysis of any data that examined the veracity of the products that the respective IR units under study indicated they provided and, moreover, the quality of such products. The report made some references to the original charge of the DAPST with an astonishing shift in language, stating that "excellence in administration depends on the quality of our decision-making, including the quality of our decision support systems." In other words, the chair conflated good data support systems with quality decision-making. This is a significant finding because it suggests that data support systems such as the IIW are a means to and end rather than a foundational starting point for knowledge creation. Perhaps Patrick Terenzini (1993) put it best when he described three tiers of intelligence—defining the nature of institutional research and its prerequisite skills, whereby technological skills is the lowest of the three tiers. According to Terenzini, "this form of intelligence is foundational: by itself, however, it is of little value." (p. 9). What is more, the report made no recommendations for reorganization of the units that were studied. Notwithstanding, the units were reorganized approximately six months after the report was drafted. Remarkably, in the absence of a public dissemination of the DAPST findings, the reorganization further contributed to an organizational culture of misinformation.

Study Team & Its Findings: Do KM Principles and Practices Emerge?

There is no conclusive evidence from the data that was analyzed that KM principles were being employed in a thoughtful manner at Western University. To the contrary there is ample evidence to suggest that the IR function is fixed in data and data systems and has yet to make the necessary transformation along the KM continuum to knowledge creation. In short, at Western, technology is viewed as the panacea for good decision-making. Moreover, from the draft report itself there are no acknowledgments or recommendations addressing policy analysis and knowledge driven activities for better decision-making. However, arguably, the most significant finding is the units that made up the IR function and were under review underwent major reorganization six months after the report was drafted. This was unexpected given that the report

Figure 2. Organizational chart post-reorganization

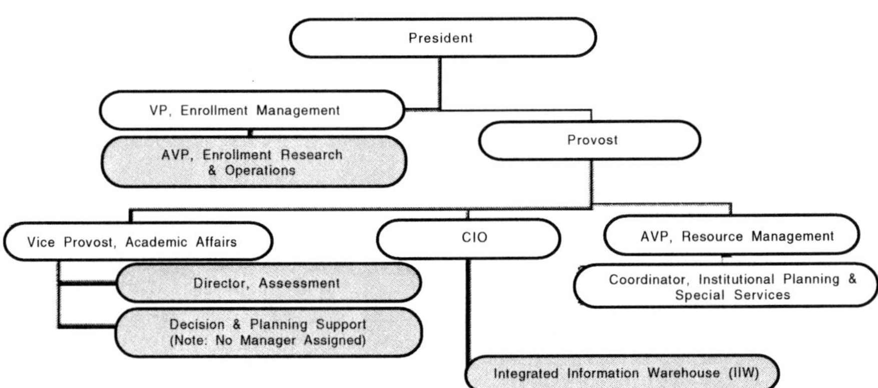

was neither publicly disseminated nor was anyone seemingly following through on any set of recommendations that would have been advanced from the draft version of the report. The question still remains as to why these units were reorganized. Certainly, there must be other private reasoning that is not captured in the data analyzed.

As a result of the reorganization, decision and planning support, institutional planning, analysis and special services, and assessment and enrollment research were separated into four distinct units reporting to three different senior administrators. The new units are as follows: decision and planning support, institutional planning, analysis and special services, assessment, and enrollment research and operations. They all remained in the academic affairs (provost's office) except for enrollment research and operations who now reported to a newly created area called enrollment management (president's office) (see Figure 2). Remarkably, in this reorganization, not a single person that was part of the original IR units under review was fired. However, two key individuals resigned and the director along with two other technical staff of the decision and planning support unit along with the IIW responsibilities were transferred out of that unit and into the CIOs area. One individual was a key architect of the IIW in the decision and planning support unit and the other was the administrator of the UIS. In addition, the former director and two systems support individuals of the decision and planning unit were reassigned to work with the IIW. In short, there was a shuffle in the organizational hierarchy with two key resignations and the transferring of a key director and other staff, none of which would be expected given the DAPST findings.

Conclusion

Western University is an example of an organization that only adopted parts of KM principles by developing the capacity for data/information systems through its IIW but failed to develop capacities in other critical areas necessary to interpret and create knowledge. That is, Western spent much of its energy discussing how to improve upon its data, data quality, and data access and invested in the people that support such systems but failed to invest in a commensurate fashion in the human capital needed to transform the information generated from these systems into knowledge in order to advise decision makers.

The DAPST and its draft report illustrate that KM principles were not at the core of its values. Its myopic focus on such a small part of KM rendered its team's report meaningless in helping to advance knowledge creation for enhanced decision-making, especially during a time when Western needed critical IR to help senior management navigate through its new and sweeping objectives and a changing higher education marketplace.

Recommendations

The DAPST team would had been better served if they focused their attention on: (1) developing a critical perspective of university colleges and departments performance and plans that are informed by a deep understanding of each unit's strategic objectives and overall operating environment; (2) executing consultative projects in close collaboration with various units to help address administrative and financial management questions and/or opportunities; (3) examining important university-wide academic/financial/physical planning issues and/or opportunities by working closely with units as well as by drawing on external data as appropriate and necessary to inform internal review processes; (4) collecting critical academic/financial/physical information from across the university for the purposes of not only supporting internal decisions-making but also to ensure timely and accessible responses to requests for data from regulatory agencies, peer institutions, and other interested parties; and (5) moving the IR function beyond information authority and into the realm of IR as policy analysis.

References

Bukowitz, J.R. & Williams, R.L. (1999). *The knowledge management fieldbook.* Upper Saddle River, NJ: Financial Times, Prentice Hall.

Firestone, J.M. & McElroy, M.W. (2003). *Key issues in the new knowledge management.* Amsterdam: Knowledge Management Consortium International Press.

Kidwell, J.J., Vander Linde, K.M., & Johnson, S.L. (2000). Applying corporate knowledge management practices in higher education. *EDUCAUSE Quarterly, 4,* 28-33.

Laudon, K. & Laudon, J. (1999). *Management information systems-Organization and technology in the networked enterprise.* Englewood Cliffs, NJ: Prentice Hall.

Saupe, J.L. (1999). The functions of institutional research. In M.W. Peterson (Ed.), *ASHE reader on planning and institutional research* (pp. 211-223). Needham Heights, MA: Pearson Custom Publishing.

Serban, A.M. (2002). Knowledge management: The "Fifth Face" of institutional research. *New Directions for Institutional Research, 113,* 105-111.

Terenzini, P.T. (1993). On the nature of institutional research and the knowledge and skills it requires. *Research in Higher Education, 34*(1), 1-10.

Volkwien, J.F. (1999). The four faces of institutional research. What is institutional research all about? A critical and comprehensive assessment of the profession. *New Directions for Institutional Research, 104.* San Francisco: Jossey-Bass.

Whitley, M.A., Porter, J.D., & Fenske, R.H. (1992). *The primer for institutional research.* Tallahassee, FL: Association for Institutional Research.

Endnotes

1 Letter from senior and influential dean to Western University provost requesting that the provost convene a high level meeting to discuss a more effective way to coordinate the three units that make up the IR function dated December 4, 2002.

2 Letter sent to prospective members of the Study Committee by the CIO and chair of the Study Committee dated June 10, 2003.

3 Draft Final Report electronically sent to the Study Committee members by the CIO and chair of the Study Committee dated December 2003.

Section III

Knowledge Management of Teaching and Learning

Chapter VII

Revealing Unseen Organizations in Higher Education: A Study Framework and Application Example

Lucie Sommer
The University of Colorado, USA

Abstract

Structuration theory, which examines the relationship between local and institutional structures, and organizational theory specific to the higher education setting, are utilized to formulate an analytical framework appropriate for "reading" educational technologies as social phenomena. Wanda Orlikowski's (2000) technology-in-use model, (a contemporary revision of Poole and DeSanctis' [1990] adaptive structuration model) and Burton Clark's (1984) taxonomy of higher education organization are applied as the foundation for the inquiry.

Introduction

In the higher education setting, changes in management practices, organizational structure, and communication technologies have provoked considerable speculation about the future of academic institutions. Many experts are asking if the centuries-old traditions of the university system will survive the information age, and if not, what the new paradigms for higher learning will be (Brown & Duguid, 1996; Duderstadt, 2000; Frye, 2002; Johnstone, 2002; Katz, 2002; Strauss, 2002; Wulf, 2003). Though often presented as vague forms that we will discover far out into some distant future, 21st century higher learning organizations already exist. Discerning their forms, however, can be challenging. Adopting a new conception of technology—one that highlights its dynamic relationship with social interaction—may help to reveal largely "unseen" higher education organizations.

Course management (CM) systems are a prime example an emerging form of higher education that has not yet been recognized as such. Generally, those who have adopted these technologies understand them as tools that facilitate communication within and between existing organizations, rather than as new forms of HE enterprise. If we consider the possibility that these technologies may represent not only new technologies but also new systems of social organization, then the dramatic increase in adoption of CM systems warrants close attention.

CM uses crosses the boundaries of diverse academic disciplines, widely divergent service sectors, and international borders. Over 50 different CM systems are currently being employed in colleges and universities—the leading system in the industry serving over 5.6 million users (Rosen, 2002)—and more systems are on the way. For instance, MIT and a select group of partners have been hard at work developing the next generation CM system: the Open Knowledge Initiative (OKI) and the companion Open Courseware (OCW) project. If we are to understand these new technologies as emerging organizational systems, rather than simply as technologies that are "external" to existing systems, we can understand MIT's work as a potentially critical influence in the current restructuring of higher education. Indeed, the group has openly stated their intention for these systems to have both a profound and far-reaching effect on the future of HE (OKI Web site, 2003). Given this goal, the development of these technologies should be accompanied by careful analysis. This paper aims to contribute to this imperative by proposing a study framework for analyzing higher education technologies and by applying this framework to MIT's emerging CM system.

I begin my discussion of MIT's system by laying the theoretical foundation necessary to consider their CM system as an organizational and social phenomenon. Reframing the technologies in this way allows me to then explore the reflexive relationship that exists between these new organizing systems and the traditional organizational structure of HE. I employ a structurational perspective of technology (Orlikowski, 2000; Poole & DeSanctis, 1990) as well as a classic understanding of HE structure (Clark, 1986) to support my investigation of MIT's system. I conclude that MIT's technologies not only have the potential to reify familiar HE forms but they may create new, controversial forms as well. A major goal of my analysis is to reveal the existence of these heretofore "invisible" organizational structures in hopes that such awareness will help to widen the participation in future discourse and decision making about the HE organizations of tomorrow.

Background

Technology as Message Transmission Tool

CM systems can be understood, first, in terms of their technical characteristics. Most systems are comprised of software templates and server software that are designed to support administrative, teaching, and learning communication via electronic means. These templates can be customized according to individual as well as institutional needs. Generally, they are distributed through either client-based or commercial-based servers, using companion CM systems software. The networking characteristics of CM systems and the technical properties associated with information distribution have greatly influenced popular conceptions of these systems.

Indeed, the view that CM systems represent a suite of message transmission tools strongly dominates the discussion about these educational technologies. This perspective is prevalent in the educational technology literature, where CM systems are routinely conceptualized as "containers" providing communication "access" to teaching and learning participants and to educational experiences (Carmean & Haefner, 2002). This understanding is common in other discussion forums as well. Recently a group of experts from myriad perspectives—from information technology, administration, research, and teaching—gathered on "Tech Talks" (a Web-based seminar addressing educational technology issues) to discuss CM systems (2002). Despite their diverse professional backgrounds, all the participants discussed CM systems as communication "tools."

The ontological assumptions that form the basis of the technology-as-tool perspective are rarely examined. Analyzing these assumptions reveals that the message transmission view rests on the notion that it is possible to separate technology from its social context (Jackson, 1996). Closely related to this idea is the assumption that these systems are neutral in terms of their impact on the communication process. The technology-as-tool view understands CM system participants as tool wielders, employing inert electronic instruments to serve their information transmission needs. Faculty members are information senders, students are receivers, and IT personnel manage the transmission exchange. In sum, separating technology from its social context encourages stakeholders to understand CM systems as mechanical vehicles that impartially transmit messages.

Technology as Social Process

An alternative perspective is to view CM systems not as neutral, context-independent tools but rather as socially embedded processes. From this perspective, these technologies are not vehicles for message transmission that exist independent from their environment, but rather fluid, communication phenomena, responsive to and constitutive of the organizations in which they exist. This perspective does not deny the understanding that CM technologies are technical tools, rather it suggests that they are, in addition, communication systems that organize (and are organized by) social interaction. From this view, technical properties such as software configurations and information protocols serve to define what is possible and what is not possible in a given communication process. In the case of CM systems, technical specifications determine the possibilities for teaching/learning activity, they:

- Guide the structural conventions for teaching/learning interaction
- Define conversation spaces for particular kinds of teaching/learning interaction

- Define who can initiate and participate in teaching/learning conversation
- Shape the ordering and sequencing of teaching/learning interaction
- Control and manage the flow of information and interchange
- Permit or deny access to teaching/learning information

From this perspective, the technical specifications are understood as integral to (rather than separate from) social process.

Different Perspectives, Different Lines of Inquiry

Regarding CM systems as message transmission tools that can be separated from the organizations that employ them permits certain questions and prevents various others. For instance, this view enables researchers to examine the changing functionality of various versions of containers as is popular in current educational technology literature. Issues of technical management and integration also follow naturally from this perspective (Luker, 1999; Twigg, 1994). These issues are often related to questions about adoption and resistance patterns or to inquiries as to how CM system "tools" are being or might be used (Carmean & Haefner, 2002; Frederickson, Clark, & Hoehner, 2002; Young, 2002). Rarely, however, does the tool-based perspective intersect with concerns about organizational process. When it does, it is usually with a functional (rather than a constitutive) understanding of the relationship.

In much of the literature investigating higher education management practices, the relationship between technology and organization is generally understood as both unidirectional and instrumental. For instance, an article appearing in the *Journal for Knowledge Management* claims that "new technologies have been developed to better enable the management of knowledge" (Ives, Torrey, & Gordon, 1998, p. 269). Likewise, early communication studies that explored the relationship between work and technology were fairly strategic in nature, aiming to discover ways in which new technologies might improve specific work tasks and processes (Contractor & Eisenberg, 1990: Nass & Mason 1990) as well as change management practices (Sproule & Keisler, 1991; Zuboff, 1998.)

Clearly, the transmission perspective encourages as well as discourages certain types of questions. Likewise, if we take the view that CM technologies are communication systems that cannot be separated from their social contexts, a different set of issues emerge. One immediate consequence of looking at technology and communication in a parallel, relational view is that the social context for these phenomena becomes more pronounced. For instance, both Bijker's (1987) ideas on social constructivism and Fulk's (1990) social influence theory highlight the relationship between technology and social contexts. This shift in emphasis enables them to make some innovative conceptual moves, and consequently, produces a novel set of research interests.

Gidden's structuration theory (1984) also strongly influences the nature of questions considered by those interested in technology. Central to Gidden's theory are his unconventional ideas about structure. In his view, there are no structures—technological or otherwise—that exist in and of themselves. Rather, structures are the "rules" and the "resources" that individuals create through the process of human interaction. Structures are patterns, but not fixed patterns. While Giddens himself did not directly address communication practices relating to technology, many find his ideas about structure to be highly relevant to the subject (Barley, 1986; Beninger, 1990; Orlikowski, 2000; Poole & DeSanctis, 1990). For these scholars, technologies are structures as Giddens describes them: socially malleable rules and resources that shape and are shaped by human communication interaction.

By highlighting social interaction, the technology-as-social-process perspective puts a "face" to previously inert "technical" issues, emphasizing that human beings are central to the organization of technology structures—and they organize them in the context of specific social settings. Specific people, in particular cultural contexts, design software interfaces and architectural infrastructures. Design structures influence the interactions in which technology users engage. In other words, technology designs have communication implications for the people who interact with them. Users also make their own decisions about how to integrate technology into existing organizations; these are largely guided by their own cultural assumptions. "Humanizing" technology structures in this way allows one to take a closer look at how individual needs and interests may intersect with technology structures. In sum, emphasizing an inseparable relationship between social and technological structuring processes opens important new doors of inquiry.

Issues, Controversies, Problems

A logical next step is to examine the inquiry of those who adopt a technology-as-process perspective in their study of higher education technology and to apply these ideas to our study of MIT's course management system. Who is considering the emerging technologies in the higher education sector from this framework and what have they found? A survey of educational technology literature reveals that although there are a handful of experts who have begun to highlight the importance of the social context of technology (Katz, Goldstein, & Dobbin, 2001; Smith, 2002), more generally, it is the absence of direct discussion about the relationship between technology and organization that is striking. In terms of the literature, it appears that those who are writing specifically about CM systems in the higher education setting greatly favor the technology-as-tool perspective.

A closer look, however, reveals that, in fact, a great deal of discourse involving the social nature of technology is taking place. Unfortunately, very few are able to recognize it as such. To do so, readers and listeners of educational technology discourse must adopt an interpretive framework that "sees" and "hears" the social dimension of what are often understood as purely "technical" conversations. For instance, in numerous educational technology journals, we find plenty of discussion concerning the architectural design of educational technologies in general, and of CM systems in particular. These highly technical conversations are being carried out by information technology experts across the nation and are generally offered and interpreted from a technology-as-tool perspective. I suggest that these technical discussions can (and should) also be interpreted from the technology-as-social-process framework.

From this perspective, the technical experts designing these systems are deliberating not just technical design structures but social processes as well—processes that will, in turn, have profound affects on the possible interactions that administrators, teachers, and learners may have. An important consideration about the conversations currently taking place about HE organization is the limited viewpoint that informs them. Those engaged in discussing these topics are mainly those who posses advanced technical knowledge of educational technology systems and can recognize and use the appropriate professional vocabulary. The cultural framework for these professionals is clearly different from many others who work in HE. Furthermore, public discussion about how the work of these professionals relates to the organizational future of HE is noticeably absent in the discourse about the architecture of these systems. To ensure that next generation HE structures are useful and desirable, more careful consideration of this heretofore "invisible" discourse is warranted.

Unfortunately, few of us know how to approach these conversations from a more inclusive and more productive standpoint. Theoretically sound yet practically useful frameworks for engaging in this kind of consideration are needed. Combining the work from several different theorists, I propose such a framework in the following sections. My goal in proposing and engaging this framework is to assist in illuminating this hard-to-recognize conversation and to encourage the possibility of broad participation as this discourse continues. It is my hope that greater attention to the social nature of CM systems and more diverse participation in future discussions will increase the likelihood of valuable and equitable HE structures for tomorrow.

Solutions and Recommendations

A Hybrid Model for Studying HE Technology as Social Process

In formulating an analytical framework appropriate for "reading" educational technologies as social phenomena, I borrow elements from two types of theory: structuration theory that examines the relationship between technology and interaction structures and organizational theory that is specific to the higher education setting. I adapt Wanda Orlikowski's (2000) technology-in-use model, (a contemporary revision of Poole and DeSanctis' [1990] adaptive structuration model) and Burton Clark's (1984) taxonomy of higher education organization as the foundation for my inquiry.

Orlikowski's approach to studying the relationship between technology and organization proceeds by first analyzing "potential" social and technological structures, then observing technology use, and finally, looking for ways in which potential structures are "enacted". Her analytical model aims to simultaneously consider:

1. The potential structuring elements of social systems (including, but not limited to those related to technology) and
2. The enacted structural outcomes produced by human engagement with (or "use" of) potential structures, in other words, "technologies-in-practice."

Figure 1.

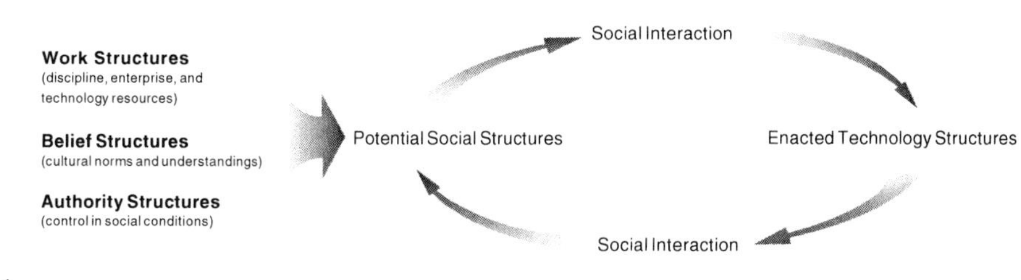

Whereas Orlikowski chooses to emphasize the enactment dimension in her analysis, I foreground the potential structuring elements specific to the HE context.[1] Like Orlikowski, I examine three different structural "dimensions" through which organizational rules and resources are enacted in MIT's CM system. I adapt the dimensions she identifies, however, to more closely reflect the particulars of HE context. I rely on Burton Clark, an expert on HE organization, to guide the formulation of these dimensions. Though his classic study is somewhat dated, *The Higher Education System, Academic Organization in Cross-National Perspective* (1983), it still represents a valuable taxonomy for understanding HE organization. In it, Clark examines three dimensions of organizational structure: (1) work (which he identifies as knowledge-based), (2) belief, and (3) authority. Marrying Orlikowski's considerations of structure with Clark's dimensions of organization produces a hybrid analytical framework.

Employing this framework for my analysis of MIT's CM system, I first discuss the potential structural properties relating to the technology, illuminating them by examining Clark's three structural dimensions of higher education organization. I then examine how the potential structures that Clark outlines might be reified (and adapted) through social interaction processes, in other words, how they may be enacted as "technologies-in-practice" (Orlikowski, 2000). My purpose in applying this framework to a tangible case study is two-fold: to provide a technology-as-process reading of MIT's important technology development and to assess the strengths and weaknesses of the proposed study framework.

Case-Study Application: Part 1

The Potential Structural Properties of HE's Knowledge-Based Work

Clark (1983) asserts that in order to appreciate the unique organizational structure of higher education, we must begin by considering the special nature of "knowledge itself" which he describes as "the prime material around which activity is organized" in the higher education setting (p. 6). He contends that the form of HE organization is closely tied to its knowledge-based endeavors: "varying efforts to discover, conserve, refine, transmit and apply knowledge" (p. 11). In understanding the potential structuring properties related to knowledge-based work, (such as disciplines, enterprises and technology), we must first acknowledge their intimate relationship with the ephemeral "material" of knowledge. Equally important is to recognize that the "activity" Clark describes is communication activity. Keeping these ideas in mind, one can examine Clark's findings along the lines of Orlikowski's framework, with the purpose of uncovering potential structuring rules and resources that might influence technology structure.

Clark found the knowledge-based activities of HE to be consistently organized into study institutions, or enterprises, and into knowledge specialties, or disciplines. Enterprise structures, extremely diverse in nature, have traditionally been localized and contained in specific geographic areas. In contrast, disciplinary forms cut across enterprise boundaries. The discipline mode of organization links together communities of experts all over the world. Both the disciplinary and the enterprise structures that Clark describes can be seen as possible structuring elements in MIT's CM system. It is important to emphasize that each of these elements are far from fixed and stable. Rather, they are continually evolving, themselves being enacted in new and different ways. Clark highlights the dynamic nature of HE rules and resources throughout his work, reminding us that both disciplinary and enterprise structures are growing ever more diverse. This same dynamism is true of the next dimension I will explore—that of belief structures.

Normative Rules as Potential Structural Properties

In analyzing the potential structural properties that are associated with normative rules in the HE setting, Clark's study again provides valuable insight. In his estimation, the normative or "symbolic side of organization... is uncommonly potent" in the knowledge-based organizations he studies (p. 7). Clark saw the norms and values that influence organizational form as being intimately linked with other structural dimensions; his approach to describing normative (or symbolic) structures reflects this belief. He examines belief norms according to the patterns he identified in terms of knowledge-based work structures, looking at four basic types of cultural norms that pervade the academic setting: the culture of the discipline, the culture of the enterprise, the culture of the profession, and the culture of the system (which he describes in terms of national traditions).

Clark notes profound differences in beliefs and values between each of the individual disciplines, an argument that is strongly supported by Tony Becher's (1989) in-depth study of disciplinary knowledge and its influence on organizational culture and structure. Clark also links the tendency towards fragmentary organization (a tendency that he describes as a distinguishing feature of HE structure), to both differences in disciplinary beliefs as well as deep cultural differences between faculty members and administrators. In contrast to his findings about the disintegrating influence of the norms associated with disciplines and enterprises, Clark finds that the norms that surround the academic profession and various national traditions tend to provide a cohesive influence to organization. Once again, these normative structures can be understood as potential structuring elements in MIT's HE-situated enactment.

Authoritative Rules as Potential Structuring Properties

In addition to the symbolic norms that affect the ways in which rules and resources are organized, formal, and informal authority structures are often involved in the structuration process as well. Clark sees this dimension of analysis—that of authority structures—as closely tied to the belief structures previously described. He asserts that the complexity of belief structures greatly contributes to the complicated nature of potential power structures in the academic setting. Unlike traditional bureaucracies, where control structures are fairly clearly, often hierarchically defined, Clark's analysis shows that in the academic setting, scholarly expertise is a huge factor in the potential structuring of authority. The result is that enactments of orderly, "clean" hierarchies are extremely rare. Much more common are messy, ill-defined, poorly articulated power structures. The highly negotiable quality of power in academic settings is a salient feature of higher education organization (Clark, 1983, p. 108) and hence, a strong potential in its technology enactments as well.

In Clark's words, "legitimate power takes many forms in academic systems. No wonder participants are often confused, laymen bemused or irritated, analysts reduced to 'organizational anarchy'" (Clark, 1983, p. 124). What then provides coordination for these disjointed authority structures? What weaves together the complex work and belief structures discussed earlier into comprehensible organizational forms? Clark asserts, "bureaucratic, political, and oligarchical forms of national authority contribute to the integration of the whole" (Clark, 1983, p. 136). In addition to these, he identified a "market-like interaction" that "undeliberately" influences how order is coordinated in higher education.

Clark (1983) explores the dynamics between three coordination and control mechanisms—(1) state authority, (2) market influences, and (3) academic oligarchy—in his "triangle of coordination" model. He applies this model to compare national systems of higher education in terms of "their primary mechanisms for control and coordination." Clark's tripartite model is interesting to my inquiry for two reasons. First, we can view the national mechanisms of control in the U.S. as macro-level structures that inform MIT's efforts. The trans-national comparison that Clark provides facilitates a clearer understanding of the U.S.'s potential structures. Additionally, macro analysis of the current dynamics of change in HE suggests that U.S. transitions are occurring in conjunction with international change, rather than independent from it. Hence, looking at the larger patterns of change is potentially useful in understanding MIT's local enactment.

While Clark's framework for comparing control mechanisms remains theoretically valuable, the data he collected is several decades old. In her more recent analysis of control and coordination trends, Barbara Sporn (1996) updated Clark's findings. Her study indicates a shift in terms of the primacy of coordination mechanisms in different national systems, "especially regarding the role of the state" (Sporn, 1996, p. 10). With regard to HE in the U.S., control has moved towards centralized coordination and away from autonomous systems of organization (Sporn, 1996).

Sporn presents new trends in policies and discussions as evidence of these changes. She writes, "In the U.S., various states have implemented policies designed to regulate academic quality, and debates in the federal government leading to the creation of State Postsecondary Review Entities (SPRES) have been characterized as inaugurating a new era of governmental control" (Sporn, p. 11). The recent boom in discussion about coordinating management practices evidences that this trend towards centrally controlled organization also exists at a local, institutional level. (Cameron & Freeman, 1991; Deem, 1998; Dill, 1982; Gale, 1999; McNay, 1995; Peterson & Dill, 1997; Sporn, 1996). From a structurational perspective, these shifts can be seen as potentially powerful organizational influences to current technology enactments.

The Disorderly Nature of HE Order

To summarize, Clark's work provides a useful outline of the major structural dimensions of HE, particularly when viewed in conjunction with related contemporary scholarship. In terms of the potential structural properties he reviews—be they related to knowledge work, belief or authority—Clark's study documents the consistent enactment of highly fragmented organizational forms. Yet, at the same time, HE structures are recognizable and functional. This tension between disorder and order, autonomy, and unity is, in Clark's estimation, a fundamental element in HE organization.

For instance, both Clark's and Becher's findings confirm that the influence of knowledge structures and their related normative control structures is central to the disorderly nature of structure in the HE context. Curiously, these profoundly fractious norms stand alongside strong cohesive belief systems. Similarly, the negotiable quality of authority in HE has previously assured a relatively high level of autonomy in terms of intellectual activity on the one hand and a healthy bureaucratic structure on the other—once again, a balance of freedom and control. With recent trends in coordination of control, there is some question as to whether this longstanding tension will continue or whether, with more centralized control, HE organization will begin to look different in the near future. Analyzing MIT's CM system is one place to explore these kinds of questions.

Underlying Infrastructure as Potential Structuring Properties

The highly centralized nature of the underlying technology of MIT's system (OKI) is quite different from the technology that Orlokowski (2000) studied.[2] To address these differences I borrow Poole and DeSanctis' (1990) ideas about "technology contexts." They understood technology contexts to be potential structuring properties just as the social contexts I described above. Following their lead, I will examine the underlying technical properties of MIT's system as a potential dimension of structural influence. To explore this dimension, I examined the descriptions of the OKI's infrastructure found on MIT's Web site. The Initiative defines structural architecture standards for the following elements of communication interaction, describing them as the ground-floor properties of the shared "delivery" technology (or the OKI):

- Access to learning resources (Authentication OSID, Dictionary OSID, Hierarchy OSID),
- Teaching and learning content administration (DBC and SQL OSIDs)
- Administration of privilege and control (Hierarchy OSID)
- Surveillance and student tracking administration (Logging OSID)
- Prioritizing and scheduling of work activities (Scheduling OSID)
- Administration of contact possibilities (Shared OSID)

The list above includes the corollary terms that the OKI uses to describe these organizing structures. While the initiative refers to these organizational components as Service Interface Definitions (or OSID's), they might be more easily recognized as fundamental administrative structures, crucially important in the flow of communication interaction. These structures represent important structural elements in MIT's CM system, particularly as they relate to the dimension of authority structures.

Application: Part 2

Moving from Potential Structural Elements to Technologies-in-Practice

Relying on Orlikowski's claim that technologies-in practice are derived in part from potential organization structures, this section will explore MIT's projects with an eye on discovering which of the structuring elements that characterize HE organization might be enacted in MIT's technology effort. While a faithful application of Orlikowski's model would involve direct study of participants' interactions with technology and organizational systems, (in order to understand the fluid and dynamic process of technologies-in-practice), she notes, that "recurrent use" can cause "enacted technology structures to become routine, even institutionalized" (p. 421). Based on this idea, I examine current descriptions and demonstrations of MIT's technologies (as presented on two websites relating to MIT's efforts), considering them to be "beginning routines" of their evolving technology practices.[3] It is my intention to provoke further discussion about these practices before they are formally enacted.

Overview of MIT's CM System

MIT's Open Courseware Initiative (OCW) and Open Knowledge Initiative (OKI) are two distinct but coordinated efforts. OCW was launched in the spring of 2001, providing free access to the media contents of MIT's courses (text, graphics, and other media). Shortly after, MIT introduced OKI, which it described as being less focused on the content of online courses and more focused on the *delivery* of these courses (Strauss, 2002). Whereas I group these two technologies together in my understanding of MIT's CM system—understanding the content applications and the infrastructure upon which they are built to be intimately related—MIT's enactment often downplays their connection.

MIT has its own learning management system, Stella. In a pilot program, 20 courses developed using Stella were "harvested" on an OKI compliant platform; these became the first of MIT's OCW. Stanford, and the University of Michigan are adapting their own learning management systems (CourseWork and CHEF) so that they will be OKI compliant as well. These higher learning institutions, along with several others, are partners in MIT's OKI. The ultimate goal is to make the OKI platform publicly available for those who want to and have the skills to adapt their proprietary learning management systems. For those who don't have such a system or the skills necessary to adapt it, MIT (and others) plan to "package their open source systems" (Tech talks, CM SYSTEMS, p. 13) and license them to interested institutions.

While MIT's OCW is, according to their description, one of many possible applications supported by OKI, it is, nonetheless, receiving a great deal of attention those interested in MIT-led effort. It is one of three pilot models being developed in conjunction with the underlying architecture for OKI's larger educational infrastructure, all of which are being closely studied as potential educational models. Hence, it is a valuable application to study, given the likelihood of its widespread influence.

Before beginning with my analysis of these companion technologies, I want to emphasize the difficulty in separately discussing the different dimensions of these systems, given their highly interrelated nature. Talking about knowledge-based work, beliefs, and authority as separate structuring elements is artificial and at times slightly awkward, yet, at the same time, useful for analytical purposes. As I examine these dimensions, I find many of the existing structures and trends in HE organization outlined earlier in this paper being potentially enacted in these new technologies. I also outline what appears to be a new form of HE organization. I explore these issues—often raising more questions than I answer—in the following three sections: knowledge-based work structures, normative structures and authoritative structures.

Enactment of Knowledge-Based Work Structures: Discipline Structures

Employing the hybrid analytical framework I proposed, this section outlines first the discipline structures, then the enterprise structures enacted in MIT's efforts. Evidence of disciplinary structures was most apparent in MIT's OCW descriptions. The structures I found there are conceived and organized along highly traditional lines. For instance, the knowledge-based work of anthropology remains almost entirely separate from linguistics and philosophy despite parallel interests and inquiries; nuclear engineering is separate from political science, women's studies separate from history. Hence, one can conclude that the disciplinary structures that Clark and Becher associate with existing HE organization are, at the moment, strongly reified in MIT's enactment of these new technologies (their Open Courseware System).

Enactment of Knowledge-Based Work Structures: Enterprise Structures

While the OCW Web site provides some description relating to enterprise structure, much of my analysis of these potential structures focused on the "delivery" side of MIT's efforts, or the OKI technology project. Again, looking at the moments of enactment captured on the OKI Web site, I discovered an interesting combination of tradition and change with regard to enterprise structure. On the one hand, the traditional enterprise structures that Clark described persist in MIT's technology systems. The creation of CMS content is defined in terms of the institution that authors it. For example Cambridge, Dartmouth, and Stanford are creating their "own" course content technologies. The collaborative technologies-in-practice effort defines institutional boundaries as more permeable—in terms of their willingness to share—but enterprise structures have clearly not disappeared.

In addition to these familiar enterprise forms, new, non-geographically-based enterprise structures are also introduced. These become clear when analyzing the description of the OKI. Indeed, the Initiative can be read as the roadmap for creating a new HE "infrastructure". Leaders of the project define this infrastructure as the technologies "that support teaching and learning" and that "support the core activity of the academy, the creation and transmission of knowledge." They liken this new infrastructure to existing administrative structures, emphasizing how it "supports education in a manner comparable to those systems that have provided fiscal, resource, and administrative services" (OKI Web site, 2003). Analyzing these descriptions (with organizational structure in mind) leads me to understand the current enactment of OKI technology as a new form of "enterprise" or "learning management system".

Enactment of Normative Structures

Clark's findings suggest an inextricable relationship between the knowledge-based work structures of HE and its belief structures. One might analyze the structures described on MIT's Web site with this linkage in mind. In the previous sections, I discussed how the CM technologies reify the separation of existing disciplinary cultures as well as many traditional enterprise structures. I also described how the technology enactment might be seen as creating new enterprise forms. Looking at the technology with an eye on belief structures sheds additional light on these enactment phenomena. Specifically, there is evidence that the developing structures not only reify the traditional separation of academic and administrative culture but also reflect broader changes occurring in the culture of the system.

I turn my focus initially towards analyzing the separation of the culture of the discipline from the culture of the enterprise in MIT's technology enactment. Examining the description reveals that not only do the enacted structures evidence the familiar lack of interaction between the culture of the discipline and the culture of the enterprise typical of HE organization, but the structures seem to intensify this separation. The OKI's organizational framework strongly emphasizes integration both at a local and an international level. "When combining OKI with on-the-wire protocols like IMS, it becomes much easier to integrate the whole lot" (Kraan, 2003, p. 2). This kind of large-scale integration is very different from traditional HE organizational structure. The structural nature of the OSID's (discussed in the previous section) also support the goal of broad-based integration. They are "designed to allow multiple OKI sites to share some common infrastructure..." (Thorne, Schubert, & Merriman, p. 4). Clearly, the cultural values of stability and reliability have strongly influenced current structure. According to Clark's research, these values are strongly prized by the culture of the enterprise, whereas the culture of the discipline favors individual autonomy and freedom. One might conclude then that the foundational structures currently enacted in the OKI over-represent the interests and values of the culture of the enterprise and under-represent those of the culture of the disciplines.

The separation of the CM system into the "content" and "delivery" components (or the OCW and OKI components) also evidences the break between cultural systems. Implied in this structural split is the assumption that the organization and administration of communication interaction does not impact educational activities. Leaders of the project openly acknowledge that the OKI Service Interface Definitions provide foundational technology structures, yet at the same time, they imply a lack of relationship between these foundations and the educational activities built upon them. They cite an advantage to OKI's organizational split as being "much greater flexibility in learning related applications". They continue, claiming that "if all the hard work is done in standardized, widely used adapters, then it becomes much easier and cheaper to make applications that are very innovative or finely tuned to teachers' and students' needs" (Kraan, 2003, p. 2). This is a curious assumption given that teaching and learning needs have informed the foundational organizational structures in an extremely limited way.

In addition to looking for evidence of disciplinary and enterprise structures in MIT's enactment I also examined the technology for rules and resources relating to the culture of profession (the system of beliefs that Clark identified as a balancing force to the fragmentation between the discipline and enterprise structure). Much of the rhetoric is clearly recognizable as enacting HE's existing professional culture. The values that the project's leaders espouse are closely aligned with longstanding traditions: "At colleges and universities, visions of learning communities fostering the open development and exchange of ideas and useful services have guided the growth of institutional culture for years. Peer review is a hallmark of this system. The revolutionary open-source software movement shares this collaborative ideal" (Moore, 2002).

But are the possibilities for individual autonomy and innovation truly reified in MIT's enactment? Leaders claim that OKI has "noble design goals" and frequently cite their intention to provide a technology system that is: "open, scalable, secure, reliable, flexible and extensible" (Thorne, Shubert, & Merriman, 2002). Three of these goals ring quite true with the traditional values of the culture of the profession—open, reliable, and flexible. But the others—scalable, secure, and extensible—seem to represent a new set of professional values.

Investigating this new trend, I found many incidents where this new set of values were emphasized. For instance, leaders of the OKI promote these values as they articulate the goal of this new enterprise: "Specifically, OKI efforts include developing the means to exchange educational content or student information and to synchronize information across the educational community" (Tansey, 2003, p. 4). The project is being developed in close connection with others who share the goals of synchronicity and extensibility. For example, the IMS has goals not only to synchronize HE's technical structures, but those of K-12 education and professional training as well. Frank Tansey (2003) does a nice job describing this grand scheme plan in his article, "The Standard Bearers Close Ranks." In it he states, "The OKI is feeding into IMS (Global Learning Consortium) the new methodology for next-generation applications ... IMS attempts to provide specifications and standards that meet the needs of many vertical efforts" (Tansey, 2003, p. 4).

How these integration/unification values may impact HE's professional culture—a culture that has long been unified by their strong commitment to autonomy and individual innovation—is an interesting question to ponder. Before moving to examine that question, however, it will be useful to round out my analysis of MIT's CM system by looking at the authority structures enacted in the collaborative effort.

Enactment of Authority Structures

To review, Clark's findings on HE's potential authority structures reveal a complex system of contested control mechanisms that combine the authority of disciplinary expertise, with guild-like experience, formal bureaucratic hierarchy, individual charisma, and trustee representation of public interests. This very untidy web of authority is, according to Clark, coordinated by bureaucratic, political, oligarchical, and market-like interactions (Clark, 1983, p. 135). At first glance, the authority mechanisms in MIT's technology enactment seem to reify the highly fragmented (though also coordinated) and widely informed structural patterns that Clark discusses. A closer look, however, reveals a dramatically different kind of authority structure being enacted in these new systems.

As mentioned earlier, the OKI technology description strongly emphasizes the diversity of participation in the structural design of MIT's proposed CM system. The title of the initiative, the "Open Knowledge Initiative", and the goals of the project underscore the importance that leaders give to uninhibited participation. According to Vijay Kumar, director of academic computing at MIT, "OKI is about creating an infrastructure to enable educational applications," applications that he and others strongly emphasize as being locally defined (TechTalks, 2002). All the publicly available descriptions about MIT's projects highlight the potential diversity of these applications, particularly with regard to design authority. Indeed, MIT's companion effort, their OCW, models the potential for broad-based participation in the structuring of the technology.

It is not until one conducts a more in-depth reading of the technology's description that the highly unified organization of the underlying infrastructure for these applications becomes clear. There are two forms of licensing available for the OKI: the "definition" license and the "implementation" license (OKI Web site, 2003). The first applies to the underlying infrastructure of the project (the Service Interface Definitions or OSID's) and the second to the "implementations and exemplar applications" associated with the OKI project.

The two licenses vary greatly in terms of the code editing freedom they allow. The definition license is strictly limited in terms of modification; the license states, "You may use, copy, and distribute *unmodified* versions of this Work..." (italics added). This language is quite clear in indicating that the underlying architecture for the OKI system is tightly sealed. The implementation license more closely relates to the project's rhetoric about "open knowledge." At the application level, "permission to use, copy, *modify* and distribute this Software and its documentation...is hereby granted" (italics added).

The technical code(s) that are "protected" by the definition license are all the Service Interface Definitions (OSID's) that make up OKI's underlying organizational structure. These structures are intended to have widespread influence, providing what leaders describe as a new "standard for application development" (Long, 2002) and the "architectural framework for a new educational infrastructure...that will shape the educational infrastructure of tomorrow" (OKI Web site, 2003). Analyzing the licensing as part of MIT's efforts suggests that the highly diverse levels and types of expertise and authority that traditionally interact in the process of HE authority structuring have been significantly adapted in MIT's enactment.

Given this fact, a look at who exactly is participating in the design of this infrastructure seems important. Though participants in the effort include a combination of public and private universities, all are well funded research institutions. The complete list of participants includes: Cambridge University, Dartmouth College, Indiana University Bloomington, Massachusetts Institute of Technology, North Carolina State University, Stanford University, University of Michigan, University of Pennsylvania, and University of Wisconsin, Madison. MIT's collaborative effort is supported by IMS Global Learning Consortium, Inc. (sponsored by Educause's NLII) and Advanced Distributed Learning (an initiative sponsored by the U.S. Department of Defense) (Tansey, 2003). Given the significant coordinating role that the IMS is playing in the technology enactment, the scope of their vision of themselves and other education institutions is relevant:

The IMS Global Learning Consortium develops and promotes the adoption of open technical specifications for interoperable learning technology. Several IMS specifications have become worldwide de facto standards for delivering learning products and services...IMS is a worldwide non-profit organization that includes more than 50 Contributing Members and affiliates. These members come from every sector of the global e-learning community...The Consortium provides a neutral forum in which members with competing business interests and different decision-making criteria collaborate to satisfy real-world requirements for interoperability and re-use (IMS Web site, 2003).

Having identified the participants in the design of authority structure, I turn my attention now to examining the different authority structures emphasized in current design. In reviewing descriptions of the CM technologies, it doesn't take long to discover a strong focus on structures relating to access privilege. The importance of who does (and who doesn't) have access permission seems greatly magnified in comparison to existing organizational structures. MIT's CM system is portrayed as opening doors to a freely available set of learning resources. This ideal stands in stark contrast to the description of OKI's Authentication Standards, which have a built-in structural emphasis on reviewing credentials and checking for access permissions (OKI Web site, 2003). In addition to a focus on access, the enactment also seems to emphasize structures related to surveillance and tracking. For example, the project's Logging OSID "records and retrieves a variety of application history...for purposes of analysis, description collection, and security." As with the increased emphasis on access structures, the surveillance structures represent an adaptation of traditional HE authority structures.

Implications

Many of the structures that Clark and his colleagues described are evidenced in the enactment of technology that is the subject of this study. To start, my inquiry indicates that MIT's OCW strongly reifies traditional disciplinary structures. These findings are not terribly surprising, given that the creation of these courses occurred within MIT's existing, discipline-based organizational context. Many might argue that they also represent only one possible "OKI compliant" application. They are more significant that this, however, given that the OCW is a "content" application designed to be a model for future applications and one of the primary applications that has informed the OKI's underlying architectural structures. Its current organizing structure, therefore, may have wider implications.

Considering this fact, the OCW enactment leads me to wonder, what are the potential benefits or consequences of reenacting existing disciplinary organization in these new technologies? Certainly, the structures enacted in MIT's OCW have longstanding traditions supporting them; in some cases, thousands of years of practice shore up their structural boundaries. One might ask, however, whose interests are served by the reification of traditional disciplinary organization? How will the current growth of interdisciplinary studies (Klein, 1996) or the increase in disciplinary fragmentation and complexity (Clark, 1983) be impacted by reenacting traditional disciplinary structures? In sum, studying the current structures enacted in MIT's OCW raises questions about whether or not new forms of knowledge organization are conceptually and/or structurally possible given the beginning boundaries these systems have defined.

My analysis of these technologies also suggests that MIT's projects represent a new form of enterprise structure. The OKI project is described in administrative terms that directly parallel traditional HE organizations. Yet the physical, geographically located boundaries of today's institutions no longer apply. Hence, the CM system can be understood as a new kind of educational enterprise. We might understand this new enterprise structure as a potential first step towards realizing the non-geographically structured "degree-granting bodies" that Brown and Deguid (1996) describe in their futuristic vision of HE: "DGB's could take on as many or as few students and faculty as they thought practical becoming smaller than the liberal arts college or larger than an entire state system. They could set degree requirements and courses as they saw fit. But a DGB would essentially be administrative..." (Brown & Duguid, 1996, p. 18). Viewing CM systems as providing a structure compatible with the DGB's confirms the authors' prediction that "emerging computational infrastructure will be crucially important in shaping an already changing system" (Brown & Duguid, 1996, p. 11).

While my investigation is limited in terms of how its conclusions might be generalized, the idea that these systems represent new forms of enterprise structure is relevant for other existing CM systems. In light of this project, we can understand systems such as Blackboard, ECollege, WebCT, not just as technological "tools" that we employ in existing organizations, but also as emerging educational enterprises. From this perspective, a closer examination of their organizing frameworks seems important. Particularly because, unlike MIT's CM system which has largely grown up in a HE context, these other systems are being developed within the context of for-profit business organizations. Looking into the different organizing structures of the business setting (typically more hierarchical than those of HE) and how they might be influencing the organization of these new educational enterprises would make for an interesting future research project.

Returning to the project at hand, the normative structures I encountered in MIT's enactment evidence a deepened separation between the culture of the discipline and the culture of the enterprise. They also seem to be biased towards the latter's professional values and interests. In analyzing the structures in MIT's system that relate to the culture of the system, I found it useful to keep in mind Sporn's (1999) research about the U.S. trend towards centralized control. The OKI's strong tendency towards system-wide integration parallels current national level trends. The assumption underlying these new organizing patterns is that the educational interactions that occur in HE are unaffected by underlying communication structures. This contradicts a significant body of communication research that finds communication organization and communication interaction to be inseparably related. Given the imbalanced representation of enterprise values in the OKI's current structures, there is a significant possibility that these foundational structures may not meet contemporary educational needs. Without more input into the organizational development process, faculty and students may end up with learning spaces that are out of synch with their unique teaching/learning values.

Analyzing MIT's descriptions of their CM system also highlights change in terms of who participates in organizational decision-making. The new enterprise structure moves from a traditionally diverse and highly contested process to one that looks quite different. Participants involved in defining the underlying structures to this CM system are not only much smaller in number than at traditional universities, but they are also a much more homogenous group.

How are the partners of the OKI project related? In large part, they are linked by their advanced knowledge of and their innovations involving educational technologies. Closely analyzing the current enactment reveals two levels of authority—those who have the power to influence the shape of the foundational structure for these technologies and those whose authority is limited to structuring individual applications. One might view this partnership as creating a new kind of "insider" community in the landscape of HE. Perceptions about the exclusive nature of the development process, which has been characterized as occurring "behind the scenes" (Tansey, 2003, p. 1) and "behind closed doors," (Kraan, 2003, p. 1) underscore this concern. This begs an admittedly contentious question: might this technology enactment represent a new kind of exclusivity with tight restraints on membership and participation that contradict the ideals of American higher education?

Another potentially related finding in my inquiry is the change in importance given to access privilege. Why has authentication for the entrance into a learning space become so important? Whose interests are protected by this kind of monitoring? What innovations might be limited by it? In an era that hails the benefits of student centered learning and that downplays the power relationships between students and faculty (who are now "guides on the side"), these hierarchical structures seem woefully out of date. Or perhaps they derive directly from the changes currently emerging in teaching/learning organization, seeking to protect the interests of those whose power might be threatened by these changes?

When so many knowledge-based businesses are actively increasing autocratic organization, documenting the productivity benefits of such structures, the OKI's emphasis of bureaucratic authority structures seems odd. The way that the centrally controlled system is being sold to faculty is through the promise of not having to "worry about infrastructure", "freeing" faculty to teach more "efficiently." Do faculty and students want efficiency in teaching? What might be lost with this shift in values?

It is interesting to note that similar structural coordinating/unifying efforts are occurring in elementary and secondary education. The Schools Interoperability Frameworks (SIF) is a project whose "goal is to provide a technical framework that will enable diverse applications to interact and share data seamlessly" (Tansey, 2003, p. 2). As with the HE projects, scalability, and extensibility are highly prized values in these efforts. While the potential benefit in coordinating highly fragmented efforts are understandable, particularly with the global increase in education needs, again, the organizational diversity (and hence the communication interaction diversity) that may be compromised by such narrowly defined authority structures is concerning.

Conclusion

The OKI project is defining an architecture designed to facilitate the construction and use of educational applications for the next decade. Though leaders of the initiative recognize that "the implications of this goal are enormous," discussion of these implications is, in my opinion, scanty. It is my hope that this paper stimulates further conversation about the issues I have raised. Towards that end, I have provided a potential model to apply towards understanding this (and other) technology proposals and used this model to analyze a national-level technology enactment that is potentially hugely significant.

With regards to the former, I have outlined a model that aims to enrich the application of structuration theory to educational technologies by grounding it in what we know about the unique organizational traditions of HE. Applying this hybrid analytical framework to a particular case study, I have attempted to model how it can be used to read and interpret new technologies. This framework, which starts from a technology-as-process perspective, draws attention to the relationship between technology and organization. In the case of MIT's system, using a structuration framework for analysis reveals how the CM system potentially influences—and is influenced by—the social organizations of HE. The hybrid analytical model I proposed, however, is not without its problems.

In particular, MIT's goals for inter-networking produce a technology infrastructure that is necessarily more standardized, and hence, less malleable than the one that Orlikowski studied. This required me to apply her structuration framework in a significantly different manner than she modeled, highlighting potential structures over enacted structures. Though she clearly anticipated the possibility of more centralized technology systems in her research[4], she did not offer suggestions for how to accommodate these differences in terms of study approach. While my revisions to her analytical framework sufficed for this discussion, the increase in these kinds of technologies suggests the need for further discussion about how to best access and study them. My application activity also highlighted the increasing need for me, as a social science researcher, as well as others who approach the study of communication technology from social science backgrounds, to become more fluent in the technical language of these systems. Given my novice level of proficiency in these languages, I offer my analysis of these technologies somewhat tentatively and invite those who are more proficient to add to my interpretations.

Based on my analysis of MIT's system as a social organizing system, I presented several claims. I suggested that MIT's CM systems represent a new form of HE and that the values of the culture of the disciplines seem to be grossly under-represented in MIT's current technology enactment. I pointed out that the new system we see by looking at MIT's technology as organization represents a highly coordinated, centrally administered organizing system, the likes of which HE has not seen in its nearly 3,000 year history. These claims and their potential implications warrant future attention, particularly from those within HE organizations who have had limited participation in these initial organizing conversations.

In the 1980's, Clark presented HE's longstanding organizational structures as phenomena which essentially "stack the organizational deck;" he saw the curious combination of fragmented and unified structures he identified as "fundamental" to an HE organization. Twenty years later, profound organizational changes have occurred, both in and outside HE. Paul Trowler (1998), a contemporary organizational scholar studying the HE context, looks at the changeable nature of organizational structure and emphasizes the importance of the often overlooked factor of individual agency in this process. Based on my analysis, I suggest that mindful, conscientious agency is indicated in the case of adopting the organizing structures associated with MIT's CM system.

Two notable scholars of organizational communication describe structures as "recipes for engaging in everyday life" (Banks & Riley, 1993, p. 177). The foundational structures currently being enacted in the OKI project (and the companion projects), can potentially serve as recipes for how educators engage in their everyday lives. That depends, in large measure, on members of the HE community: "...the success of OKI depends almost entirely on the support it gets. If a sufficient amount of people start demanding OSID slots in their MLE components, and writing adapters, the benefits can quickly scale. If not, the benefit of implementing OSID's will be limited to just a nice clean insulation of the application from the network" (Kraan, 2003, p. 3). My caution to all in the HE community is to engage in diverse conversation before they decide whether to ask for these organizing structures. My hope is that this chapter provides a preliminary model for those interested in doing so.

References

Banks, S.P. & Riley, P. (1993). Structuration theory as an ontology for communication research. In Deetz, S. (Ed), *Communication yearbook*, 16 (pp. 167-196). Newberry Park, CA: Sage.

Barley, S.R. (1986). Technology as an occasion for structuring: Evidence from observations of CT scanners and the social order of radiology departments. *Administrative Science Quarterly*, *31*(1), 78-108.

Becher, T. (1989). *Tribes and territories: Intellectual enquiry and the cultures of the disciplines.* Philadelphia: Society for Research into Higher Education and Open University Press.

Becher, T. & Trowler, P. (2000). *Tribes and territories: Intellectual enquiry and the cultures of the disciplines.* Philadelphia: Society for Research into Higher Education and Open University Press.

Beniger, J.R. (1996). Who shall control cyberspace? In Strate, L., Jacobson, R., & Gibson, S.B. (Eds.), *Communication and cyberspace: Social interaction in an electronic environment.* Hampton Press.

Beninger, J.R. (1990). Conceptualizing information technology as organization and vice versa. In Fulk, J., & Steinfield, C. (Eds.), *Organizations and Communication Technology.* Newbury Park: Sage Publications, 29-45.

Bijker, W.E., Hughes, T.P. & Pinch (Eds.) (1987). *The social construction of technological systems: New directions in the sociology and history of technology.* Cambridge, MA: MIT Press.

Brown, J.S. & Duguid, P. (1996). Universities in the digital age. *Change*, July/Aug, 11-19.

Carmean, C. & Haefner, J. (2002). Mind over matter: Transforming course management systems into effective learning environments. *Educause*, Nov-Dec, 27-34.

Clark, B.R. (1983). *The higher education system: Academic organization in cross national perspective.* Berkeley: University of California Press.

Contractor, N.S. & Eisenberg, E.M. (1990). Communication networks and new media in organizations. In Fulk, J. & Steinfield, C. (Eds.), *Organizations and communication technology.* Newbury Park: Sage Publications, 143-172.

DeSanctis, G. & Fulk, J. (1999). Articulation of communication technology and organizational form. In DeSanctis, G. & Fulk, J. (Eds.), *Shaping organizational form: Communication, connection, and community* (pp. 5-32). Thousand Oaks: Sage.

Duderstadt, J. (2000). *A university for the 21st century.* Ann Arbor: University of Michigan Press.

Dutton, W.H. (1999). The virtual organization: Tele-access in business and industry. In DeSanctis, G. & Fulk, J. (Eds.), *Shaping organizational form: Communication, connection, and community* (pp. 473-496). Thousand Oaks: Sage.

Frederickson, S., Clark, B., & Hoehner, P. (2002). A primer for the online instructor: Part 1: Getting started. *Learning and Leading with Technology, 29*(6), 6-12.

Frey, B.E. (2002). Reflections. *Educause*, Jan/Feb, 8-14.

Fulk, J., Schmitz, J., & Steinfield, C. (1990). A social influence model of technology use. In Fulk, J. & Steinfield, C. (Eds.), *Organizations and communication technology* (pp. 117-140). Newbury Park: Sage Publications.

Giddens, A. (1984). *The constitution of society: Outline of the theory of structure.* Berkeley: University of California Press.

Jackson, M.H. (1996). The meaning of "communication technology": The technology-context scheme. In Burleson, B. (Ed.), *Communication yearbook 19* (pp. 229-268). Beverly Hills, CA: Sage.

Jackson, M.H., Poole, M.S. & Kuhn, T. (2002) The social construction of technology in studies of the workplace. In Lievrouw, L. & Livingston, S., *New media handbook* (pp. 236-252). Sage.

Johnstone, S.M. (2002). Sign of the times: Change is coming for e-learning. *Educause*, Nov/Dec, 15-24.

Katz, R.N. (2002). An interview with Neil Gershenfeld, director for the Center for Bits and Atoms at MIT. *Educause*, March/April, 34-38.

Kraan, W. (2003). IMS and OKI, The wire and the socket. *CETIS News*. The Center for Educational Technology Interoperability, July 17.

Kumar, V. & Long, P. (2002). MIT's Open Courseware Initiative and Open Knowledge Initiative. Transcript from *CREN Tech Talks*, March 7.

Luker, M. (1999). Preparing your campus for a networked future. *Educause leadership strategies series*. Jossey-Bass Publishers, November, No. 1.

McOmber, J.B. (1999). Technological autonomy and three definitions of technology. *Journal of Communication, 49*, 137-153.

Moore, A. (2002). Open-source learning. *Educause Review*, September/ October, 43-51.

Nass, C. & Mason, L. (1990). On the study of technology and task: A variable-based approach. In Fulk, J. & Steinfield, C. (Eds.), *Organizations and communication technology* (pp. 46-68). Newbury Park: Sage Publications.

Olson, F. (2001). Getting ready for a new generation of course-management systems. *The Chronicle of Higher Education, 48*(17), 25.

Orlikowski, W. (2000). Using technology and constituting structures: A practice lens for studying technology in organizations. *Organization Science, 11*(4), 404-428.

Poole, M.S. & DeSanctis, G. (1990). Understanding the use of group decision support systems: The theory of adaptive structuration. In Fulk, J. & Steinfield, C. (Eds.), *Organizations and communication technology* (pp. 173-193). Newbury Park: Sage Publications.

Rosen, J. (2002). Blackboard nears profits. *Publishers Weekly, 249*(22), 20.

Sampler, J. (1996). Exploring the relationship between information technology and organizational structure. In Earl, M.J. (Ed.), *Information management: The organizational dimension* (pp. 5-22). Oxford, UK: Oxford University Press.

Smith, N. (2002). Teaching as coaching: Helping students learn in a technological world. *Educause*, May/June, 38-45.

Sporn, B. (1999). Adaptive university structures: An analysis of adaptation to socioeconomic environments of US and European universities. In Kogan, M. (Ed.), *Higher education policy series*. London: Jessica Kingsley Publishers.

Sproulle, L. & Keisler, S. (1991). *Connections: New ways of working in the networked organization.* Cambridge, MA: MIT Press.

Strauss, H. (2002). The right train at the right station. *Educause Review*, May/June, 30-36.

Strauss, H., Kerns, C., & Boettcher, J. (2002). Course management systems and learning tools: Where are we at the end of 2002? Transcript from *CREN Tech Talks*. November 7.

Tansey, F. (2003). The standard bearers close ranks. *Syllabus Magazine*, March.

Trowler, P.R. (1998). *Academics responding to change: New higher education frameworks and academic cultures.* Buckingham: Open University Press.

Twigg, C.A. (1994). The need for a national learning infrastructure. *Educom Review, 29(4, 5, 6).*

Winner, L. (1986). Do artifacts have politics? In *The whale and the reactor: A search for limits in an age of high technology* (pp. 19-39). Chicago: University of Chicago Press.

Wulf, W.A. (2003). Higher education alert: The information railroad is coming. *Educause*, Jan/Feb, 12-21.

Young, J.R. (2002). Designer of free course-management software asks: What makes a good Web site? *The Chronicle of Higher Education*, February 8.

Endnotes

1 Not only is my ability to observe the potential enactments of MIT's technology quite limited but the enactments themselves are, by nature, not as malleable as those that Orlikowski studied. This is a result of the centralized nature of the CM system's underlying architecture. As Orlikowski (2000) writes, "It is likely that the increased complexity and internetworking accompanying the growth in global infrastructures will require these artifacts to be more standardized, interconnected, and interdependent (and hence, their use may be less malleable)" (p. 409). This, as well as the other reasons discussed in the previous section, motivates my decision to foreground the potential rather than the enacted structures of these systems.

2 It is these differences, in part, that led to me foreground the potential rather than the enacted structures in my analysis. This approach, however, is not without its problems. In privileging potential over enacted structures, I run the risk of distancing myself from the social interaction process I have proposed to examine. And yet the infrastructure issues of MIT's efforts—what some might understand as "embodied" rather than enacted structures—are a critical element of the technology. In order to solve this theoretical problem, I barrow from Poole and DeSanctis's approach in order to examine the underlying infrastructure of the CM system, looking at the technical properties of the proposed architecture as an additional kind of "potential" structure (much like the authors analyzed the technology contexts along with social contexts of the technology they studied)

(Poole and DeSanctis, 1990, p). Though my inclusion of these structures diverges from Orlikowski's insistence that structures "have only a virtual existence" and not a "material existence" (Orlikowski, 2000, p. 406), it is not necessarily inconsistent—particularly since I consider these as potential structural elements.

3 Given that MIT's technologies are still in the development phase and are currently being used by only a small number of pilot participants, my ability to observe these technologies as technologies-in-practice is severely limited. In lieu of this kind of observation, I examine the information that is publicly available about these systems: the current descriptions of MIT's efforts that exist on their OKI and OCW Web sites. I interpret these descriptions as evidence of practices that are being *considered* as opposed to truly enacted. I employ the language of Orlikowki's framework, interpreting these descriptions as "enactments", but I do so with a cautionary reminder to readers. The descriptions to which I refer do not represent technologies-in-practice in a strict sense. Rather, perhaps, the reader might understand these descriptions as beginning phases or "moments" of practice that are currently being discussed. Hence, the enactment section of my analysis is necessarily more speculative and less developed than the example Orlikowski presents.

4 Orlikowski (2000) anticipates the centralization of technology infrastructures saying, "Organizations wishing to link to other businesses or to the Internet will need to provide standard interfaces and consistency of performance across a range of technological platforms to ensure the interoperability of multiple artifacts. Providing for such interconnections increases interdependence and complexity, coupling the artifacts more tightly together in larger technological systems or infrastructures. Such integration is likely to reduce the degrees of freedom available to users to experiment with and modify their technological artifacts in use" (p. 424). These ideas are highly relevant with regards to MIT's efforts.

Chapter VIII

Distributed Learning Objects: An Open Knowledge Management Model

Veronica Diaz
The University of Arizona, USA

Patricia McGee
The University of Texas at San Antonio, USA

Abstract

This chapter analyzes the emergence of learning objects as a dynamic and interactive relationship between technology and the organization. We examine the way that organizational objectives are embedded within selected technologies. In other words, how is the selected technology addressing the organization's needs? Further, we argue for a socially-constructed model of knowledge management. Specifically, we utilize Demarest's (1997) four-step process of the construction of a knowledge economy. From these processes, via a constructed technological system, a learning object economy emerges, which includes various constituents: the 21st century learner, the subject matter expert (university professor), vendors who support or enable knowledge management, and populaces that harvest and benefit from the collection of knowledge.

Introduction

As state and federal funds diminish and as higher education resources and university budgets become more restricted, postsecondary institutions are becoming increasingly entrepreneurial in pursuing and developing technological solutions. Meyer (2002) describes a changing marketplace, increasingly global in orientation, where technology enables the provision of adult education, executive training/retraining, competency-based programs, and education to remote geographical areas. Knowledge management,[1] in higher education, is a way to retain and manage knowledge products. As higher education organizations increasingly interact with other organizational types, such as corporations, consortia, and other educational institutions, knowledge products become critical in the exchange process. Technological systems are designed to manage knowledge and are situated in social systems with corresponding cultures, values, and beliefs. As such, higher education, as an organizational structure and a social system, must consider processes, policies, and embedded assumptions about technology, teaching, and learning, not only within their own institution, but also across those with which they interact.

The trend toward knowledge management is evidenced in the myriad of technological artifacts that have emerged to capture, categorize, and manage learning objects. During their evolution, learning objects have come to be defined in a number of ways, depending on the context and culture from which they emerge, for example, computer science, education, instructional technology, and so on. For our purposes, we define a learning object as any digital asset that is intended to be used to achieve a learning objective and can be re-used in different contexts. Learning objects may be data or data sets, texts, images or image collections, audio or video materials, executable programs, courses offered through Learning/Course Management Systems (L/CMS), or other resources that can be delivered electronically. Learning objects should be re-useable and re-purposeable over time and location and interoperable across systems and software (see Downes, 2002; Robson, 2001; Wiley, 2000). Additionally, learning objects can be combined or aggregated in different ways providing the potential for individualized learning experiences for specific learners in which their learning styles, prior knowledge, and specific learning needs are accounted for. They may also offer great value in terms of saving time and money in course development, increasing the reusability of content, enhancing students' learning environment, sharing knowledge within and across disciplines, and engaging faculty members in a dynamic community of practice (Bennett & Metros, 2001). Learning objects may be created by individuals or institutions and therefore require consideration of digital rights as well as storage and distribution.

How learning objects are stored and subsequently accessed has been primarily addressed through technology systems known as digital learning object repositories. Thomas and Home (2004) have identified four rationales, not only for the development of learning objects, but also for their storage in these digital containers.

1. **The Efficiency Route:** The more institutions work together, the less likely replication of efforts and therefore reduced costs based on the idea that learning objects "deliver industrial economies of scale" (p. 12).
2. **The Teacher-Centered Route:** The more that educators share resources and best practices, the more likely teaching will improve. In this manner learning object "creation [is] co-production" (p. 12).
3. **The Pupil-Centered Route:** Learners who have access to a variety of objects designed with different learning needs in mind, can be better supported. In this sense, learning objects become "scalable and networked" (p. 13).
4. **The Freedom Argument:** Educators should take ownership and be able to disseminate freely to the larger educational community without struggling with or against issues of institutional ownership, intellectual property or even censorship.

These rationales serve to illustrate the value structures within organizational cultures that determine how technology is used to make knowledge accessible and the reasons for doing so. Such positions are reflected in organizational policies and are particularly critical within cross-institutional interactions.

This chapter analyzes the emergence of learning objects as a dynamic and interactive relationship between technology and the organization. We examine the way that organizational objectives are embedded within selected technologies. In other words, how is the selected technology addressing the organization's needs? Further, we argue for a socially-constructed model of knowledge management. Specifically, we utilize Demarest's (1997) four-step process of the construction of a knowledge economy. Next, we examine the way that knowledge is transmitted through a selected technological system. From these processes, via a constructed technological system, a learning object economy[2] emerges, which includes various constituents: the 21st century learner, the subject matter expert (university professor), vendors who support or enable knowledge management, and populaces that harvest and benefit from the collection of knowledge. We discuss four current models of knowledge management found in higher education: the traditional model, the intellectual capital/appropriative model, the sharing/reciprocal model, and the contribution pedagogy model. We propose a new, relativist model of knowledge management for higher education that accommodates cross-institutional cultures and beliefs about learning technologies, construction of knowledge across systems and institutions, as well as the trend toward learner-centered, disaggregated, and re-aggregated learning objects, and negotiated intellectual property rights.

A Starting Point: Thomas's Theory of Organizational Technology

Thomas (1994) argues that a technical system utilized within an organization can be objective, but also infused with objectives, reflective of the interests or goals of particular groups within the social system. A technological system, he contends, has the ability to define and redefine tasks, responsibilities, and relationships or to evoke or reinforce change. Further, the eventual selection of a specific technology reflects the interests and ideologies of the organizational structure. Organizations are composed of interdependent social and technological systems where changes in one usually occasion adaptation in the other (e.g., a course management system many interact with a registration system). However, the relationship between technology and the organization is dynamic and interactive, that is, technology may cause organizational change and organizational objectives may produce a change in the technological system. Thomas explains that in order for the technology to be incorporated into organizational life, it must be transformed from a physical object into a social one. In other words, organizational members must recognize that the technology exists and then negotiate a set of understandings about what it is, what it means, and how it defines and redefines tasks, responsibilities, and relationships. Thomas proposes a model of organizational technology whose adoption and use is shaped or determined, to some extent, by the organization that selects it. While he acknowledges that the technological system interacts with the organization and its objectives and vice versa, this model is limited to some extent by those very things: the organization and its objectives.

Current knowledge management models are organizationally-centered and are thus limited by the values and interests of their constituents. However, others are arguing for a transformation of the knowledge economy from one that is proprietary to a freestanding, shared knowledge community (Norris, Mason, & Lefrere, 2003). Norris et al. point to eight external and internal forces that are producing this shift: (1) Investments in infrastructure and best practices by "early adopters" of e-knowledge (e.g., associations, governmental agencies, corporations, universities) deliver results that encourage wider adoption, and also facilitate new generations of enterprise applications; (2) Global enterprises that increase competitiveness by developing faster ways to manage their knowledge and strategic learning by creating tools that non-experts can use; (3) Growth in expert networks and easier, more productive participation in communities of practice that push e-knowledge practices and competencies; (4) Increasing sophistication by users, who develop an appetite for services that provide significant gains in their capacity to access and assimilate knowledge; (5) Advances in Internet and intranet-based capabilities that enable jump shifts in creating and accessing knowledge stores; (6) Innovations in mobile communications that provide ubiquitous access to perpetual learning solutions, as well as new ways to meet demands for e-commerce in any place or time; (7) Insight into new and more effective ways of experiencing how knowledge drives innovation; and (8) Increased understanding about how to deploy international standards in ways that ensure useful return on investments (e.g., through interoperability) that stimulates continued investment. We believe that these are just some of the local and global changes occurring that are motivating higher education to explore a system of knowledge management that is socially-constructed rather than organizationally-determined. As this trend unfolds, there is an increasing demand for collaborative discourse and negotiation, not just about what technology means, but also how it is designed and how artifacts such as learning objects are shared. This trend is evidenced by such efforts as the IMS Global Learning Consortium, Inc., in which members from around the world work together to develop specifications for e-learning technologies.

Social Construction of Knowledge and Learning Objects

The global nature of education within a distributed learning context requires that higher education, particularly considering learning objects as a valuable commodity that can be traded and exchanged, is part of an evolving knowledge economy. Texts, videos, and other materials have proven the value of institutionally-generated knowledge, but traditionally these products have produced revenue for an individual with value capital for the institution. Learning objects are forcing institutions to examine the economic exchange of the knowledge capital they are generating as they search for strategies to manage and negotiate value.

Following Thomas's theory of the social or organizational construction of technological systems and drawing from an economic business perspective, Demarest (1997) postulates that organizations value knowledge based on "what works." Business uses resource capital in order to develop processes and structures that result in increased sales and revenue. Davenport, DeLong, and Beers (1998) found four distinct types of knowledge management initiatives in corporations that were intended to:

1. Provide repositories for internally generated policy and informational knowledge;
2. Provide access to knowledge or transfer among individuals;
3. Facilitate the generation and use of knowledge; and
4. Manage knowledge assets in such a way that value is apparent.

Corporate knowledge management comes from an economic model that is based on a knowledgeable workforce that increases the organization's return on investment. Davenport, et al. believe an economic model is appropriate for learning objects in higher education in that they are, by definition, designed to be re-used and shared. Whether or not they have a monetary value assigned to them is incidental, it is the investment of development and dissemination that belies their institutional value. In higher education, "what works" is similar to that of business, but involves "human capital," which may result in increased enrollments, higher post-graduation employment rates, and academic recognition and prestige for the knowledge generated and disseminated. It is the latter that applies most directly to learning objects in that academic recognition comes from the intellectual production of knowledge that is to be disseminated across institutions, and to a large extent contributes to the knowledge base of those institutions.

Higher education values philosophical and scientific knowledge that is generated by the scholarship of its members. Such knowledge has traditionally driven innovation and production (Lyotard, 1984). The commodification of knowledge through information distributed through technologies such as the Internet has expanded the power of university-generated knowledge that can reach beyond business and government to everyone with access to the Internet. However, the value of philosophical and scientific knowledge may be confused with knowledge that keeps the organization performing. For Demarest (1997) this includes:

- A shared understanding of how value is determined, assigned, maintained, and communicated throughout the organization and with external groups or individuals with whom the organization interacts.
- A set of processes and systems—technical or human—that support and help channel the [organization's] value-creating activities (p. 1).
- A set of indicators that associate the value-creation process with the measures of the organization's success.
- A set of systems that as a part of the "knowledge management infrastructure that monitor the efficiency and effectiveness of that value creation process, indicate opportunities for performance improvement and generally signal the relative rise or decline in value creation" (p. 1).

Higher education has parallel types of performance knowledge manifested in standards for knowledge acquisition by the learner (program requirements, degree audits, grades), standards of academic knowledge (criteria for merit and tenure, peer review of intellectual property), structures and processes for control of organizational knowledge (publications, events, training), and standards for institutional knowledge (internal reviews, accreditation). The sum total of these types of knowledge and the mechanisms through which their value is determined and tied to performance is what allows the institution to function and yet varies among institutions, challenging the cross-fertilization and reciprocation that goes hand-in-hand with exchange of resources. Demarest believes organizational knowledge is socially constructed, and shared. This occurs through four processes: construction, embodiment, dissemination, and use.

Construction is "the process of discovering or structuring a kind of knowledge" (p.6). Organizations that are learning-focused (i.e., K-12, higher education, and workplace professional development departments) utilize specific processes of identifying valued knowledge. Value propositions in such organizations, and to a certain extent in industry where learning is seen as training, may come from external events or forces (community needs, governmental mandates, etc.) or from experience through interaction with client populations (focus sessions, course or training evaluations, documented complaints, etc.). Valued knowledge emerges through an iterative process of examining and implementing the governing body's mandates (government, professional organization, and certifying agencies), determining community- or client-based values and needs, and identifying best practices and policies that support the identified organizational outcomes.

Embodiment is "the process of choosing a container for knowledge once it is constructed" (p. 6). The container may take a variety of forms, most typically a document: manual, memoranda, report, tutorial, or speech. In higher education, such embodiments may be captured as learning objects and stored in a repository or learning content management system (L/CMS). How the embodiment is conceptualized may reflect the organizational cultural beliefs about the social relationships, communication processes, and the structures of authority. For example, L/CMSs that are course-based and only accessible to registered members of the course may indicate intellectual property controls or return on investment as indicated by course registration.

Dissemination "refers to the human processes and technical infrastructure that make embodied knowledge, such as documents, available to the people that use the documents and the bodies of knowledge" (p.6) that serve a function to achieve the organizational goals. Such knowledge dissemination is increasingly digital, although issues of access through systems and (perhaps) limitations of user's technical skills may be why some educational organizations rely on printed media. Digitization has enabled knowledge updates, re-organization, and re-purposing to be quickly and easily possible. Communication about such changes however must be made to the population who uses the knowledge.

Use refers to the ultimate objective of any knowledge management system: the "production" (p. 6) of value. At this point, Thomas's value proposition is most evident. Organizational knowledge may be constructed, embodied, and disseminated but until it is used, its value is only a construct. Use, it can be argued, is what determines the value of any knowledge. Learning objects stored in repositories or located by "Googling," but finding out by whom, when, or for what reason (much less for what outcome) is marginally addressed through metadata, but more directly addressed through strategies such as Digital Rights Management (DRM). DRM identifies the rights of holders, permissions, and tracks usage. The Digital Object Identifier (DOI®) system identifies and tracks use of digital objects, primarily to protect and document how intellectual property is being used, but not to discover the knowledge value of an object. As tracking strategies become adopted and uniformly used, we suspect value will be determined more by frequency of use than by other indicators, such as return on investment (ROI), or by the knowledge value to the user. Most importantly, the social construction of organizational knowledge does not address knowledge acquisition, which is a primary function of higher education.

Technology-Supported Knowledge Acquisition and Construction in Higher Education

The US history of funding technology as a strategy for reform illustrates the theory of technological determinism[3], but belies the reality of the application and adoption of technology and the difficulty, if not impossibility of its predictability and control (Hughes, 2001). Technological relativism[4] embraces this ambiguity and better reflects what actually occurs in the post-structuralist learning environment where faculty conduct scholarship and the learner engages in social learning through a variety of technologies, in a variety of ways, in different contexts that support the institutional goals and philosophy. Sørensen (1996) discusses the prevailing discourse about learning through doing, using, and interacting by which a learning economy is produced, based on the notion that learner actions involve production that is supported by various technological systems. As learners increasingly access objects within structured learning experiences they are also generating objects that document, describe, illustrate, or share their own knowledge acquisition. This process reflects Demarest's focus on performance enacted through his social model of knowledge management. In higher education, performance outside of pedagogically-driven environments is less valued because it occurs outside of the economy. The organization assigns value based on the source of the knowledge. Because the learner can access knowledge anywhere or anytime, value propositions erode and are relative, at least for the learner.

The nature of learning object construction and re-use as disaggregated[5] course content that may be re-aggregated in different ways reflects current thinking about the social construction of knowledge espoused in pedagogical models of online learning (Simonson, Smaldino, Albright, & Zvacek, 2003), the commodification of the course (Diaz, 2004), and the instructional use of learning objects (Higgs, Meredith, & Hand, 2003). Figure 1 below illustrates learning designs in distributed learning systems. Linear learning designs are more content-driven with little deviation from the instructional path and low interactivity with others or the content that is predetermined and a strategy for sharing knowledge. Such designs are highly re-usable and functional when concept, principle, and procedural knowledge are the goal. As the learner moves to the right of the continuum they are afforded more choices about the path of instruction, information formats, and sources, and how they will demonstrate and document their knowledge acquisition. The learner becomes, to a degree, a designer of their own instruction and a generator of knowledge. Difficult to replicate and re-use, this design holds more promise for transfer of knowledge to other contexts and deeper learning (Carmean, 2002). The generation of knowledge and eventual dissemination via learning objects represents a shift, not only in who generates and how generation occurs, but also in how constituencies receive the knowledge. Didactic instruction is a universally used approach to teaching in classroom settings. The traditional approach to instruction in higher education is instructor-dependent, content-driven, and situated in knowledge transfer (Gibbons & Wentworth, 2001). This is at odds with what is known about adult learning in college and the workplace (Mentkowski, 2000) and in research indicating that as educators use technology in general, their role as subject matter expert shifts to that of guide and facilitator, reflecting an epistemological shift with a variety of associated

Figure 1. Learning designs in distributed learning systems

• Rote • Memorization • Habitualization • Routinization			Deeper learning • Transferability • Relevance/applicability • Guided Discovery
Linear ⟷ *Single user*	Branched ⟷	Hyper-content ⟷	Learner-centered Multiple users
• High re-usability • ID design • Instructor/trainer as designer/director			• Low reusability • Emergent design • Instructor/trainer as facilitator/resource
Knowledge Sharing Technological determinism	⟷		Knowledge Generation Technological relativism

outcomes (Reeves, 2002). A learning object pedagogy, unlike the traditional model, is one in which the learner makes decisions and choices about a task or problem as they locate relevant information, and construct and generate knowledge eventually embodied in a learning object. The instructor and LCMSs, serve as guide and facilitator.

Objects that are used within larger pedagogical frameworks, classrooms, L/CMSs, or blended learning environments, have embedded systems which determine or sanction the function of the object and which operate within the instructional designer's pedagogical determinism. Although objects that are learner-centered achieve multiple objectives and are more likely to be generative, they are also confined to some degree by the system, process, and technology within which they operate. The disaggregation of the course has provided a natural opportunity for the learner to modify existing objects or create new ones that become a part of the knowledge used by others to learn (Collis & Stijker, 2003). It is the opportunity for knowledge generation that informs the social model of knowledge management through knowledge management learning designs that operate across institutions, through cross-fertilization, be it intentional (determinist) or selected (relativist).

Transmission of Knowledge Across, Through, and in Spite of Organizations

The challenge of any institutionalized knowledge base and system of transmission, transferal, or adoption is that no learner remains within the organizational context throughout their day-to-day life, and they move between contexts across their learning and working life. As workers who are engaged in continual learning, we move between and among organizations that use technologies, the use of which, for the most part, is defined for us by the organizations in which we are situated. Learning environments, rules, procedures, and intended outcomes change as we move from school to work to training. Thus within an institution, the individual acts and interacts from a personal point of view.

In post-secondary education, technology is used to support learning, primarily as an Information Communication Technology (ICT) through which knowledge is constructed, learning is managed, or learning objects are disseminated. E-learning has become standard in higher education, as evidenced by the burgeoning and robust market for course management systems, Web-based tutorials and simulations, and mobile computing. Of course, learners in formal educational environments also acquire knowledge from family, social groups, and other social, religious, or civic organizations (Bransford, Brown, & Cocking, 2000). Social learning is ill-structured and not necessarily outcome-driven, while learning that is not situated in work or education is typically uniquely structured and without conditional assessment measures. For most of us, our preparation to learn strategically in formal and organized settings begins at an early age in traditional educational institutions. The nature of this type of learning is so institutionalized that it crosses most cultures, economic groups, and generations. Yet when we leave an educational setting and are required to learn in workplace environments, the nature of learning shifts.

In the workplace, technology is also used as an ICT although the focus is more on job skills training for just-in-time, just-in-need, or just-in-case learning that relates to job tasks, seen as performance support. Designs for workplace knowledge management systems are equally recommended to be learner-oriented in interface and content as well as management design (Raybould, 2002). Over the developmental life of the learner, then, the organizational uses and expectations of technology shifts at the macro level as well as the micro level as discussed by Thomas (1994).

An often-missing component from the decision to implement a technology-mediated learning strategy is evaluation or effectiveness studies to determine if the selected technology has the ability to address institutional goals and concerns. The literature in this area looks at "satisfaction" in a way that does not always address actual learning outcomes and overall, there exists a lack of empirical studies showing that the use of instructional technology actually improves learning regardless of the context (Arbaugh, 2002; Buckley, 2002; McClelland, 2001; McGorry, 2003; Neal, 1998). Studies conclude that the full potential of instructional technology is reached only by a full transformation of the learning process, faculty development, and institutional systems (Buckley, 2002; Jamieson, Fisher, Gilding, Taylor, & Trevitt, 2000; Moore, 2002). The research on the effectiveness of distance education or online learning programs shows difficulty with student-instructor communication, lack of socialization both with the instructor and other students, student engagement and interaction, innovation in teaching, and technical difficulties or support (McGorry, 2003; Salisbury, Pearson, Miller, & Marett, 2002). Finally, the instructor's actual technological expertise (Lea, Clayton, Draude, & Barlow, 2001; Webster & Hackley, 1997) along with their ability to overcome interaction problems (Berger, 1999) has been found to be important both in faculty member's decisions to adopt instructional technology and in students' satisfaction and learning outcomes. These findings are at odds with return on investment (ROI) arguments that distributed education can serve large populations without denigrating effectiveness, a trend seen in higher education.

Technology has shifted the nature of traditional learning and training by removing the learner from contexts, such as school and workplace. Taylor (2001) has developed a model that describes the shift in distributed learning from linear and print-based to flexible and modular/digital based:

- The "correspondence model" relies on print-based resources.
- The "multimedia model" provides learning resources through a variety of media including print.
- The "tele-learning model" incorporates modes of presentation of materials to include audio or video-conferencing and broadcast TV or radio.
- The "flexible learning model" requires that students engage in interactive, online computer-mediated resources and activities.
- The "intelligent flexible learning model" is the next generation model in which the learner accesses learning processes and resources through portals.

Learning through and with learning objects enables the learner to self-direct their experiences and engage with others for purposes that best support their learning, while utilizing objects that best match their needs. Diaz (2004) notes that the more complex and autonomous the system, the more it allows the learner to manage their own learning, but the higher the degree of technical skills necessary, and the larger the institutional investment. Conversely (or perversely), the more the learner is engaged in making choices and directing learning experiences, the greater the likelihood they will generate knowledge. Personally constructed knowledge is then influenced by the organizational knowledge that shapes our behaviors, values, and norms that we bring to learning or working context. The process of knowledge construction is reflected in the way organizations approach knowledge management. Learner- or worker-generated knowledge is not without limitations and barriers within certain models of knowledge management.

Four Models of Knowledge Management

Existing models of knowledge management have emerged from policy and practice. Although the tradition of distributed instructional materials is not new for higher education, the shift toward digitalization has affected the nature of distribution, as well as policy decisions. Learning objects are a relatively new concept with regard to knowledge management, and the idea of re-use and re-purposing has necessitated specific management and ownership considerations. Typically, learning objects originate with ideas generated by faculty members and are created with supports from the university, then distributed through a local or external repository. Rights of ownership and attribution are critical as are permissions to re-use, revise, and maintain the objects. Pre-learning object policy has not fully accounted for the unique provisions of reuse. In this evolving context of learning objects, we have identified four models that address control and ownership in varying ways: traditional pre-digital, intellectual capital/appropriative, sharing/reciprocal, and contribution-pedagogy.

Traditional Pre-Digital Model

The traditional model of ownership in the area of copyright predates technology. Up until the passing of the Digital Millennium Copyright Act of 1998 (DMCA), and perhaps after, long established legal principles grant to employees, such as faculty members, the inherent right of ownership to their inventions (Chew, 1992). Intellectual property policy language, especially in the area of digital works such as learning objects, can sometimes be ambiguous. McMillen (2001) finds that academic custom, the informal principles of university practice, impact copyright ownership in two ways. First, if there is ambiguity in a faculty member's contract or other written document that expressly assigns copyright ownership, courts may look at custom and usage to determine the university and professor's intent regarding ownership. In other words, courts could decide to take into account an institution's established practices in deciding who should retain property rights. Second, if no contract, policy, or written document regarding copyright ownership exists, courts are permitted to use the academic custom and usage within or outside the institution to determine what the parties would have agreed to had they addressed copyright ownership.

In Rhoades (1998) examination of the actual ownership of faculty products, he found that, of the contracts analyzed, a majority of them had extensive provision for faculty ownership; in fact, the institution does not always claim ownership, even when it is a "work for hire." The "conditions" of production or use of resources are pivotal in determining ownership and assigning profits. In her analysis of intellectual property ownership in the institution of higher education in the United States, Chew (1992) reexamines ownership via social tradition and case law. Surprisingly, her findings reveal that, despite common assumptions, long established legal principles grant to employees, such as faculty, the inherent right of ownership to their inventions. Faculty members' claims on their inventions and the enforceability of university policies are unclear. However, as distributed learning technology evolves and requires greater use and infusion of institutional resources, ownership, and control may begin to away from individual creators and contributors and toward resource providers. Further adding to the ownership ambiguity is the vast array of digital products that are being produced within commercial and non-commercial collaborations and partnerships.

Intellectual Capital/Appropriative Model

The intellectual capital or appropriative model holds that ownership, control, and maintenance of intellectual property, especially in the area of distributed learning, is important. Under this model, institutional resources expended are carefully monitored and among other factors, become the criteria for ownership and control. Further, the vast majority of higher education institutions' intellectual property policies are increasingly based on this model (Diaz, 2004). The arrival of technology into the area of copyright has created a new market for products that previously had little or no commercial value. In fact, many copyright sections of intellectual property policies differentiate between digital and non-digital property and contain specific and substantial rights over these economically viable products. The intersection of intellectual property rights, specifically in the area of copyright, and technology in higher education is the realm of distributed learning, including distance education, learning objects, digital repositories, and electronic courseware products.

Consistent with previous studies in the area of intellectual property copyright policy transformation and the corresponding commodification of educational products (Chew, 1992; Lape, 1992; Packard, 2002; Slaughter & Rhoades, 2004), Diaz (2004) finds that policies are evolving to further address distributed learning products in a variety of ways. Findings indicate that institutions are revising policies to further deal with and capture instructional products. Policies are aligned with the organizational change that is occurring in higher education within a larger context of an information-based economy (Castells, 2000). Additionally, the new instructional model is heavily dependent on information technology in the form of network connectivity, infrastructure and support staff, thus making it resource intensive. Policies reflect this change by mimicking the shift in ownership conditions away from those required in a traditional setting to those required in a high technology setting. Use of institutional resources in the instructional process has been nominal (i.e., secretarial support, libraries), compared to those required now: media specialists, instructional designers, and so on. Ownership terms changed to address the new instructional model, but claims on instructional products have appeared where there were previously none.

Institutions are asserting ownership where they previously had not because online courses and course materials present a potential source of revenue from which the institution could benefit. Several explanations exist for this increasingly appropriative behavior. Faculty-developed electronic content and courseware materials (especially in specialized academic areas where the market is deficient) present a potential source of revenue and savings, as the institution will not have to pay costly licensing fees to purchase or utilize externally developed products. Increasing "contracted" education serves the dual purpose of producing salary savings while providing one-on-one attention to students and improving their performance (Twigg, 2000). The appropriation of digital knowledge may also be a preemptive move on behalf of universities that fear faculty members will package their courses and make them available to multiple markets (while employed at the present institution or after they have left), perhaps in competition with the college or university that employs them.

Sharing/Reciprocal Model

The sharing reciprocal model is based on shared value and the exchange of learning objects and other digital materials across organizations and institutions (Diaz & McGee, 2004). The focus here is on the support of learning activities. Individual institutions support the assembly of learning objects, which may be shared across departments but, more commonly, objects are imported from many other places. Table 1 illustrates the many partners that may be involved

Table 1. eLearning Partnerships

Organizational partnership	Partners
EDUCAUSE Corporate Partner Program (http://www.educause.edu/partners/about.html)	• IT professionals (public/private) • Technologists • Managers • Higher education executives
Massachusetts Institute of Technology DSpace Federation (http://dspace.org)	• Columbia University, Cornell University, Ohio State University, and the Universities of Rochester, Toronto, and Washington • Hewlett-Packard • MIT Libraries
The Fedora Project (http://www.fedora.info/)	• University of Virginia • Andrew W. Mellon Foundation • Cornell University

in these consortia. Organizational support mechanisms and systems moderate costs. Many institutions join consortium in order to create a system for storing and distributing objects in what becomes a mutually beneficial learning object economy (Learning Content eXchange, 2003). Consortia often articulate content and evaluation standardization as a strategy to increase the market value of an object. DRM, Royalty Rights Management (RRM), index, and search functions as well as supporting technologies are collectively addressed and operated through a well-organized consortia initiative. Such collaboration allows members to establish pre-determined policies and procedures that articulate a negotiated value and standard of quality for the objects that are shared.

Learning object registries can provide standards and access for institutions that may not be interested in partnerships. One example is the Learning Object Network (LON) (http://www.learningobjectsnetwork.com) that uses Digital Object Identifier (DOI) as the identifier mechanism and collects object metadata and location information so they can direct potential users to the source. Institutions or consortia must determine the degree of access and set policy that sets the rights of the owner of the object. One approach to DRM is the Creative Commons Project[6] that provides no-cost licenses so that copyright holders can inform potential users about copyright restrictions. Knowledge management systems that can serve consortia provide customizable interfaces that can meet the unique needs and preferences of a group regardless of their funding level or size. For example, EZ Reusable Objects (EZRO) is an open source, free Web application that requires little to no technical expertise to configure and operates to manage learning objects. EZRO is scalable and responds to the specific needs of consortia driven by a variety of goals and directed by institutional policy.

The first three models discussed above fail to address the value of knowledge acquisition acquired through learner-object interaction, which should be an expectation and criteria in the learning object economy. Instead, they focus specifically on the exchange of goods in terms of the agreed-upon market value rather than the knowledge value that informs the "buyer" of whether or not, as Demarest would argue, the product "works." For higher education the value should reside in the object's actual knowledge value.

Contribution Pedagogy Model

The focus of the contribution-pedagogy model is that learners contribute to object development or generate objects themselves, thereby contributing to the knowledge base of the institution. This reflects the shift toward a learning object pedagogy in which learners, not only learn from experience by participating in the generation of the object, but by contributing to the learning of others through object development and re-use. Collis and Striker (2003) suggest that by having learners generate learning objects, and contribute to a course repository that grows with each offering of the course, the burden of producing objects is shifted away from the institution and the instructional process. This results in a variety of benefits: time is saved for the instructor or content-generator, resources are designed by the population for which they are intended by providing a locally better "fit" with the intended audience, learners can contribute and revise objects over time by updating content or presentation, and the tacit knowledge of the learner is transparent and can be shared or studied by the institution (Collis & Winnips, 2002).

Laurillard and McAndrew (2003) illustrate the contribution-pedagogy model in their design of generic learning activities that shift teaching from a transmission model to a construction model. A design of generic learning activities shifts teaching from a transmission model to a construction model as illustrated by Laurillard's "Conversational Framework" for learning. This iterative process requires the learner to engage, act, and reflect upon what they know and how they come to learn. An analysis of scalable (individuals or groups) and sustainable (efficient and economic) learning designs address how to design for diversity of learner experiences, goal-based learning, re-use of objects, use of online learning tools for learning outcomes, clear and succinct instructions, and dynamic technology function. Specific recommendations are made for the design of objects to be used in multiple courses. When multiple applications are considered at the design stage, there is an increased likelihood of increased re-use across disciplines. Additionally, objects can be easily re-versioned depending on the needs of new or revised courses and pedagogy is wrapped around objects, activities, and supports. The Sharing/Reciprocal and Contribution-Pedagogy models impact how value is attributed, estimated, and assigned to learning objects and reflect Thomas and Home's (2003) Student-centered Route and Freedom Argument for the distribution and access of learning objects that suggests a new economy.

Learning Object Economy

Higher education's new approach to its knowledge products has led to the emergence of a learning object economy. Johnson (2003) notes that the learning object economy has at least five markets of exchange: proprietary, commercial, free, shared, and peer-to-peer. Each of these "markets" has a corresponding culture and has been met with varying degrees of success. He argues that a fully functioning learning object economy would satisfy the needs and requirements of its constituents: market-makers (repository builders), instructors, end users, assemblers, regulators, publishers, resellers, and authors. Figure 2 illustrates the way that various constituents intersect and exchange in this new economy (Johnson, 2003).

Figure 2. Learning object economy (Learning Object Economy adapted from Johnson, 2003)

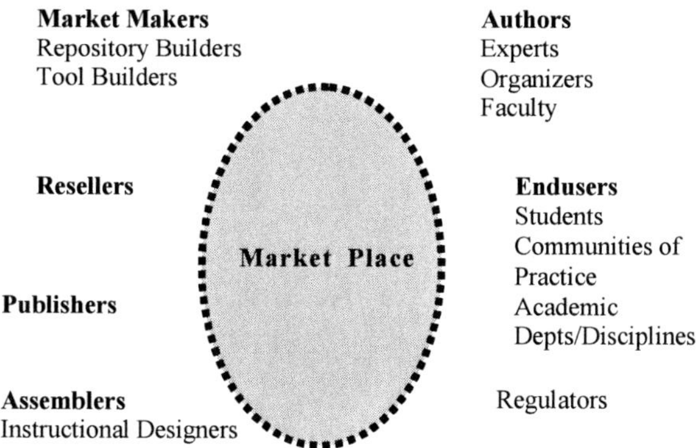

Table 2. Learning object economy and the five markets

Market	Product example
Proprietary	Private company training repository
Commercial	E-learning companies selling learning objects
Free	MERLOT or the Educational Learning Object Exchange
Shared	Higher education LO consortia
Peer-to-peer	Sharing systems between higher education institutions

Technologies, if they resonate and are adopted, can generate an economy that is derived from the value placed on them by a social group. Groups may have different interpretations of the basis of the value. Since learning objects require group collaboration, represent knowledge construction, and are disseminated across populations, there is a high level of mediating variables and processes.

Technological systems, if they resonate with the organization and are adopted, can generate an economy that is derived from the value placed on them by a social group. Groups may have different interpretations of value, and since learning objects require group collaboration, represent knowledge construction, and are disseminated across varied populations, a high level of mediating variables and processes exist. Johnson (2003) describes five markets, each with a different exchange approach, in which learning objects operate. These markets—proprietary, commercial, free, shared, and peer-to-peer—are described in Table 2.

Each of the aforementioned four knowledge management models (traditional-pre digital, intellectual capital/appropriative, sharing/reciprocal, and contribution pedagogy) intersects with one or more of Johnson's learning object economy markets. For instance, the traditional-pre digital, intellectual capital/ appropriative models exist within the value system of the proprietary and commercial markets. The last three markets, free, shared, and peer-to-peer, also exist in higher education settings. It is possible for appropriative and non-appropriative models to coexist, for instance within a college or department. Each market satisfies those constituents' needs and is aligned with a set of culture-specific values. Implicit needs must also be met in order for exchange to flourish. For instance, learning objects must be credible or carry some quality assurance regardless of the system within which they operate.

Although the literature (Hart, 2004; Kidwell, Vander Linde, & Johnson, 2000; Norris et al., 2003) suggests a maturing of knowledge management practices that have resulted in a myriad of systems, the learning object economy in all markets is still weak at best. As Johnson (2003) points out, the current level of

Table 3. The learning object economy: Drivers, enablers, and mediators (Adapted from Johnson, 2003)

	Definition	Higher education example
Drivers	Knowledge, productivity, competition, readiness, infrastructure	Faculty-, student-, staff-produced knowledge; L/CMSs; wireless learning environments.
Enablers	Learning technologies, learning design, standards	A menu of learning technologies available to educators; learning technologists as support staff to enhance learning and teaching functions.
Mediators	Resources, policies, perceived value	Learning technologies centers; flexible and adaptable intellectual property policies.

activity has not yet reached a "tipping point." The solution, he postulates, is an "economy of content in which individuals and organizations can acquire, adapt, and repurpose content" (p.7). Table 3 presents a summary of Johnson's drivers, enablers, and mediators to a thriving learning object economy.

Several of these drivers, enablers, and mediators are present in the models discussed earlier and suggest some explanation for the under use of learning objects. For instance, higher education intellectual property policies governing the control and ownership of digital instructional products or learning objects are often structured in such a way as to inhibit development and sharing outside of the originating institution (Diaz, 2004). This type of behavior, evident in the Intellectual Capital/Appropriative Model, also prohibits the sharing of resources and distribution of costs: mediators in the economy. The Appropriative Model and other models discussed are limited, to some extent, by their social context. Each is operating within the boundaries of their organizational context and corresponding values and is thus limited by those constraints. In response to these limitations, we propose a new relativist model. We argue that in order for a learning object economy to succeed, it must be able to take advantage of and utilize its drivers, enablers, and mediators independently of a social or organizational context.

Open Knowledge Model

Knowledge sharing and re-construction with intellectual property rights attribution and learner-owner intellectual property rights are necessary in an increasingly globalized and distributed learning ecosystem.[7] The Open Knowledge Model embodies trends in a variety of disciplines: computer science (see

OKI and OSPI), education (see McGee & Robinson, 2004), science (see Cottey, 2003), and social justice (see Open Knowledge Network) in that it utilizes a relativist construction and accommodates cross-institutional cultures and beliefs about learning technologies, the construction of knowledge across systems and institutions, as well as the trend toward learner-centered e-learning, disaggregated and re-aggregated learning objects, and negotiated intellectual property rights.

We build on Thomas' and Demarest's conceptual frameworks in an attempt to address the emergent model of knowledge management in higher education that reflects current beliefs about the learner, the function of the institution, the trend toward knowledge generation, and the evolution of existing models. In that the function, definition, and value of technology are relative to organizational culture and values, we assert that no organizational position is more or less valid than another (Wescott, 2001). The Open Knowledge Model provides for this caveat. This is not to say that value is not shared across higher education systems, but rather that individual organizations and their members have come to contribute to the value given to the knowledge that is generated within them.

The first component of the Open Knowledge Model addresses how the culture and actions of higher education tacitly and explicitly determine the value, purpose, and role of knowledge for the institution at large. The culture of each higher education institution determines the value and use of knowledge, rather than the technology. This is clearly reflected in institutional efforts such at MIT's OpenCourseWare project in which course syllabi and materials are accessible to all in an effort to support their "mission to advance knowledge and education, and serve the world in the 21st century. It is true to MIT's values of excellence, innovation, and leadership" (MIT, 2004). MIT has chosen to share intellectual property that represents the values, norms, and standards of learning of their unique and specific mission. We see such efforts as supporting the inherent purpose of higher education: as a primarily generator of bodies of knowledge that should be made freely available to the public. Traditional models of knowledge dissemination that are tied to processes of tenure and promotion (peer-referred journals with limited circulation) restrict knowledge access. In the Open Knowledge Model, intellectual property is digitized and distributed with rigorous standards of review, but made available to anyone who is interested, rather than a privileged few through repositories (Crow, 2002).

Traditionally, intellectual property rights policy has indicated the market value higher education has placed on learning objects, however, documented knowledge acquisition (through learner generation) and use of learning objects (through tracking) is a more authentic indicator of value. In the Open Knowledge Model, intellectual property rights are determined by the generator and negotiated by the end user who may choose to re-purpose the content through licenses allowed through systems. The growing number of repositories and referatories indicates that learning objects are a valid and valued knowledge source both within and outside of any one institution. Additionally, we propose that knowledge value is reflected in use and re-use of learning objects.

The second area of focus deals with the ways in which knowledge is created, embodied, disseminated, and used in higher education; the relationship between knowledge and technological innovations; and the relationship between knowledge, innovations, and performance standards that higher education requires in order to meet its strategic objectives. Higher education, as an institution, embodies cultures that are both shared and not shared. For instance, sharing and collaboration in a learning object economy can occur within and across disciplines, departments, and the institution as a whole. In this sense, the academic setting is unique in that cross-cultural/organizational generation, sharing, and re-purposing, is possible and brings the added benefit of greater innovation and diffusion of knowledge. Further, repositories and referatories, as technological systems, make this possible as learning objects grow and become more meaningful with use and reuse. With successful cross-pollination comes increased funding; consortia and leveraged resources and capital, standardization by industry in accordance with established values to support reuse.

The third area of focus deals with the strategic and material commercial benefits that higher education expects to gain from more effective knowledge management practices and performances. These may include increased revenue, prestige, partnerships, cross-organizational fertilization, and higher skilled faculty and graduates. Several factors have contributed to the development of knowledge management. The literature in the area of globalization in higher education points to information technology, organizational change, and productivity growth (Castells, 1997, 2000; Tiffin & Rajasingham, 2003). The development of new intellectual property policies, and the extensive revision of existing ones (Olivas, 1994), is one signal of the organizational transformation and the effort to harness productivity to the benefit of the institution. Globalization, increased competition among non-profit and for-profit educational entities, and changes in funding structures has all contributed to changes in the way higher education institutions deliver services and leverage their instructional products.

Table 4. Stages of organizational learning

Precipitating Jolts	▪ Proliferation of information technology (IT) in higher education (HED) ▪ Increased entrepreneurial behavior in HED ▪ Increased competition or economic pressure
Learning Stage I	▪ Emerging HED IT profession ▪ Established HED entrepreneurial behavior (patents) ▪ Collaborative HED/IT professional organizations (EDUCAUSE) ▪ Elite organizational behavior (MIT's OKI, DSpace)
Learning Stage II	▪ Higher education develops L/CMSs ▪ Current technology is expensive and insufficient ▪ Organizations seek to "retain" knowledge
Diffusion	▪ Social consensus via organizational leaders (in process) ▪ Lower level orgs mimic behavior
Institutional Copyright Policy Transformation	▪ Whole policy revisions ▪ Addendums to existing policies ▪ Instructional technology/software clauses

The utilization of distributed learning technologies and systems has several benefits for the academy: increased research productivity, generation of tuition revenue via increased access, institutional acquisition of instructional products, and improved learning. While some of these outcomes are yet unproven, they are well documented in the language that surrounds policy. Several studies have suggested higher education's move toward commercializing instructional products (Anderson, 2001; Slaughter & Rhoades, 2004; Welsh, 2000). One can speculate on what has prompted such activity in this area. Organizational learning theory tells us that a number of precipitating jolts, both external and internal to the organization, can prompt such changes (see Table 4). Such jolts can come from the changing economy, changing technology, and pressure to improve learning outcomes (Castells, 2000).

The Open Knowledge Model represents the drivers of knowledge management: the methods for management and the conceptual framework that guides processes of knowledge generation. It supports a new economy based on authentic knowledge value in which human capital is embraced and recognized as the core of educational institutions and that which higher education can best support and sustain.

References

Anderson, M. (2001). The complex relations between the academy and industry: Views from the literature. *The Journal of Higher Education, 72*(2), 226-246.

Arbaugh, J. (2002). Managing the online classroom: A study of technological and behavioral characteristics of Web-based MBA courses. *Journal of High Technology Management Research, 13*(2), 203-223.

Becker, H. (2001). *How are teachers using computers in instruction?* The Center for Research on Information Technology and Organizations. Retrieved February 12, 2004, from *http://www.crito.uci.edu/2/pubdetails.asp?id=292*

Bennett, K. & Metros, S. (2001). *The promise and pitfalls of learning objects: Current status of digital repositories.* Retrieved from *http://itc.utk.edu/educause2001*

Berger, N. (1999). Pioneering experiences in distance learning: Lessons learned. *Journal of Management Education, 23*(6), 684-690.

Bransford, J., Brown, A., & Cocking, R. (2000). *How people learn: Brain, mind, experience, and school.* Washington DC: National Academy Press.

Buckley, D. (2002). In pursuit of the learning paradigm. *Educause Review,* January/February.

Carmean, C. (2002). *Learner-centered principles.* Retrieved on March 11, 2004, from *http://educause.edu/nlii/keythemes/lcp/*

Castells, M. (1997). *The power of identity.* Oxford: Blackwell Publishers.

Castells, M. (2000). *The rise of the network society* (2nd ed.). Oxford: Blackwell Publishers.

Cavanaugh, C. (2001). The effectiveness of interactive distance education technologies in K-12 learning: A meta-analysis. *International Journal of Educational Telecommunications,* 7(1), 73-88. Retrieved June 15, 2004, from *http://www.unf.edu/~ccavanau/CavanaughIJET01.pdf*

Chandler, D. (1996). Shaping and being shaped: Engaging with media. *CMC Magazine,* (3), 2. Retrieved June 15, 2004, from *http://www.december.com/cmc/mag/1996/feb/toc.html*

Chew, P. (1992). Faculty generated inventions: Who owns the golden egg? *Wisconsin Law Review, 2,* 259-314.

Clark, T. (2001). Virtual schools: Trends and issues. *Distance Learning Resource Network and WestEd.* Retrieved on March 14, 2004, from *http://www.wested.org/online_pubs/virtualschools.pdf*

Collis, B. & Striker, A. (2003). Re-useable learning objects in context. *International Journal of E-learning, 4*(2), 5-16. Retrieved October 13, 2004, from *http://dl.aace.org/14190/*

Collis, B. & Winnips, K. (2002). Two scenarios for productive learning environments in the workplace. *British Journal of Educational Technology, 33*(2), 133-148.

Cook, J. & Cook, L. (1998). How technology enables the quality of student-centered learning. *Quality Progress,* July, 59-63.

Cottey, A. (2003). Open Knowledge: A proposed adaptation of Open Science, focusing on guidelines for knowledge claims. *SGR Newsletter, 26*, 17-8.

Creative Commons (2004). *"Some rights reserved": Building a layer of reasonable copyright.* Retrieved April 15, 2004 from *http://creativecommons.org/learn/aboutus/*

Crow, R. (2002). *The case for institutional repositories: A SPARC position paper.* Washington, DC: The Scholarly Publishing and Academic Resources Coalition.

Curren, L. (2004). MIT's Double-Secret Hidden Agenda. *eLearn.* Retrieved June 15, 2004, from *http://www.eLearnMag.org/subpage/sub_page.cfm?article_pk=11125&page_number_nb=2&title=FEATURE%20STORY*

Davenport, T., DeLong, D., & Beers, M. (1998). Successful knowledge management projects. *Sloan Management Review, 39*(2), 374-84.

Demarest, M. (1997). *Knowledge management: An introduction.* Retrieved March 1, 2004, from *www.noumenal.com/marc/km1.pdf*

Demarest, M. (1997). Understanding knowledge management. *Long Range Planning, 30*(3), 374-384.

Diaz, V. (2004). *The digitization and control of intellectual property: Institutional patterns of distributed learning behavior and the organizational policy response.* Unpublished doctoral dissertation, University of Arizona.

Diaz, V. & McGee, P. (2004). *Policies for success on the new learning object frontier.* Presentation at the National Learning Infrastructure Annual Meeting. San Diego, CA.

Downes, S. (2002). *Design and reusability of learning objects in an academic context: A new economy of education?* Retrieved June 15, 2004, from *http://www.usdla.org/html/journal/JAN03_Issue/article01.html*

EZRO (2004). Retrieved June 15, 2004, from *http://ezro.devis.com/*

Gibbons, H. & Wentworth, G. (2001). *Andragogical and pedagogical training differences for online instructors.* Paper presented at DLA 2001, Callaway, Georgia. Retrieved March 9, 2004, from *http://www.westga.edu/~distance/ojdla/fall43/gibbons_wentworth43.html*

Higgs, P., Meredith, S., & Hand, T. (2003). Technology for Sharing: Researching learning objects and digital rights management. *Flexible Leader 2002 Report.* Retrieved January, 10, 2003, from *http://www.flexiblelearning.net.au/leaders/fl_leaders/fll02/finalreport/final_hand_higgs_meredith.pdf*

Hughes, T. (2001). Through a glass darkly: The future of technology-enable education. *EDUCAUSE Review.* Retrieved April 13, 2004, from *http://www.educause.edu/ir/library/pdf/ffp0111s.pdf*

Jamieson, P., Fisher, K., Gilding, T., Taylor, P., & Trevitt, C. (2000). Place and space in the design of new learning environments. *Higher Education Research and Development, 19*(2), 221-237. Retrieved June 17, 2004, from *http://www.oecd.org/els/pdfs/EDSPEBDOCA027.pdf*

Johnson, L. (2003). *Challenges impeding the learning object economy.* Macromedia White Paper. Retrieved June 15, 2004, from *http://download.macromedia.com/pub/solutions/downloads/elearning/elusive_vision.pdf*

Joy, L. (2004). *Training versus learning.* Retrieved on March 18, 2004, from *http://www.structured-training.com/asp/trainingvlearning.asp*

Kidwell, J., Vander Linde, K., & Johnson, S. (2000). Applying corporate in higher education. *EDUCAUSE Quarterly.* Retrieved June 17, 2004, from *http://www.educause.edu/ir/library/pdf/EQM0044.pdf*

Lape, L. (1992). Ownership of copyrightable works of university professors: The interplay between the copyright act and university copyright policies. *Villanova Law Review, 37,* 223-269.

Laurillard, D. & McAndrew, P. (2003). Reusable educational software: A basis for generic e-learning tasks. In A. Littlejohn (Ed.). *Resources for networked learning.* UK: Kogan-Page.

Lea, L., Clayton, M., Draude, B., & Barlow, S. (2001). The impact of technology on teaching and learning. *EDUCAUSE Quarterly, 24*(2).

Learning Content eXchange. (2003). *A new industry model for the e-learning market.* Retrieved June 17, 2004, from *http://www.learningcontentexchange.com/LearningObjectEconomy.pdf*

Lyotard, J. (1984). *The postmodern condition: A report on knowledge.* (Trans. G. Bennington and B. Massumi). Minneapolis: University of Minnesota Press.

McClelland, B. (2001). Digital learning and teaching: Evaluation of developments for students in higher education. *European Journal of Engineering Education, 26*(2), 107-115.

McGee, P. & Robinson, J. (2004). The digital divide: Making a case for open source. Paper published in the *Proceedings of the Education and Information Systems: Technologies and Applications (EISTA)* Conference, Orlando, Florida.

McGorry, S.Y. (2003). Measuring quality in online programs. *The Internet and Higher Education, 6*(2), 159-177.

McMillen, J. (2001). *Intellectual property: Copyright ownership in higher education, university, faculty, & student rights.* Asheville, NC: College Administration Publications, Inc.

Mentkowski, M. & Associates. (2000). *Learning that lasts: Integrating learning, development, and performance in college and beyond.* San Francisco: Jossey-Bass.

Meyer, K. (2002). Quality in distance learning. *ASHE-ERIC Higher Education Report, 29*(4), 1-121.

MIT (2004). OpenCourseWare. Retrieved from *http://ocw.mit.edu/index.html*

Moore, M. & Kearsley, G. (1996). *Distance education: A systems view.* Wadsworth Publishing.

Neal, E. (1998). Using technology in teaching: We need to exercise healthy skepticism. *The Chronicle of Higher Education,* B4.

Nichols, R. (1996). The value of education and training. *Discourse, 2*(1), 13.

Norris, D., Mason, J., & Lefrere, P. (2003). *A revolution in the sharing of knowledge: Transforming e-Knowledge*. Ann Arbor, Michigan: Society for College and University Planning.

Olivas, M. (1992). The political economy of immigration, intellectual property, and racial harassment: Case studies of the implementation of legal changes on campus. *Journal of Higher Education, 63,* 570-598.

Open Knowledge Initiative (OKI) (2004). *http://web.mit.edu/oki/index.html*

Open Knowledge Network (OKN) (2004). *http://www.openknowledge.net/*

Open Source Portfolio Initiative (OSPI) (2004). *http://www.theospi.org/*

Packard, A. (2002). Copyright or copy wrong: An analysis of university claims to faculty work. *Communication Law and Policy, 7,* 275-315.

Perdue, P. (1994). *Technological determinism in agrarian societies.* In M.R. Smith & L. Marx, (Eds.), *Does technology drive history? The dilemma of technological determinism.* Cambridge, MA: MIT Press.

Por, G. (1997). *Designing knowledge ecosystems for communities of practice.* Paper presented at the *Advancing Organizational Capability via Knowledge Management Conference*, Los Angeles, California. Retrieved February 10, 2004, from *http://www.co-i-l.com/coil/knowledge-garden/dkescop/index.shtml*

Raybould, B. (2002). Building performance-centered Web-based systems, information systems, and knowledge management systems in the 21st century. In A. Rossett (Ed.), *The ASTD e-learning handbook,* 338-353. New York: McGraw-Hill.

Reeves, T. (2002). *Evaluating what really matters in computer-based education.* Retrieved June 15, 2004, from *http://www.educat io nau.ed u.au/archives/cp/reeves.htm*

Rhoades, G. (1998). *Managed professionals: Unionized faculty and restructuring academic labor.* Albany: State University of New York Press.

Robson, R. (2001). *All about learning objects.* Retrieved June 15, 2004, from *http://www.eduworks.com/LOTT/tutorial/learningobjects.html*

Rossett, A. & Donello, J. (1999). *Knowledge management for training professionals.* Retrieved February 3, 2004, from *http://defcon.sdsu.edu/1/objects/km/map/index.htm*

Rossett, A. & Marshall, J. (1999). Signposts on the road to knowledge management. In K.P. Kuchinke (Ed.), *Proceedings of the 1999 AHRD conference: Vol. 1* (pp. 496-503). Baton Rouge, LA: Academy of Human Resource Development.

Salisbury, W., Pearson, R., Miller, D., & Marett, L. (2002). The limits of information: A cautionary tale about one course delivery experience in the distance education environment, *e-Service Journal, 1*(2).

Sieczka, K. (n.d.). *Workplace training versus traditional classroom training.* Retrieved February 16, 2004, from *http://www.ideamar kete rs.com/library/article.cfm?articleid=25789*

Simonson, M., Smaldino, S., Albright, M., & Zvacek, S. (2003). *Teaching and learning at a distance: Foundations of distance learning* (2nd ed.). Upper Saddle, NJ: Pearson Education, Inc.

Slaughter, S. & Rhoades, G. (2004). *Academic capitalism in the new economy.* Baltimore: Johns Hopkins Press.

Smith, M. & Marx, L. (Eds.) (1994). *Does technology drive history: The dilemma of technological determinism.* Cambridge, MA: MIT Press.

Solmon, L. & Wiederhorn, J. (2000). *Progress of technology in the schools 1999: Report on 27 states.* Milken Foundation. Retrieved February 12, 2004, from *http://www.mff.org/publications/publications.taf?p age=277*

Sørensen, K. (1996). *Learning technology, constructing culture: Socio-technical change as social learning.* STS working paper no 18/96, University of Trondheim: Centre for technology and society. Retrieved June 15, 2004, from *http://www.rcss.ed.ac.uk/SLIM/public/phase1/ knut.html*

Taylor, J. (2001). Fifth generation distance education. *Higher Education Series, 40.* Retrieved June 15, 2004, from *http:// www.dest.gov.au/ highered/hes/hes40/hes40.pdf*

Thomas, G. & Home, T. (2004). *Using ICT to share the tools of the teaching trade: A report on open source teaching.* Becta ICT Research. Retrieved April 9, 2004, from *http://www.see veaz.mys chools.net/Bestpractice/OSDDB6.pdf*

Thomas, R. (1994). *What machines can't do: Politics and technology in the industrial enterprise.* Berkeley: University of California Press.

Tiffin, L. & Rajasingham, L. (2003). *Global virtual university*. London; New York; Canada: Routledge.

Twigg, C. (2000). *Who owns online courses and course materials: Intellectual property policies for a new learning environment.* The Pew Learning and Technology Program, Center for Academic Transformation at Renssalaer Polytechnic Institute.

Webster, J. & Hackley, P. (1997). Teaching effectiveness in technology-mediated distance learning. *Academy of Management Journal, 40,* 1282-1309.

Welsh, J. (2000). Course ownership in a new technological context: The dynamics of problem definition. *The Journal of Higher Education, 71*(6), 668-699.

Wescott, E. (2001). *The Internet encyclopedia of Philosophy.* Retrieved March 18, 2004, from *http://www.iep.utm.edu/r/relativi.htm*

Wiley, D. (2000). Connecting learning objects to instructional design theory: A definition, a metaphor, and a taxonomy. *The instructional use of learning objects: Online version.* Retrieved June 15, 2004, from *http://www.reusability.org/read/*

Wiley, D. (2003). *Learning objects: Difficulties and opportunities.* Retrieved June 15, 2004, from *http://wiley.ed.usu.edu/docs/lo_do.pdf*

Winner, L. (1977). *Autonomous technology: Technics-out-of-control as a theme in political thought.* Cambridge, MA: MIT Press.

Endnotes

1 "Knowledge management involves recognizing, documenting, and distributing the explicit and tacit knowledge resident in an organization" (Rossett & Marshall, 1999).

2 A learning object economy requires that individual objects are created and shared across institutions (Johnson, 2003).

3 Technology drives change and events. In teaching and learner this means that pedagogy and learner's actions are determined by technology and indeed effect changes in practice. The authors see this more as a result of technological drift (Winner, 1997) through which organizations have been

inattentive to the determinism that has become enculturated (see Perdue, 1994).

4 In our view, technological relativism means that the function, definition, and value of technology are relative to the organizational culture and values and the beliefs about the value within the higher education community. Additionally, we assert that no organizational position is more or less valid than another (Wescott, 2001), but equal consideration must be given to each value position. Additionally, individuals choose what and how they use and adapt technologies to their own purposes (Chandler, 1996).

5 Learning objects typically are parts of a larger course or unit of study. Aggregation involves combining objects to create a scope of learning content.

6 Creative Commons (2004) is a free licensing service that "uses private rights to create public goods: creative works set free for certain uses. Like the free software and open-source movements, our ends are cooperative and community-minded, but our means are voluntary and libertarian. We work to offer creators a best-of-both-worlds way to protect their works while encouraging certain uses of them—to declare "some rights reserved."

7 An ecosystem is a combination of systems that interact to support the survival and generation of organisms that exist within it. The authors see the tools, resources, people, and experiences accessible to the higher education student as constituting a digital learning ecosystem that contributes to a digital knowledge ecosystem (Por, 1997).

Section IV

Case Studies

The following section of this volume presents six case studies. Each is a presentation of a real-world situation of information management in a higher education setting. As the authors of the previous chapters and I have broadly conceptualized the field of Knowledge Management (KM) to be any information technology or information management process that is implemented in the knowledge-intensive setting of postsecondary education, the case studies do not necessarily pertain to the direct application of KM techniques. Rather, the case studies present situations where the social, political, and economic realities of higher education organizations intersect with knowledge and information management.

The first case study, by Richard Smith, Brian Lewis, and Christine Massey of Simon Fraser University (Canada), is titled, "Policy Processes for Technological Change." The authors present concepts of organizational change and strategic IT planning as related to online learning policy in Canada. This case has been included because it highlights that information management, KM in particular, is reliant upon the development of sound organizational policies. In higher education, IT policy is often intertwined with strategic planning, the method by which academic leaders attempt to prepare for the future. Often the process of strategic planning is information-centric, relying on demographic projections of future students, forecasts of endowment payouts based on market trends, and institution-specific data such as faculty retirements, etc. Planning for the future IT needs of an institution is also an important task, one that is often connected to the instructional function of the organization.

Next, Bongsug Chae (Kansas State University) and Marshall Scott Poole (Texas A&M University) present a case titled, "Enterprise System Development in Higher Education." The authors highlight the challenges faced by educational organizations when enterprise systems from the corporate sector are introduced. In particular they find that the unique circumstances presented in the nonprofit postsecondary education sector, such as state mandates and requirements, make the implementation of enterprise systems difficult. The case illustrates why KM principles and structures that were created in the private sector need to be adapted to higher education settings.

Third, Kandis M. Smith of the University of Missouri presents "Higher Education Culture and the Diffusion of Technology in Classroom Instruction." Using Roger's theory of innovation diffusion, the author presents evidence of the various attitudes faculty hold toward the use of instructional technology. As an example of theory-driven research, this case provides a useful induction to Roger's concepts. Students of KM will find that the case also provides an excellent introduction to the notion of academic cultures, including the academic profession, the various scholarly disciplines, specific institutions, and institutional types.

In the fourth case study, "Wiring Watkins University: Does IT Really Matter?" Andy Borchers of Kettering University questions whether or not various technologically-intensive initiatives at a particular university were successful in achieving the desired organizational effects. The case documents what happened when a university asked, "Could a strategic advantage be found through IT?" As KM is often directly tied to strategic planning issues, this case provides an understanding of some of the perceived benefits and actual challenges that are weighed during the process of change management.

The fifth case is titled, "Challenges of Complex Information Technology Projects: The MAC Initiative" by Teta Stamati, Panagiotis Kanellis, and Drakoulis Martakos of the University of Athens (Greece). The case presents the difficulties encountered when a consortium of universities in Britain attempted to integrate their data systems. The integration posed several challenges in the areas of student information systems, financial systems, the staffing model, the physical resources of the universities, research computing and consulting services, payroll, and a management information system. The case provides an account of large-scale information restructuring and some issues to consider when systems from different higher education institutions are to be integrated.

Finally, the sixth case, by Bing Wang and David Paper of Utah State University, is titled, "A Case of an IT-Enabled Organizational Change Intervention: The Missing Pieces." The setting of the case is a university-owned research foundation, which allows readers to consider the various ancillary programs that are affiliated modern universities and the information relationship that exists between a main campus and an external research unit. Also of note in this case is the focus on intellectual property management, a key component of academic KM at research institutions. The authors present a compelling story of information management, change resistance, and power structures within the research foundation.

At the end of the case studies is a set of questions for use in an instructional setting. The questions may be used in conjunction with the case studies, or with the earlier chapters in this volume. Instructors might wish to utilize the case studies as examples for research papers as well.

Chapter IX

Policy Processes for Technological Change

Richard Smith
Simon Fraser University, Canada

Brian Lewis
Simon Fraser University, Canada

Christine Massey
Simon Fraser University, Canada

Introduction

Universities, among the oldest social institutions, are facing enormous pressures to change. There have always been debates about the university, its purpose, its pedagogical program, and its relationship to other social and political structures. Today, these debates have been given renewed vigor and urgency by the availability of advanced information and communication technologies for teaching and learning. These include computers and computer networks, along with the software and telecommunications networks that link them together. When these technologies are used to connect learners at a distance, they are called "telelearning technologies." When referring to their use more generally, to include local as well as remote teaching innovations, they are sometimes called "technology mediated learning" (TML).

Despite much media attention and recent academic criticism, pressures on universities are facilitated, but not caused, by telelearning technologies. Change in universities is not simply a result of forces acting upon universities, but is the result of a complex interaction of internal and external drivers. The use of telelearning technologies intersects with a host of social, political, and economic factors currently influencing university reform. Technology, in this context, has become the catalyst for change, reacting with other elements in a system to spark a reaction and a change in form and structure.

This chapter examines policy processes for the introduction of technology-mediated learning at universities and colleges. It is based on the results of a two-year research project to investigate policy issues that arise with the implementation of telelearning technology in universities and colleges. The focus was on Canadian institutions of higher learning, but the issues raised are common to higher educational institutions in other countries. The study scanned a large number of institutions, reviewed documents, and interviewed key actors including government and institutional administrators, faculty, and students, to discover the range of issues raised by the implementation of telelearning technologies. This chapter discusses these issues and findings.

CASE Questions

- What policies or processes are in place to guide change in colleges and universities? Who knows about these policies and participates in them?
- What are the forces behind technological change in higher education organizations? Are they external or internal?
- Can technology be used as a tool for achieving meaningful and positive change or is it an end to itself?
- In what ways can technology be used to increase access to education?

Doing the Right Thing and Doing Things Right

Organizations implementing telelearning technologies often find themselves facing a variety of new issues not encountered when delivering courses in traditional formats. For example, telelearning technologies can provide access to courses for a broad range of new users. What kind of new or different support services will these new students require? On the flip side of the access issue, students are often concerned about who will have access to files that have stored their electronic discussions, how their identities are safeguarded, and how long these files will be stored. These concerns regarding the implementation of telelearning technologies can be broadly classified as concerns on how to implement these technologies, or "doing things right."

These micro issues of implementation, however, quickly raise questions about "doing the right things," the larger, often politically charged questions that form the policy environment for telelearning technologies. These issues are about why telelearning technologies are used and often evoke preconceived notions of economy, society, and education. These issues are concerned with power relations and the very nature of educational institutions. Examples of these issues would be the purpose of education, the role of professors/trainers, and the goals of business-education partnerships—not only "how" a subject is taught, but what, when, why, by whom, and for what purpose. These broad policy debates, while easily becoming polarized, can help to define an institution's goals so that choices about implementing telelearning technologies become clearer.

Clearly, the two aspects of telelearning policy, "doing things right" and "doing the right things," are linked and both must be dealt with in organizational policies and practices. The importance of sound policy processes that can deal effectively with both aspects cannot be overstated.

One could argue that universities already have well-established mechanisms in place to make these kinds of decisions. After all, universities have long traditions of collegial decision-making. But it is a peculiar feature of decisions about technology that these well-worn processes are seldom respected, as the wisdom of how and why to use technology is expected to be apparent to all.

The issues raised by telelearning technologies suggest a need for a systematic approach that honors collegiality while ensuring that the difficult questions can be dealt with in ways that do not overwhelm the process but serve to facilitate choices about implementation. One danger is that policy processes focus solely on "doing things right," trying to avoid controversy with broader political questions. The decisions that result from such processes risk being dismissed by those affected as ill considered and will not be supported. Another danger is that "doing the right thing" questions can overwhelm all discussion, with no progress made on making any decisions for the institution. In the end, decisions are often made anyway, but without consultation, behind the scenes, and as surreptitiously as possible, to avoid getting caught up in an endless and unproductive process.

Policy Processes

Drivers for Policy Processes

Telelearning technologies serve to amplify a variety of pressures acting on universities and colleges today. For example, the post-secondary sector is experiencing greater competitive pressures than ever before. Institutions can no longer count on their geographical "turf" as being safe from poaching by other institutions. New public and private institutions are emerging to offer popular programs. Telelearning technologies serve to magnify these competitive pressures as online courses attract students from all over the world and as entirely "virtual" institutions are created with no campus infrastructure and no tenure.

At the same time, the demand for post-secondary education is increasing. This demand is coming increasingly from adult workers who are returning to school to upgrade their skills and seek higher professional degrees. These students are seeking more flexible schedules, up-to-date curriculum, and high levels of support services. The more traditional student cohort is seeking similar flexibility as more of these students have part-time jobs and are taking longer to complete their degrees. In this case, telelearning can be an opportunity for universities and colleges to expand their student base and to create new revenue streams through the remote delivery of courses.

The temptation for university administrators in the face of these threats and opportunities is to try to respond quickly, that is, without consultation with their existing constituencies in faculty and students. Consultation, as seen later in the chapter, takes many forms but it is first and foremost an attempt toward inclusiveness in the decision-making process. It is more important than ever that universities establish policy processes that can help them establish priorities and directions to guide planning and to enable rapid responses to threats and opportunities.

Strategic Planning

Strategic planning is a business concept that has migrated recently to universities and colleges as they seek processes to direct their future development. The process can be initiated for a number of reasons. Many institutions feel the need to identify a "niche" for themselves in an expanding marketplace by identifying specific areas where the institution will focus its efforts. In other cases, a strategic plan is useful for convincing others—the Senate, faculty members, and students—that change is necessary (Tamburri, 1999, p. 10).

But the translation of strategic planning from business practice to one appropriate to post-secondary institutions is not automatic. Strategic planning cannot be applied in universities and colleges in the same way in which it is applied in the private sector. Organizational goals in higher education are often vague and, even when well defined, contested. The division of responsibility for priority setting between disciplinary units and the organization as a whole is unclear. But vagueness can be a virtue within post-secondary institutions. Individual units are continually scanning their own discipline's environment and are making informed judgements about their specialized unit. These judgements may conflict with judgements made for the organization as a whole. In the end, contradicting strategies may coexist in the university at the organizational level and at the level of the individual unit (Norris & Poulton, 1991).

Cynthia Hardy argues that many university strategic plans display a fatal lack of emphasis on implementation. She shows how an "executive management" model of strategic planning cannot be imported into universities since it assumes a unitary organization with a common goal. In fact, universities are pluralist organizations where different groups often have competing visions. This means that difficult decisions, such as the reallocation of funds or the elimination of programs, never occur or are made in ways that treat everyone equally since the plan avoids conflict by ignoring how power is distributed and how decisions are really made within the institution (Hardy, 1992).

In light of these concerns, Olcott (1996) suggests a variation on strategic planning specifically designed for aligning institutional academic policy with distance education practice. The need for alignment will become more important as distance education continues to move progressively from the periphery to the core of institutional functions. Olcott argues for a reciprocal adaptation of both distance education units and institutional policy and practice; distance education systems must adapt to create an environment that values mainstream academic norms, and institutional practices must recognize the advantages of the distance education approach. This rapprochement can be achieved by avoiding traditional areas of discontent and agreeing on a commitment to educational values such as quality, access, and responsiveness. He suggests a range of areas where policies can be reformed: recognition of distance education teaching for tenure and promotion purposes, academic residency requirements, and intellectual property.

Strategic Planning for Technology

While strategic planning has begun to play an important role in university and college planning processes, what is different today is the addition of a new function for information technology—teaching and learning.

All too often, computing plans are focused on technology itself, rather than on how technology enables faculty and students to achieve some of the key instructional or research goals of the institution. (Hawkins 1989, cited in Nedwek, 1999)

Still, while many universities may be aware of the need for planning, fewer have successfully extended this process to information technology. The 1998 Campus Computing Project report is instructive. Just under half of U.S. colleges reported having a strategic plan for information technology:

[Fully] 60 percent do not have a financial plan for information technology and less than a third have a plan for using the Internet in their distance learning initiatives. (Green, 1998)

While information technology planning for educational technology is still not widely observed, there are some lessons that we can draw from information technology planning generally. A study of 150 technology officers in universities in the U.S. found that approximately 10 percent of respondents participated in no technology planning at all, saying that it was a frustrating, time-consuming endeavor that distracts instead of contributes to their day-to-day tasks. Nonetheless, this study found that a majority of technology officers devoted a considerable amount of time to strategic planning. The successful processes were able to distinguish between the two functions of technology planning: socioeconomic goals and strategic goals (Ringle & Updegrove, 1998). Socioeconomic goals for technology planning were issues concerned with process. In this case, the goals for a planning exercise were to:

1. Align technology with other institutional priorities
2. Disseminate knowledge about technology needs and constraints
3. Build alliances with key decision-makers
4. Lobby for and obtain financial and other resources
5. Address existing technology needs
6. Keep an eye on the leading edge

These process goals were the most important function of technology planning for these technology officers. The second function of technology planning — the strategic — is concerned with technical issues. Given the speed at which the technology is changing, few technology officers were confident in being able to predict their institution's needs two or three years down the road. For this reason, technology planning needed to focus primarily on the process issues and not get bogged down in technical details (Ringle & Updegrove, 1998).

Ringle and Updegrove's (1998) findings correspond to this chapter's findings about the important role of policy processes for institutional telelearning policy. Technology needs will change quickly and unpredictably. It is crucial, however, that a forum exists for addressing the role and function of technology in the institution. This same study found that the least successful technology plans were those that were marginalized and set apart from overall institutional strategic planning (Ringle & Updegrove, 1998).

John Daniel addresses the development of technology strategies for teaching and learning extensively in his book, *MegaUniversities and Knowledge Media: Technology Strategies for Higher Education.* He makes the point that change works best if it is supported by peer groups and training and if research results are used to demonstrate the reasons for change. It is unrealistic to expect single technology decisions for entire universities. However, the organization as a whole can support technology in strategic ways while allowing units to determine the best way in which to carry out this priority for their students and discipline (Daniel, 1996).

Alberta's Learning Enhancement Envelope program, which provides funding to that province's post-secondary institutions for technology-enhanced learning, makes an institutional technology plan a requirement of funding. As a result, institutions in this province are developing a body of knowledge about technology planning for teaching and learning.

In Canada, the Standing Committee on Educational Technology of BC has developed a guide to educational technology planning. Their plan describes an inclusive process with advisory and communication processes to assist in getting "buy-in" from different internal groups. They avoid the common pitfalls of strategic planning by focusing on implementation. A regular process of revision ensures that any plan is not set in stone for a period of longer than two years, allowing for negotiation and adaptation to new circumstances. The plan is meant to be flexible and adaptable to the specific cultural and institutional circumstances of different colleges and universities (Bruce et al., 1999).

Fair Process

Another danger of strategic planning within universities is that they fall prey to internal lobbying and opposition. As a result, controversial proposals are eliminated before they reach fruition (Tamburri, 1999, p. 11). This is not to say that it is necessary to create division in order to create change. Kim and Mauborgne (1997) note that it is more important that decision-making processes be fairly carried out than that they accommodate everyone's interests. Fair process was the key factor in the cases they studied on the diffusion of new ideas and change in organizations. Kim and Mauborgne identify three key elements to fair process: first, it engages people's input in decisions that directly affect them; second, it explains why decisions are made the way they are; and third, it makes clear what will be expected of organizational members after the changes are made (1997).

Clearly, fair process can only do so much. Policy processes must negotiate between a set of prior normative issues and a set of practical issues associated with achieving a particular outcome or decision. A successful policy process for change achieves a balance between these two elements, satisfying employee needs for procedural justice with the organization's need to reach decisions and to move forward.

Organizational Change

Much of the discussion so far has concerned organizational change in our universities and colleges. According to Hanna, for change to occur in established organizations, three conditions must be met: (1) enormous external pressures; (2) people within the organization who are strongly dissatisfied with the status quo; and (3) a coherent alternative embodied in a plan, a model, or a vision (Hanna, 1998, p. 66).

It is this third condition that presents perhaps the greatest challenge to higher education institutions as they chart their course in this emerging environment. Sound policy processes are a crucial part of the development of this alternative plan since "the collegial tradition of academic governance makes it unlikely that a technology strategy developed without extensive faculty input would have any impact" (Daniel, 1996, p. 137).

It has been suggested that the challenge to using educational technology effectively in universities and colleges is threefold (Morrison, 1999):

1. **Technical:** adequate support and training
2. **Pedagogical:** helping faculty reorient their teaching to best exploit the technology
3. **Institutional:** reorienting the institution to the effective deployment of educational technology

The first two issues can be addressed with changes in policy and funding. The final step, however, requires something more difficult—leadership and vision.

Organizational change in universities and colleges, therefore, requires a delicate balance of collegial and collaborative policy processes that are championed by a leader with a vision for the institution. Such grandiose organizational change projects are clearly not suited to all institutions—most would surely fail. All, however, are capable of beginning to address the place of educational technology in their teaching and learning.

Part of the process is simply to allow innovation to make its way through the institution more effectively. Universities and colleges have been described as organized along a "loose-tight" principle. That is, as long as an organizational member's behavior is generally aligned with organizational values, individual creativity and innovation are supported. If the individual's behavior moves outside the realm of these core values, the organization "tightens" as a response to guide behavior back to the core values (Olcott, 1996).

Part of the challenge for post-secondary institutions in finding their way with telelearning is to create an environment in which it is not only safe to experiment on the periphery, but also where it is safe to fail in the center; where it is "safe to take the risks needed to improve learning and teaching in times of constant, accelerating change" (Gilbert, 1998). The alternative is to have innovation continually at the margins without ever affecting the core. Kay McClenney observed this trend about innovation in U.S. colleges. She notes that despite mounting pressures for change, most innovative practices are kept at the margins of institutions, thus relieving pressure on the college to truly transform the institution (Gianini, 1998).

Putting It All Together: Teaching and Learning Roundtables

One of the most useful models for introducing pedagogical and technological change is the Teaching, Learning and Technology Roundtable (TLTR) program coordinated by the Teaching, Learning and Technology Group (TLT Group), an affiliate of the American Association for Higher Education (http://www.tltgroup.org). The TLTR program provides a set of tools for institutions to help shape goals, facilitate discussion, and organize the implementation of strategies, outside of the bureaucratic structure. A set of structured activities helps evaluate institutional values and pedagogical principles over the use of technology. For example, participants are asked what it is they most value about their institution and would hate most to lose. Only then is technology examined to see how it might support stated values and principles.

A TLTR-style committee should approach its membership strategically. In general, it should be broadly representative of key units in the institution. It is important to have the support of senior-ranking individuals, but they need not be members. The most useful members will be at the operational levels—those who either work with technology or would be expected to.

One of the strengths of the TLTR model is that it places telelearning issues firmly within the context of "doing the right thing" questions. Many technology-planning exercises have failed because they were marginalized from broader questions of institutional mission and purpose. A TLTR group ensures that there is a forum within the institution for those with concerns about the use of technology to have their issues dealt with.

Another strength of the TLTR model is that it is a broad set of organizing and operating principles that can be adapted to local circumstances. Steven Gilbert suggests that TLTR groups not assume a formal policy function in their institution. Some TLTR groups, however, have found that over time, their credibility within the institution is such that they are asked to take on a policy role. Each group will establish itself differently. The TLT Group sponsors national events to help local TLTRs get started and to allow established Roundtables to share experiences and strategies. In this way, local strengths are supplemented by a national network of support.

Finally, the greatest contribution that TLTRs seem to make to institutional telelearning policy is in their communication function. Staff and faculty from dispersed units in the institution discover shared experiences and learn about useful innovations. Support units discover ways in which they can more effectively support telelearning activities. For decentralized institutions, like many universities and colleges, this is an important achievement.

The University of Ottawa and Carleton University jointly sponsored a TLTR workshop in 1998 to begin these processes at their institutions. They have developed an excellent resource on TLTR at (http://www.edteched.uottawa.ca/ottacarl/TLTR/). Although it is still early in the process, several other Canadian institutions have expressed interest in the model and are considering adopting it or trying parts of it in their own sites.

Conclusion

This chapter has shown that policy processes are critical to the development of sound policies and strategies for telelearning technologies. Based on this research, the following institutional policy processes should be considered:

1. Use a transparent process of deliberation and implementation.
2. Make decisions based on research. Since academic culture values research, the basis for technology decisions needs to be clearly communicated and documented.
3. Enable faculty to feel in control of the technologies and that they fulfill an academic purpose.

The issues associated with online learning are quickly and easily polarized, linked as they are to fundamental ideas about the purpose of education, the role of professors, and the sharing or wielding of power.

Based on this research on policy processes, there are two key areas that need further study. First, there is a need for more research on the impact of policy processes. In the area of telelearning technology, studies are being done to evaluate the technology in terms of cost-benefit, learning outcomes, and pedagogical approaches. More research is also needed on the most effective way to enable universities and colleges to make decisions in this area.

Second, on a broader scale, there is a need for research on the management of change in universities that recognizes and works to uphold those values that make universities unique public institutions—including an unfamiliarity with and even an abhorrence of "management" itself. It is also important that whatever guidelines are developed, these must be sensitive to the variations and differences between universities.

As higher education administrators, teachers, and students seek to maneuver their way through the challenges ahead, they will need to find ways to negotiate change, identify priorities, and find solutions that work. In this context, policy processes become critical. This study has shown that the selection and application of appropriate policy processes for the introduction, application, and use of technology-mediated learning plays a key role in managing technological change in an institution.

Discussion Questions

1. Which of the policy processes discussed here seem to fit with your organization? What steps would you take to see these processes put in place?

2. Who is involved in the technology planning process in your organization? Could more people be involved in the process?
3. Is the process of technology planning regarded as legitimate by the members of your organization? What role do students play? What about teachers? Others?
4. What are the drivers of change in your organization?
5. Should organizational change be included as part of an information technology strategic plan?

References

Bruce, R., Bizzocchi, J., Kershaw, A., Macauley, A., & Schneider, H. (1999, May). Educational technology planning: A framework. Victoria, British Columbia: Centre for Curriculum, Transfer and Technology. Available at *http://www.ctt.bc.ca/edtech/framework.html*

Daniel, J. S. (1996). *Mega-universities and knowledge media: Technology strategies for higher education.* London: Kogan Page.

Gianini, P. (1998, October). Moving from innovation to transformation in the community college. *Leadership Abstracts, 11*(9).

Gilbert, S. W. (1998). AAHESGIT Listserv, Issue 195. See *http://www.aahe.org/technology/aahesgit.htm*

Green, K. C. (1998, November). *The campus computing project: The 1998 National Survey of Information Technology in Higher Education* Encino, CA. Available online *http://www.campuscomputing.net/*

Hanna, D. E. (1998, March). Higher education in an era of digital competition: Emerging organizational models. *Journal of Asynchronous Learning Networks, 2*(1), 66-95.

Hardy, C. (1992). Managing the relationship: University relations with business and government. In J. Cutt & R. Dobell (Eds.), *Public purse, public purpose: Autonomy and accountability in the groves of academe* (pp. 193-218). Halifax & Ottawa: Institute for Research on Public Policy and the Canadian Comprehensive Auditing Foundation.

Kim, W. C., & Mauborgne, R. (1997). Fair process: Managing in the knowledge economy. *Harvard Business Review, 75*(4), 65-75.

Morrison, J. L. (1999). The role of technology in education today and tomorrow: An interview with Kenneth Green, Part II. *On the Horizon, 7*(1), 2-5.

Nedwek, B. (1999). Effective IT planning: Core characteristics. *Presentation to the Society for College and University Planning Winter Workshop, Information Technology Planning*, Hawaii, March 21-24.

Norris, D. M., & Poulton, N. L. (1991). *A guide for new planners*. Ann Arbor, MI: Society for College and University Planners.

Olcott, D. J. Jr. (1996). Aligning distance education practice and academic policy. *Continuing Higher Education Review*, *60*(1), 27-41.

Ringle, M., & Updegrove, D. (1998). Is strategic planning for technology an oxymoron? *Cause/Effect, 21*(1), 18-23. Accessed April 20, 1999, from *http://www.educause.edu/ir/library/html/cem9814.html*

Tamburri, R. (1999). Survival of the fittest. *University Affairs*, 8-12.

This case was previously published in Case Studies on Information Technology in Higher Education: Implications for Policy and Practice, pp. 34-42, edited by L.A. Petrides, published by Idea Group Publishing (2000).

Chapter X

Enterprise System Development in Higher Education

Bongsug Chae
Kansas State University, USA

Marshall Scott Poole
Texas A&M University, USA

Executive Summary

"One system for everyone" has been an ideal goal for information technology (IT) management in many large organizations, and the deployment of such systems has been a major trend in corporate world under the name of enterprise systems (ES) (Brown & Vessey, 2003; Davenport, 2000; Markus, Petrie, & Axline, 2000). Benefits from ES use are claimed to be significant and multidimensional, ranging from operational improvements through decision-making enhancement to support for strategic goals (Shang & Seddon, 2002). However, studies (Hanseth & Braa, 2001; Rao, 2000; Robey, Ross, & Boudreau, 2002) of the deployment of ES in private sector organizations show that the ideal is difficult to accomplish. This chapter reports a case in which a major

university system in the U.S. attempted to develop an in-house enterprise system. The system is currently used by more than 4,000 individual users in almost 20 universities and state agencies. This case offers a historical analysis of the design, implementation and use of the system from its inception in the mid 1980s to the present. This case indicates that ES design and implementation in higher education are quite challenging and complex due to unique factors in the public sector—including state mandates/requirements, IT leadership/resources, value systems, and decentralized organizational structure among other things—that must be taken into account in planning, designing and implementing ES (Ernst, Katz, & Sack, 1994; Lerner, 1999; McCredie, 2000). This case highlights (1) the challenges and issues in the rationale behind "one system for everyone" and (2) some differences as well as similarities in IT management between the private and public sectors. It offers some unique opportunities to discuss issues, challenges and potential solutions for the deployment of ES in the public arena, particularly in higher education.

Organizational Background

The Land Grant University System (LGUS) is one of the more complex systems of higher education in the nation. Currently, LGUS consists of nine universities, eight State agencies and a medical science center that serves over 100,000 students and reaches more than four million people each year through its service outreach mission. Research projects underway by system universities and research agencies total roughly $400 million. The system employs more than 23,000 faculty and staff members located throughout the state and serves all counties in the state. The annual budget for the LGUS is approximately $2.0 billion.

The state established its first college in 1876, and this marked the beginning of LGUS. During the 1970s and 1980s, LGUS experienced tremendous growth in terms of its major activities of teaching, research, and public service. The system experienced a 27% growth in its student population, and more growth was expected. In 1986, the system achieved recognition as one of the top 10 National Science Foundation (NSF) ranked research universities in the U.S. In addition to teaching and research, LGUS provided significant services to the citizens of the state through practical application of research-based knowledge.

Table 1. Land Grant University System

The Universities	The Agencies	Health Science Center
• Big Campus (the largest campus) • West Campus • Southeast Campus • South Campus • Northwest Campus • Four other campuses	• Agricultural Research Station (ARS) • Agricultural Extension Service (AXS) • Veterinary Extension Service (VXS) • Engineering Research Station (ERS) • Engineering Extension Service (EXS) • Forest Service (FS) • Transportation Research Station (TS) • Wildlife Management Service (WMS)	• College of Dentistry (CD) • College of Medicine

At the outset of our case, in October 1988, LGUS consisted of four universities and seven associated agencies:

1. Central System Administrative Office (HQ)—the university system's headquarters;
2. Big Campus;
3. West Campus;
4. Southeast Campus;
5. South Campus;
6. Agricultural Research Station (ARS);
7. Agricultural Extension Service (AXS);
8. Veterinary Extension Service (VXS);
9. Engineering Research Station (ERS);
10. Engineering Extension Service (EXS);
11. Forest Service (FS); and
12. Transportation Research Station (TS).

In 1989, LGUS experienced another period of significant growth when three universities joined the system. In 1990, another university (Northwest Campus) joined the system. The growth continued, and in 1996, four additional institutions joined the system (two universities and two research agencies). In 1999, a medical center (MC) was established.

The LGUS itself is relatively new in comparison to many systems of higher education in the U.S. Many of the system's universities had long histories before joining LGUS, but have been part of the system for a decade or less. The units in LGUS also vary greatly in mission and purpose. Each unit has its own goals, traditions, and culture. The system values diversity and honors the principle that "one size doesn't fit all". Traditionally, there has been a decentralized culture within the system. Even though every unit is under a single umbrella, each is regarded as different and desires to maintain its uniqueness and independence.

Setting the Stage

In the 1980s, three currents of change—technological, institutional and organizational—were gaining momentum in LGUS as well as in the U.S. higher education as a whole. Together, the three forces set the stage for the emergence of the University System-Wide Management Information System (USMIS).

Technological Currents

The USMIS project cannot be properly understood without considering events in the computing industry in the 1980s. During this period, a number of new concepts and technologies, including model-oriented Decision Support Systems (DSS), query and reporting tools, On-line Analytical Processing (OLAP) and Executive Information Systems, emerged and were adopted by many organizations. These were all very attractive to organizations and their management, since they seemed to promise an increase in productivity and efficiency. In the 1980s these computer systems were mainframe-based. Building on the concept of Manufacturing Resource Planning (MRP) that was developed in the 70s and mid 80s, the idea of enterprise-wide software, today called ERP, spread rapidly through the vendor community, and SAP, Baan, JD Edwards, and PeopleSoft, among others, introduced major offerings in this area. The development of the SQL relational database management system in the late 1970s fostered the emergence of the concepts of enterprise-wide integration and enterprise software, which become popular among users that included private businesses and institutions of higher education. One vendor in particular, SCT, was prominent in the higher education sector. Established in 1968, SCT marketed a commercial student records system for higher education. In the 1980s, SCT began to promote the concept of enterprise software for higher education, and in 1989, SCT integrated an ERP system on RDBMS-Banner.

The initial sponsors of USMIS—top officials of Big Campus and the HQ who later served on the IT steering committee — were aware of these technology trends and planned to develop an enterprise information system. The system was intended to support not only financial management but also other administrative functionalities, including contracts and grants management, purchasing, office automation and communication, cashiering, requests for travel advances, enterprise and departmental accounting, state interfaces, ad hoc reporting, and information management. They also planned to create a centralized staff (later called the MIS project team) to develop and maintain this ERP so that each unit would no longer need to dedicate computer/information systems personnel to support its financial information systems. The initial sponsors believed that, with centralized IT staff, modification of LGUS accounting systems to respond to environmental changes such as new state laws and regulations could be handled efficiently and uniformly. This would eliminate multiple, difficult-to-integrate versions created by each unit, as was required by fragmented pre-USMIS systems. One large-scale information system for all units was a very attractive idea to the senior administrators of LGUS.

Calls for increased efficiency and productivity had found expression in a variety of changes in many college and university business and finance programs and practices (Jonas et al., 1997). The LGUS IT plan submitted to the state in 1984 stated:

The application of modern automated information systems' technologies to the solutions of fiscal and administrative problems ... LGUS will continue to take advantage of new technologies to increase efficiency and effectiveness in fiscal operations, administration, programming, and communication.

Prior to the USMIS project, there had been two major IT initiatives: BPP and SIMS. The Budget/Payroll/Personnel (BPP) System is an integrated data management system for human resources, payroll, and personnel operating budgets. The primary users are the administrative functions supported by the LGUS. The design concept for the BPP system was developed in the mid-1970s, with full implementation occurring on July 1, 1979. The BPP system was developed using COBOL and IBM's Information Management System (IMS) data management software. Data from BPP could be electronically transmitted to the State Comptroller's office in batch mode, thus offering the state better oversight of LGUS. By 1986, the Student Information Systems (SIMS) project had also been implemented. The SIMS supports administrative processing of student records for Big Campus and South Campus. The system uses Software AG's ADABAS as the main database system. The main development languages are COBOL and NATURAL. The SIMS later played an important role in USMIS design.

Organizational Currents

During the two decades from 1970 to 1990, the LGUS grew rapidly, attaining an annual budget of $800 million. The LGUS Board of Regents and system administrators felt a pressing need for consolidated information to facilitate coordination and control among (and over) member institutions. However, the existence of separate financial management systems supporting diverse accounting rules and practices throughout LGUS created a major barrier to enterprise-wide integration. In the mid-1980s, the business offices of the 11 units of LGUS were employing 11 different financial accounting systems. Most were modified versions of an in-house accounting information system developed by Big Campus in the 1970s. Departments within each unit had also developed or purchased their own departmental accounting systems. These functioned as shadow information systems, running in parallel with the main financial systems in each unit.

In the mid-1980s, the President and financial officers of Big Campus initiated a project to develop a large-scale fiscal and administrative information system with capabilities for decision support, executive reporting, online purchasing, budgeting and planning, investment management, and streamlined integration across departments and colleges, among other functions. Initially their idea was to develop this system solely for Big Campus. LGUS administration was impressed by this plan and decided to expand its scope to include all units of the system. One highly-placed administrator at Big Campus commented that this was the most significant change in the history of USMIS. It was a change that later created many political issues and fostered resistance from other units.

Two considerations drove this change in scope. First, there was the issue of development cost. The initial acquisition cost for the Big Campus information system was expected to be over $1 million. At the time, this seemed too high to justify for only a single university. An enterprise system that would serve all units in LGUS was an appealing idea to Big Campus because it would enable the cost to be distributed among all units. Second, the development of an "integrated large-scale fiscal and administrative information system" was part of LGUS's strategic plan, and the expanded enterprise system was viewed by LGUS administration and the Board of Regents as a means of pursuing this plan.

Institutional Currents

Institutional forces also influenced the development of USMIS. In general, public organizations have more legal restrictions on their actions than those in the private sector (Guy, 2000). During the 1980s and through the 1990s, state after state mandated more stringent reporting requirements and accountability for higher education (Ernst et al., 1994). And such a mandate seemed necessary for LGUS. In the early 1980s, State auditors found that several units in LGUS had not followed proper fiscal procedures and that there were inconsistencies in the way the various units reported financial transactions on their annual financial reports.

The use of automated information systems by governmental bodies had strong support in both the legislative and executive branches of the state. Information systems were viewed as a means to improve productivity and efficiency. Financial information systems in particular were regarded as a means to improve coordination, integration and control. Legislators and administrators also believed that a uniform information system could help ensure that state-mandated changes in accounting and other procedures were implemented quickly and uniformly and followed faithfully throughout the state.

In 1987, the legislature mandated the State Comptroller's office to develop a Unified Statewide Accounting System (USAS) for the collection and reporting of statewide payroll and personnel data. The USAS was intended to meet state agencies' general accounting requirements and thus reduce the number of separate accounting systems. In fact, the ideal scenario would be to have a single financial information system based on USAS which would replace all current financial information systems. However, cooler heads recognized that in reality this was not feasible because of the variability among state agencies in terms of their size and the diversity and uniqueness of their needs. Thus, the Comptroller's office proposed two approaches for state agencies: Either use USAS or maintain your own information systems and interface them with USAS. The latter approach was selected during discussions between the USAS development team and LGUS. This requirement offered a compelling reason to replace existing in-house computer systems with a large-scale fiscal and administrative information system. The USMIS project was welcomed by the USAS project team since it was expected to provide the Comptroller's office with a single channel to communicate with all LGUS units.

These technological, organizational, and institutional currents led the LGUS Board of Regents and chancellor to recognize the strategic role information systems would have in the future of LGUS. They delivered a directive for the development of USMIS that was aimed to insure compatibility and consolidation of accounting and fiscal information, analysis, and reports from all system units. The challenge now was to build it.

Case Description

Overview

First introduced in 1990 for Fiscal Year 1991, USMIS is an enterprise information system that incorporates financial regulations applicable to the units of LGUS. It integrates 30 databases that function as a unit across five independent modules or subsystems, including a financial accounting system, a purchasing system, a fixed assets management system, a system for sponsored research accounting, and annual financial reporting. The MIS project team has been responsible for the development and support of USMIS since the late 1980s. This team reports directly to the Department of Information Resources (DIR) within the central system administration office (HQ), the DIR in turn reports to the Office of the Vice Chancellor for Business Services who is under the Chancellor, the highest ranking officer of LGUS.

Design Process

The director of the MIS project was hired in October 1987. In November 1987, a survey questionnaire was distributed to all of the units of LGUS and the major departments within each unit to solicit input on their management information system needs. The survey demonstrated wide agreement on the need for substantial improvements in financial accounting management information within LGUS. In March 1988, an implementation team to work on the

Table 2. Options for system design

1. Install a system currently in use at another institution of higher education within State
2. Use the Uniform Statewide Accounting System
3. Install a public domain software accounting system from out-of-State that could be altered to fit the LGUS system's needs
4. Install a general purpose commercial system and adapt it into a college, university, and agency accounting system
5. Install one of the systems currently in use within the LGUS and tailor it to meet the system's needs
6. Do nothing at all
7. Design and develop a system in-house
8. Install a college and university financial system that was designed and written by an outside vendor, with no modifications to the package
9. Modify and enhance a packaged system purchased from a vendor specializing in college and university systems
10. Install a college and university financial system designed and written by an outside vendor but enhanced and modified to meet the LGUS requirements and the Uniform Statewide Accounting System and other State requirements.

development of the USMIS was formed. The core members of the team were four senior systems analysts, three of whom had worked on SIMS project since 1979 and one of whom worked for the CIS department at Big Campus.

The team's first task was to interview approximately 75 key users. The interviews resulted in the compilation of a Needs Inventory, the baseline requirements for LGUS. Ten alternative approaches to satisfy these requirements were investigated (Table 2).

The team made site visits to other universities and conducted detailed evaluations of existing information systems. Option #10 was selected on the basis of functionality, risk, time to implementation, flexibility, LGUS policy, interface/state, user involvement and technology. According to the former director, the MIS project team was asked to complete the project in one year, which was regarded as a reasonable time frame. The team was required to make regular progress reports to the steering committee, which consisted of 11 top administrators representing the units of LGUS and the Board of Regents.

In June 1988, the team prepared a requirements document which formed the basis of the Request for Proposal (RFP). In October 1988, the team submitted a 300+ page Advanced Certification Document for the USMIS to the state's Automated Information and Telecommunications Council (AITC) for approval. In the same month, the RFP was finalized, and in November, the team received the state AITC approval to purchase a software package.

Following the evaluation of vendor proposals, a contract was signed in 1989 with Information Associates for the Software AG NATURAL/ADABAS version of the Financial Records System (FRS), a popular financial information system among colleges and universities. This represented a three-way agreement among LGUS, Information Associates, and Software AG. LGUS requested this agreement in order to acquire a NATURAL/ADABAS version of the COBOL-based FRS. It was redesigned and re-engineered using NATURAL, Software AG's fourth generation language and the ADABAS data management systems. The redesign of NATURAL/FRS was completed in 1991.

This redesign of FRS was necessary in order to bring it into line with existing information systems and the Big Campus computing environment. As previously noted, in the mid-1980s, Big Campus made two major information system procurements to support administrative computing: SIMS (the Student Information Management System) and an IBM 3090-200E mainframe. The system underlying SIMS was purchased in 1984 and implemented by 1986. It included processes supporting admissions, registration, student financial aid, billing, grading, transcripts, degree audit, and loan repayment. The system employed Software AG's ADABAS as the principal database system and COBOL and NATURAL as development languages. This procurement cost over $1.6 million. The project was also committed to NATURAL because its system analysts and programmers were trained and experienced in NATURAL from their work on the SIMS project. USMIS also had to utilize the IBM 3090-200E mainframe computer, which was purchased and installed in August 1987 and cost over $8.2 million. This commitment was further solidified by an upgrade to an IBM 3090-400E, planned for 1992. Existing information systems served as critical constraints on the project.

These commitments combined with time pressure from the Board of Regents and the steering committee to produce a rather restrictive development environment. The former project director noted that:

... [p]eople (users) had little tolerance for changing. Flexibility does not mean much to users. It is not something what users want. They want what they are familiar with, so we tried to do as few changes possible ... IS implementation has to be fast. A reasonable time for system implementation to me is one year. Why? Because key players leave and are changed. That's a big problem. You lose focus and then give up.

In late 1988, the administrators of LGUS, Big Campus, and other units grew concerned about delays in the implementation of USMIS. This increased time pressure on the MIS team. Final vendor selection, completed in April 1989, increased confidence that USMIS would be implemented in a meaningful way. After modification of the purchased software package, USMIS went live with the FRS subsystem for three units—Big Campus, HQ, and VXS—in September 1990 for the fiscal year 1991. In September 1990, the Sponsored Research (SPR) subsystem went live with limited functionality. In September 1992, the Fixed Assets (FFX) subsystem went live for four campuses and two research agencies. In 1993, the purchasing system went live for LGUS, and in 1998, the Annual Financial Reporting (AFR) system went live. Following are some of the major milestones for the project:

- 03/88 – Hiring of four Senior Systems Analysts for the Project;
- 06/89 – Contract signed with Information Associates for the Software AG NATURAL/ADABAS version of the software;
- 09/89 – Hiring of four entry-level programmers;
- 11/89 – Initial code delivered;
- 09/90 – System went live with FRS (Financial Record System) and FAR (Accounts Receivable) for three units;
- 09/90 - SPR (Sponsored Research) module went live with limited functionality;
- 09/93 – Commence implementation of first phase of purchasing module at Big Campus Purchasing Department (Requisitioning and Purchase Orders); and
- 02/98 – Commence Budget Module implementation.

Implementation Process

Implementation turned out to be the most difficult task in the development of USMIS. At the outset, the MIS project team and the initial sponsors expected that full implementation of USMIS would take four years. The initial projection assumed an implementation schedule as follows:

- Year 1 – Implementation in Big Campus (Fiscal Year 1990-91);
- Year 2 – Implementation in a second university and one research agency;
- Year 3 – Implementation in a third university and a second research agency; and
- Year 4 – Implementation in the entire LGUS.

As this schedule indicates, the goal was for USMIS to be implemented in all units of LGUS. The advanced certification document explicitly stated the importance of the "full implementation" to realize substantial savings and the many benefits that would follow from USMIS. The initial position—set by the chancellor and Board of Regents of LGUS—was that no waivers of this requirement would be allowed and that no other option for financial management would be offered other than use of USMIS.

In pursuit of this goal, the MIS project team visited each member's institution and informed them of the mandatory nature of implementation for all units of LGUS. However, when Chancellor Jones left LGUS, his successor, Chancellor Smith, decided that implementation of USMIS would be optional, rather than mandatory. Changes in implementation policy, discussed in more detail in the following text, undercut the MIS project team's ability to hold to the schedule. Additional complications were introduced by local politics, leadership changes, resistance from some units, state-mandated rule and policy changes, user requests regarding system maintenance and enhancements, and lack of resources. The diffusion of USMIS through LGUS actually occurred as depicted in Figure 1.

Several of the issues faced by the MIS team have much in common with the experiences of enterprise system development in private sector organizations (Brown & Vessey, 2003; Davenport, 1998; Robey et al., 2002). However, the contexts of IS management in the public sector and in higher education pose unique challenges and also intensifies some traditional private sector problems. Research on public organizations and management indicates that there are some differences between public and private sector organizations in terms of goal complexity, authority structure, accountability, and the role of rules and regulations (Allison, 1983; Guy, 2000; Rainey, Backoff, & Levine, 1976).

Figure 1. USMIS transition schedule

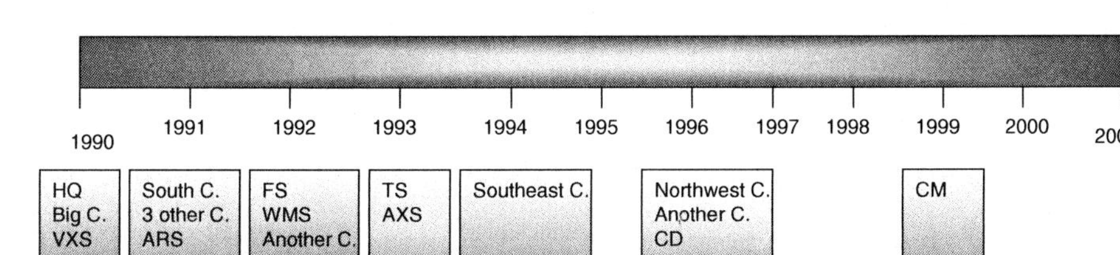

Note: C. denotes campus.

Research on IT in the public sector also indicates differences in IT management and planning between private and public sectors (Dufner, Holley, & Reed, 2002; Gauch, 1993; Mohan, Holstein, & Adams, 1990; Rocheleau & Wu, 2002). Furthermore, research on strategic planning and IT management in higher education indicates that the contexts of IS planning, development, implementation and use in higher education differ from those in private entities (Ernst et al., 1994; Lerner, 1999; McCredie, 2000). Interviews pointed to four major categories of challenges and issues that have significantly affected the USMIS over the years.

1. Politics and Organizational Resistance to Change: The Battle

The value system in higher education differs from that of the business arena. The guiding principle of the university—long term investment in the educating of citizens—is different from the business's bottom line approach. Unlike the business model, which generally emphasizes a management-driven approach, university management is based on shared governance by faculty and administrators that is for the most part temporarily drawn from the ranks of faculty. A university is a loosely-coupled system in which units and employees recognize the need to work together for a mutually beneficial future, but understand that their differences will often create tensions (Lerner, 1999).

Initially, units of LGUS had two sorts of reactions to USMIS. The smaller universities and agencies, which lacked computer and financial resources, were relatively favorable toward USMIS, since it provided them with an interface with the State's Comptrollers' office, a legislated requirement. However, other units were more negative. Despite the fact that they realized the need for consolidated reports for system level management, they preferred to use their own financial systems and interface them with USMIS.

For example, one campus had just developed a new student information system and a financial information system and did not want USMIS. Two research agencies—Engineering Research Station and Engineering Extension Service—were strongly against USMIS adoption. They advocated the need for maintaining their own information systems based on two arguments. First, they pointed out functional deficiencies in USMIS to support their needs for contract and grant management and other research related functionalities. Their second argument was that as engineering agencies they differed from other units in LGUS.

The Engineering Research Station in particular rejected the vision of "one system for everyone" and expressed concerns about USMIS. Top administrators and the IT manager of engineering research argued that USMIS was inferior to their own computer system, which was based on the Oracle database. During vendor selection in 1988, the MIS project team was less interested in a brand new system, but searched for a system compatible with existing information infrastructure (Star & Ruhlender, 1996), including SIMS, NATURAL, ADABAS and IBM 3090-200E. Engineering research had advocated a different alternative, SCT using Oracle DB. The MIS team argued that SCT was a riskier choice than Information Associates, exhibiting an attitude toward IT planning characteristic of the public sector. In general, public sector organizations tend to be more cautious and more concerned with rules and regulations, whereas private organizations tend to be more comfortable with risk (Bozeman & Kingsley, 1998). Competition is much less significant in the public sector, which tends to be concerned with service delivery and continuity, as well as with protecting the public interest (Rocheleau & Wu, 2002). The view of IT in private and public organizations also tends to be different. For the public sector IT is not a proprietary resource to be exploited for competitive advantage (Dufner et al., 2002), but more often is regarded as a cost-cutting device, a way of doing more with the same number of staff (Rocheleau & Wu, 2002). Risk avoidance is evident in public IT management (Mohan et al., 1990).

Engineering research also argued that the MIS team and steering committee initially designated research (e.g., research contract and grant management subsystem) as a low priority in the implementation plan. A top administrator of the engineering research agency insisted that "we will be asked to pay for a system we do not need nor want. We will be asked to pay for a system that at the very best will be mediocre." A top administrator of a different research unit emphasized the importance of autonomy and distinctiveness in LGUS in a memo to the HQ:

It is important to clarify the directives of the LGUS Board of Regents ... ***Centralization*** *seems to be effective in smaller state systems with less diversity of missions. But the size and complexity of LGUS make centralization a formidable task at best ... Traditionally, the HQ had maintained a very workable interpretation of its role by providing* *overview and governance where a global perspective is necessary and where shared services reap benefits to the LGUS members. But the autonomy of the System members to exercise their authorities and means in order to do a good job is one that members have long cherished. In my opinion, the current USMIS* ***philosophy*** *threatens the traditional role of the HQ and threatens to share service even when such services are costly to some system members. Such a change in philosophy could not be implemented overnight. If such as a change was in order, then it should be communicated as such and simply not be the results of the [USMIS] initiative ... the* ***autonomy*** *of the LGUS members is their strength and their means of attaining their goals.*

Most respondents recognized the conflict between these agencies and the MIS project team and HQ over the issue of USMIS adoption. They referred to it as "The Battle". The result of The Battle was that in 1995 two units, engineering research and engineering extension, and the newly joined Northwest Campus were officially allowed to establish an interface with USMIS rather than adopting it as their primary system.

2. Top Management Commitment: Leadership and Politics

The Battle was tightly interwoven with changes of leadership in the system. Among many events in the history of USMIS, the resignation of the former director of the MIS project team had significant impacts on the process of USMIS implementation. The former director had been in charge of the MIS team from the beginning in 1987 and left LGUS on July 1991. His resignation caused serious problems in the continuation of USMIS implementation. A second leadership related event compounded the difficulty of USMIS implementation. One of the initial sponsors of USMIS, the Executive Deputy Chancellor, left LGUS. This loss of two key sponsors led to a loss of direction in the implementation effort. These departures made it more difficult for the MIS team and LGUS leadership to resist the efforts of units that wanted to opt out of USMIS.

Another complicating factor was change in chancellors. From 1986 to present, there have been five chancellors. Each chancellor had different visions for USMIS, and these had significant impacts on USMIS implementation (Table 3). One interviewee noted that "Every time a new chancellor is in office, things

Table 3. Policy of USMIS implementation and change of leadership

Chancellor	Background	Term	Policy on USMIS Implementation
Smith	Formerly Dean of College of Agriculture at Big Campus	1986-1990	Mandatory
Jones	Formerly Dean of College of Engineering at Big Campus	1991-1993	Favorable to engineering agencies and neutral toward USMIS
Brown	Formerly President of Big Campus	1993-1994	Mandatory
White	Formerly President of Northwest Campus	1994-1999	Favorable toward Northwest Campus and neutral toward USMIS
Green	Hired from outside	1999-Present	No Interest

change. USMIS shifts depending on who the chancellor is at that time. The vision of chancellor is a powerful influence."

The MIS project was officially established during Chancellor Smith's regime. The chancellor and the board were very supportive of USMIS design and implementation. He strongly supported a mandatory policy for USMIS implementation. In 1990, three units implemented the USMIS as it went live.

In 1991, Chancellor Jones, formerly the Deputy Chancellor for Engineering of Big Campus, assumed office. One of the initial sponsors of USMIS noted that:

Chancellor Jones initially saw USMIS as bad, and I had to convince him not to stop what we had done so far. After becoming the chancellor, he changed his view a little bit and put his foot on both sides (us and engineering). He tried to take a neutral position but understood the engineering side more. That's why the two research agencies could avoid using USMIS.

Unlike the first chancellor who advocated USMIS, Chancellor Jones was not as strong an advocate of USMIS, and this weakened pressure for implementation. During Chancellor Jones's term implementation of USMIS was widely regarded as optional. However, the HQ and the MIS team continued to push for adoption. In 1991, six more units of LGUS became users of USMIS, and in 1992, three units implemented it.

The optional status for USMIS implementation changed dramatically when Chancellor Brown, formerly President of Big Campus, took over. Brown had been on the steering committee of the original MIS project at Big Campus and thus was very supportive of USMIS. He made implementation mandatory again and announced that all units must be on USMIS. This led to conflict between HQ and the MIS project team and those units that wanted to avoid using USMIS. A top IT administrator at one university campus recalled that "it was not a happy time for everyone".

However, Chancellor Brown's term lasted for only one year. In 1994, the Board of Regents appointed the president of the newly added Northwest Campus as the fourth chancellor during the period of LGUS implementation. Chancellor White stressed the importance of uniqueness and autonomy of each university and agency in LGUS. While White was not against USMIS implementation, he decided that units could choose not to use USMIS. Notwithstanding, acceptance of USMIS continued to spread. During Chancellor White's term of office, all units except the two engineering agencies and the chancellor's former university implemented USMIS as their primary financial and accounting system.

This led a number of those involved in the development and implementation of USMIS to believe that USMIS implementation was very "political." Several respondents said, "If you want to understand USMIS implementation you need to see how politics has played over time in the history of USMIS ... A lot of local politics was played in USMIS adoption ... Politics was very powerful in the implementation of USMIS."

While the importance of top management commitment for large IT projects in the private sector can never be overstated (Brown & Vessey, 2003), the complex, often discontinuous, and fragmented power and leadership structure intensifies the challenge in obtaining continuous top management commitment in the public sector (Watson, Vaught, Gutierrez, & Rinks, 2003). In the private sector, the process of setting objectives and carrying them out are closely integrated, whereas in the public sector these processes are loosely coupled (Rocheleau, 2000). The loosely-coupled structure of public organizations impedes consideration of operational issues at the time objectives are established. For example, an objective might be "management information systems that will insure compatibility and the ability to consolidate accounting and fiscal information, analysis, and reports from all system units". When elected top administrators negotiate to set objectives such as these, feasibility and operations aspects may not be fully considered (Dufner et al., 2002). Detailed IT issues and related topics have often not been considered relevant for consideration by university presidents or chancellors (Ward & Hawkins, 2003).

Experience with developing EIS shows that "In the private sector, once the chief executive wants an EIS, it will move. In the public sector, wanting is not enough. Movement can stop at any of a number of stages" (Mohan et al., 1990).

3. Rules and Regulations from a Public Constituency

Public organizations have many legal restrictions on their actions and operate under public scrutiny (Guy, 2000). Higher education faces calls for increased accountability and regulations imposed by multiple social institutions and governing bodies, including legislators and Generally Accepted Accounting Principles (GAAP) (Ernst et al., 1994; Jonas et al., 1997).

In the 1980s and 1990s, several state audits had shown deficiencies in LGUS and other universities, and many new rules and policy changes were mandated by the state. These were very influential in the design and implementation of USMIS. The USAS that went into effect on September 1, 1993 for a number of small state agencies has been influential in the maturity stage of USMIS implementation. Since this date, all units of LGUS had to report information to the central USAS database daily. This database, controlled and managed by the State Comptroller's office, was designed to maintain accounting data consistent with GAAP and National Association of College and University Business Officers (NACUBO) standards. The system provides accounting services to all state agencies using a *uniform* chart of accounts. Also, USAS reflects any changes in the state legislatures and policy. Thus, in the implementation and maintenance of USMIS, priority had to be given to processing requirements and maintenance requests that were mandated by law or policy changes.

For instance, in 1999, the Governmental Accounting Standards Board (GASB) Statements No. 34 and No. 35, "Basic Financial Statements" and "Management's Discussion and Analysis for State and Local Governments and Public Colleges and Universities," were issued. For the first time, accrual accounting was required for all government activities and all capital assets had to be depreciated. Starting in fiscal 2002, the state is required to implement these new rules. In response to this requirement, USMIS had to develop depreciation capabilities to report the depreciation of fixed assets. Priority had to be given to these sorts of mandated requirements and policy changes rather than user requests.

USMIS was also required to respond to state auditors' recommendations of management controls. The sate audit report in 1995 pointed out that USMIS did not provide useful information at the departmental level. USMIS responded to the audit's recommendations in a number of ways. Immediately after the state audit the MIS team began the implementation of departmental download capability. LGUS finalized licensing agreements for a software package that allowed end users to download USMIS data to their microcomputer environments so that data could be processed to meet the end user's needs. In 1998, USMIS began the implementation of budget and automated Annual Financial Report (AFR) subsystems. Recently, there has been an effort to convert the BPP system to the same processing environments (ADABAS) as the USMIS system in order to develop the interface between the two systems.

4. Diversity of Internal Constituencies and Their Needs: No CIO?

Like other public organizations (Guy, 2000; Rainey et al., 1976), LGUS serves a large number of constituencies whose goals and needs are diverse and sometimes even compete with one another. As the original objective of USMIS—one IS for everyone—indicates, USMIS was directed by a desire for centralization. The Board of Regents and the initial sponsors of USMIS believed that one IS for all units in LGUS was desirable and could be realized. However, as the design and implementation were proceeding, the size and diversity of LGUS emerged as a critical issue.

Every unit had its own chart of accounts, and the accounting practices throughout LGUS were very diverse. Few wanted to change their accounting. Some feared losing control. USMIS had to adapt to the diversity of their accounting practices. Also each unit had different priorities. For example, the research agencies required contracts and grants/research accounting capabilities in order to administer programs and to assure compliance on sponsored research projects. Big Campus, which had initially made a significant investment in the acquisition of the software package for USMIS, used this leverage to request that many other functionalities and subsystems (e.g., purchasing, department-level accounting, and administration) be added into USMIS.

The diversity of needs and requests and their sheer number resulted in problems in attaining the full design and implementation of USMIS. According to the state audit report in 1996, as of 1995 there was a backlog of over 250 user requests for system maintenance and enhancement, some of which dated back to 1990 and 1991. From September 1995 until June 1996, the USMIS support staff had completed 219 service requests. During the same period, an additional 271 maintenance items were identified by various system users. Similar to the situation in the broader public sector (Mohan et al., 1990; Rocheleau & Wu, 2002), most academic institutions have a shortage of IT related resources and skills for user-support and system maintenance (Ernst et al., 1994).

Needs at the top of LGUS also forced the MIS team to adapt. One of the original objectives of USMIS was to provide the capability of executive information systems to meet the information needs of system-level users, such as the Board of Regents and the Central System HQ. However, the 1996 state audit of management controls at LGUS pointed out the lack of a comprehensive management information system. The report recommended that:

System management should reevaluate the overall intent and purpose of USMIS and how best to meet the management reporting needs of the board and executive management. Consideration should be given to the depth of accounting functions that USMIS will provide, including general ledger, project accounting, and management reporting. Alternative methods for meeting management reporting needs should be fully identified and evaluated.

To respond to the recommendation that alternative methods be adopted, LGUS initiated the data warehousing project to develop an executive information system, rather than altering USMIS. This system went into operation in 2000. The system is loosely-coupled with USMIS and other systems at Big Campus and the system-level. Also, there are several other needs that USMIS does not support such as departmental financial management and reporting. Thus different parts of LGUS had developed or purchased "shadow information systems" to make up for the deficiencies of USMIS to meet their specific, local needs.

Until 1991, the 11-person steering committee, composed of members from universities' fiscal management, system units, and the MIS team, set priorities for development. Starting in late 1991, a different committee consisting of the five top administrators from the university fiscal management, HQ and the USMIS team, took on this task and tried to set priorities for USMIS. However, the complex and interwoven elements in USMIS design and implementation made it difficult for the group to perform this task. This is partly because every unit in LGUS, including Big Campus, wanted their project to be the top priority. However, it was difficult to manage prioritization because the group did not have the same authority as a CIO in the corporate world. Public managers tend to have less authority over subordinates and less decision-making autonomy (Rainey et al., 1976). A top IT administrator in LGUS commented:

Higher educational institutions differ from the private sector as far as IS is concerned. The university is governed by committees so the attitude is "convince us" of why we need such an information system. Therefore design and implementation become tougher. There is a lot less commitment by members.

Since 1991, the MIS team's position has been that priority was to be given to those projects that result in improved reporting and/or processing for all users of USMIS. With the recognition of the diversity of LGUS the MIS team adopted a "customer-oriented" rather than "enforcing" approach and tried to accommodate different needs of different members. The diversity of LGUS led the MIS project team to design an "average" system for all units, no matter whether they were large or small universities or research agencies, while different parts maintained "shadow systems" to meet local needs not satisfied by USMIS. The research agencies over that USMIS is for universities, not for them, while the smaller universities say it is too big for them. Reflecting on this, a key initial sponsor of the project commented "one system for everyone is nothing for nobody."

Current Challenges and Problems Facing the Organization

As finally-realized, USMIS diverges considerably from the grand vision of the project initiators and the Board of Regents. The final system is not the fully integrated large-scale information system the MIS team set out to build, but it has certainly served critical functions for LGUS. After more than a decade of service, USMIS is now regarded as an aging legacy system. Currently LGUS and the MIS project team face the same three sets of forces—technological/functional, organizational and institutional—which demand important decisions and actions on the future of USMIS. The critical question is whether USMIS needs to be replaced or extended; if extended, in what way; if replaced, when is the right time and by what?

Technological Issues

Aging administrative, financial information infrastructure is one of the most critical challenges to universities today (McCredie, 2000). Functional pressures that raised doubts about the instrumental value of USMIS came from both inter-organizational and environmental levels. At the inter-organizational level, different user groups had pointed out functional deficiencies with USMIS. At a more general level, users complained that USMIS was not user friendly, did not utilize advanced databases, and had slow response time. At the environmental level, the emergence of new technologies such as GUI, fourth generation programming languages, and client-server architecture led to functional pressures. More recently, there have been some other functional pressures due to changes in the environment. For example, the industry has clearly moved to embrace SQL as the standard query language. SQL databases like Oracle and Microsoft SQL Server are becoming much more popular than ADABAS. Also it is very difficult to find programmers familiar with ADABAS. Currently LGUS is engaged in an effort to replace SIMS, the payroll system, and the human resource system with an ERP, which is expected to cost approximately $35 million. This project is becoming another source of technological/functional pressures to either replace USMIS with an ERP or significantly enhance it through utilizing Web technologies. Most recently, the project team is considering the utilization of middleware technologies such as the EntireX Broker for Web-based services for USMIS.

Organizational Issues

Given the state of the U.S. economy in 2003, the number-one IT-related issue in higher education is funding (Crawford & Rudy, 2003). LGUS is no exception. Considering the magnitude of the ERP project, LGUS has concluded there is no way to replace USMIS in the short term. Key decision makers noted that people agree that "USMIS plays a large role in reporting to the state ... USMIS works." However, a backlog of requests for functional improvements from departmental and individual user groups and cumbersome user interfaces ("Green Screens") are acknowledged as major issues. Currently, the organization has decided to keep the legacy system, but the remaining question is for how long? And how can the USMIS be extended and renewed to meet new users and business requirements? Another issue may arise when LGUS decides to replace USMIS in the future. A top administrator commented:

Some people have been talking about the replacement of USMIS, but they don't know what they are talking about. In my opinion, they have no idea of the complexity and scope of USMIS. If they knew it they would never talk about the replacement of USMIS. You know what? ***USMIS cannot be easily pulled back. It has its own life!"***

In the late 1980s and early 1990s, USMIS was recognized as an alternative to the individual systems running in different units of LGUS. However, USMIS is now perceived to be part of the installed base, something that is exogenously given and resistant to willful change.

Institutional Issues

Institutional pressures have come from the state and the higher education community. Over the last decade, the state audit reports pointed out several limitations of USMIS, including lack of departmental support and reporting capabilities. They have questioned the appropriateness of further developing and maintaining USMIS since the mid-1990s. As an example, the state audit report of 1996 recommended that:

System management [of LGUS] should reevaluate the overall intent and purpose of USMIS and how best to meet the management reporting needs of the Board and executive management ... Implementation of USMIS at other system components should continue to be delayed until decisions are reached about the overall intent and purpose of USMIS ...

In addition to the state, the recent trend of deploying ERP in higher education is another powerful institutional pressure. Today information technology is increasingly becoming important for higher educational institutions to remain competitive (McCredie, 2003). ERP implementations are among the single largest investments in dollars and resources ever made by higher education institutions. Almost half of the major universities are using ERP systems. Of those that have not implemented an ERP, 10% are currently or will implement in a year, and an additional 25% are expected to do so within the next three years (King, 2002). A member of the steering committee for replacing SIMS with an ERP estimates that the replacement of USMIS will cost almost $50 million.

References

Allison, G. T. (1983). Public and private management: Are they fundamentally alike in all unimportant respects? In J. L. Perry & K. L. Kraemer (Eds.), *Public Management: Public and Private Perspectives* (pp. 72-92). Palo Alto, CA: Mayfield.

Bozeman, B., & Kingsley, G. (1998). Risk culture in public and private organizations. *Public Administration Review, 58*, 109-118.

Brown, C. V., & Vessey, I. (2003). Managing the next wave of enterprise systems: leveraging lessons from ERP. *MIS Quarterly Executive, 2*(1), 65-77.

Crawford, G., & Rudy, J. A. (2003). Fourth annual EDUCAUSE survey identifies current IT issues. *EDUCAUSE Quarterly*, 12-26.

Davenport, T. H. (1998). Putting the enterprise into the enterprise system. *Harvard Business Review,* July/August, 121-131.

Davenport, T. H. (2000). The Future of enterprise system-enabled organizations. *Information Systems Frontiers: Special Issue of the Future of Enterprise Resource Planning Systems Frontiers, 2*(2), 163-180.

Dufner, D., Holley, L. M., & Reed, B. J. (2002). Can private sector strategic information systems planning techniques work for the public sector? *Communications of AIS, 8*, 413-431.

Ernst, D. J., Katz, R. N., & Sack, J. R. (1994). *Organizational and technological strategies for higher education in the information age.* CAUSE Professional Paper Series #13.

Gauch, R. R. (1993). *Differences between public and private management information systems.* Paper presented at the *Proceedings of the 1993 conference on Computer personnel research*, St. Louis, Missouri, USA.

Guy, M. E. (2000). Public management. In J. M. Shafritz (Ed.), *Defining Public Administration* (pp. 166-168). Boulder, CO: Westview Press.

Hanseth, O., & Braa, K. (2001). Hunting for the treasure at the end of the rainbow. Standardizing corporate IT infrastructure. *The Journal of Collaborative Computing, 10*(3/4), 261-292.

Jonas, S., Katz, R. N., Martinson, L., Plympton, M. F., Relyea, S. W., Rennie, E. D., Rudy, J. A., & Walsh, J. F. (1997). *Campus financial systems for the future.* The National Assocation of College and University Business Officers and CAUSE.

King, P. (2002). The promise and performance of enterprise systems in higher education. *EDUCAUSE Quarterly.*

Lerner, A. (1999). A Strategic planning primer for higher education. Online: *http://www.des.calstate.edu/strategic.html*

Markus, M. L., Petrie, D., & Axline, S. (2000). Bucking the trends: What the future may hold for ERP packages. *Information Systems Frontier: Special Issue of on The Future of Enterprise Resource Planning Systems, 2*(2), 181-193.

McCredie, J. (2003). Does IT matter to higher education? *EDUCAUSE Quarterly.*

McCredie, J. W. (2000). Planning for IT in higher education: It's not an oxymoron. *EDUCAUSE Quarterly,* (4), 14-21.

Mohan, L., Holstein, W. K., & Adams, R. B. (1990). EIS: It can work in the public sector. *MIS Quarterly,* December, 435-448.

Rainey, H., Backoff, R., & Levine, C. (1976). Comparing public and private organizations. *Public Administration Review, 36*(2), 233-244.

Rao, S. S. (2000). Enterprise resource planning: Business needs and technologies. *Journal: Industrial Management & Data Systems, 100*(2), 81-88.

Robey, D., Ross, J. W., & Boudreau, M. (2002). Learning to implement enterprise systems: An exploratory study of the dialectics of change. *Journal of Management Information Systems.*

Rocheleau, B. (2000). Prescriptions for public-sector information management: A review, Analysis and Critique. *American Review of Public Administration, 30*(4), 414-435.

Rocheleau, B., & Wu, L. (2002). Public versus private information systems: Do they differ in important ways? A review and empirical test. *American Review of Public Administration, 32*(4), 379-397.

Shang, S., & Seddon, P. B. (2002). Assessing and managing the benefits of enterprise systems: The business manager's perspective. *Information Systems Journal, 12*, 271-299.

Star, S., & Ruhlender, K. (1996). Steps towards an ecology of infrastructure: Design and access for large scale information spaces. *Information Systems Research, 7*(1), 111-134.

Ward, D., & Hawkins, B. L. (2003). Presidential leadership for information technology. *EDUCAUSE Review,* May/June, 36-47.

Watson, E., Vaught, S., Gutierrez, D., & Rinks, D. (2003). ERP implementation in state government. *Annals of Cases on Information Technology, 5.*

Appendix

- **Information Associates:** The Information Associates software, a company based in New York State, is now owned by the SCT Corporation (www.sct.com) since 1992.
- **Software AG NATURAL/ADABAS:** Launched in 1979, NATURAL now has an installed base of more than 3,000 corporations. It was designed specifically for building mission-critical applications. Natural applications support many leading platforms and can be integrated with many major database systems (ADABAS, DB2, Oracle, etc.). Developed in 1969 by Software AG, ADABAS is a popular database management system, which is currently installed on many organizations including FBI, EPA's Office of Information Resources Management, UPS, Merrill Lynch, and University of Texas.

This case was previously published in the Journal of Cases on Information Technology, 7(2), April - June 2005, pp. 82-101.

Chapter XI

Higher Education Culture and the Diffusion of Technology in Classroom Instruction

Kandis M. Smith
University of Missouri, USA

Introduction

The diffusion of an innovation takes, on an average, 25 years in an educational setting. Many factors contribute to this slow acceptance rate. Rogers' (1995) theory on the diffusion of innovation and the influence of culture on such diffusion is used to shed light on the causes for this slow diffusion. While not a full explanation of this slow rate of change, this case study shows that the academic culture, within which faculty function, has a strong influence on the diffusion of the use of technology in classroom instruction. This case study provides a point of reference for further study of diffusion of technology in classroom instruction.

This case focuses on a Research I institution in the Midwest that has made a number of commitments to the integration of technology into the curriculum and has channeled many resources into this campaign. While the institution has invested large sums of money in the development of the infrastructure, the rate at which faculty have adopted the use of technology in their teaching has remained low. In order to determine the perceptions of faculty and develop some framework for understanding why the infusion of technology into classroom instruction was so low, faculty members on the campus were interviewed, focus groups were conducted, and meetings between faculty and administrators concerning technology issues were observed. Because additional issues exist with distance education, the scope of this case study research was limited to on-campus classroom instruction and support.

Case Questions

- Do the values and beliefs of academic culture promote or discourage a pro-innovation social climate?
- What aspects of academic culture hinder or promote the diffusion of innovation, specifically, the process for adoption of the use of technology in higher education?
- How do disciplinary differences affect the adoption of technology?
- What roles do faculty play in the diffusion of technology in the classroom?
- What tools and support structures drive successful technology integration into the classroom?

Case Narrative

History of Technological Innovations in Higher Education

As an innovation, technology has been diffusing throughout institutions of higher education since 1946 (Heterick, 1993). Some of the earliest research in higher education resulted in the development of ENIAC at the University of Pennsylvania in 1946. By 1965, Thomas Merrill, Lawrence Roberts and Leonard Kleinrock had developed and implemented the first wide-area computer network, operating between Massachusetts and California (Leiner et al., 1998). By 1969, ARPANET was operational at the University of California-Los Angeles, Stanford Research Institute and the University of California-Santa Barbara, and was connected to the University College of London in England and the Royal Radar Establishment in Norway by 1973. In the 1980s, BITNET was connected between City University of New York and Yale University and the National Science Foundation established five super-computing centers, enabling connections for many universities.

During the 1950s and 1960s, funding from agencies such as the Ford Foundation, the Carnegie Foundation, and the Kettering Foundation enabled institutions of higher education, usually research institutions, to acquire large computers (Saettler, 1990). Many of these were used for administrative purposes and were not available to the general faculty or to students. With the passage of the National Defense Education Act and the Elementary and Secondary Education Act, the federal government became a primary source of funds for institutions of higher education desiring to integrate technology into education (Saettler, 1990). By the late 1960s, spurred by these federal research grants, more faculty were investing in technology (Knapper, 1988). Katz (1993) stated that by the 1970s most of the research institutions were using mainframe computers extensively for three major activities: "... numerically intensive research, ... instruction in computer science, and ...administration" (p. 15).

By the 1980s, desktop computers were available to individual faculty and students (Mason, 1996). Cartwright (1993) indicated that the first uses of technology in the classroom were demonstrations of how a computer could analyze data. However, faculty also began to develop interactive processes of using technology in teaching. One example was Patrick Suppes and Richard Atkinson's program of computer-assisted instruction in mathematics and reading, which was designed for "...individualized, instructional strategies that allowed the learner to correct his [the student's] responses through rapid feedback..." thereby allowing active participation by the student (Molnar, 1997, p. 3). By 1992 the World Wide Web made access to information around the world possible from desktop computers. Today in some classrooms, faculty are using multimedia, integration of text, video, audio, animation, or graphics, which are often interactive in design. They are also using technology for simulations, acquiring information, communicating with others in the classroom and outside the classroom, and transmitting assignments electronically. According to Ringle (1996), technology is now a part of the curriculum. Usage by faculty and students is found across a wide spectrum and includes:

[...] access to literary and historic databases, simulations in the social sciences, digital imagery in art, theater and architecture, virtual laboratories in chemistry, biology, and physics, and many other things. (p. 6)

Higher education institutions are undergoing some major changes as they incorporate technology into the curriculum. Gilbert (1995) stated that although the changes occurring in education are not the result of technological changes, the character of the changes may be guided "...by our own thoughtfulness of the role of technology in education" (p. 1). Based upon this premise, Gilbert (1995) listed several indicators of changes that are already happening. First, faculty report that their best teaching efforts do not appear to be working with today's students. Second, one-third of college students do not purchase required textbooks for classes. Third, in 1994-95, over 50 percent of all freshmen had used technology in their academic endeavors, and approximately one-fourth of all students owned personal computers. Fourth, approximately five percent to 15 percent of faculty reported that by using technology in instruction, significant improvements in the quality and effectiveness of their teaching were achieved. Fifth, students on many campuses have voted to increase student fees by up to $150 per student in order to subsidize computer-related purchases and services. Sixth, more and more faculty are developing customized course packs, often in CD-ROM or Internet/Web format, in conjunction with traditional textbook publishers.

Another development, which is having an effect on American higher education, is the national technology plan. The plan, *Getting America's Students Ready for the 21st Century*, is aimed at elementary and secondary education, but has some far-reaching implications for higher education. The thrust to have all teachers trained to help students learn through the use of computers with adequate support and resources implies that institutions of higher education must train the elementary and secondary education teachers to use technology, and that the students entering institutions of higher education will expect to use technology in their college classes (Clinton, 1996). According to Plotnick (1996), society is insisting that teachers become "technologically literate" and educational technology is one of the top policy issues in education. Green (1996) said that students in institutions of higher education expect technology to be incorporated into their learning experiences.

Alvarez (1996) stated that the use of technology is changing expectations to the extent that institutions that do not incorporate technology into classroom education will not be able to attract good faculty and good students. Additionally, a 1996 Campus Computing survey showed that the most important technology issue for institutions of higher education was helping faculty to integrate technology into educational instruction (Green, 1997).

Lever-Duffy (1991) noted that most institutions of higher education have made significant resource commitments toward supporting technology, that unit costs of technology have declined, and that technology has become increasingly easy to use. With these changes, faculty in higher education are adopting technology, but at a slower rate than would be expected, especially given the popularization of technology through the media and the expectations of society, parents, and students.

As indicated by increased budget allocations for implementation of technology projects, expectations of students, parents, legislators and business executives concerning the importance of technology in education are increasing. However, Lee (1996) stated technology integration in higher education is failing and one of the main reasons for the failure is that the perspectives of faculty are ignored. According to Neal (1998) this lack of integration of faculty perspective was one of the main reasons for the failure of Instructional Television in the 1960s and 1970s. Whitaker and Ekman (1998), in discussing the potential for the application of technology to instruction, stated that such efforts must be faculty driven in order to be successful; they cannot be imperatives from the top. Ely et al. further stated that "...the individual teacher or professor is the single most important factor leading to appropriate implementation of media and technology for learning" (Ely et al., 1992, p. 7). In her introduction to *Rethinking University Teaching*, Diana Laurillard (1993) stated that the impetus for changes in higher education should be from within the system. She argued that academic values, which promote the advancement of learning, continued research and freedom, must be the driving force behind changes in higher education. The implication of such an assertion is that faculty must be the impetus behind change in order to protect and promote those academic values which make higher education unique as an institution. Although the culture of the institution frames the perspectives of the faculty who are the primary impetus for changes that occur within the institution (Ely et al., 1992; Laurillard, 1993), prior research on diffusion of innovation has not concentrated on aspects unique to a given culture (Walsh, 1993).

Diffusion of an Innovation

Rogers (1995) defined diffusion as a process which incorporates four specific elements: (1) the innovation, (2) communication channels, (3) time, and (4) a social system. Each of these components interacts with and reacts to the other three components. Therefore, no single element may be fully considered outside the context of the other elements.

An innovation, idea, process or object is defined as something new to an individual, department, or institution. An innovation need not be a new or recent discovery as measured by time, but is considered new based on the perceptions of the individual or other organizational unit. In this study the innovation was defined as a computer-mediated tool for communication. This included multimedia, electronic mail, commercial courseware, CD-ROM materials, computer simulations, World Wide Web-based resources, and Internet-based resources.

As Rogers (1995) indicated, two types of communication channels have been studied: (1) mass media and (2) interpersonal. At different stages of diffusion, the different channels have varying impacts upon decision making. In the early stages of beginning knowledge, mass media may provide the initial information to spark interest in the innovation. As an individual moves through the decision-making process, channels of communication with peers usually have a greater effect on the process.

The time element begins with the period of initial awareness of the innovation and progresses until the individual either implements or rejects the innovation and confirms the decision. In diffusion research in the field of education, innovations such as kindergartens and team teaching have been the subjects of study. Although the rate of diffusion in education appears to be accelerating, Miles (1964) cited several studies that indicated a relatively slow rate of diffusion of innovations in education. Research on innovations in higher education by Getz, Siegfried and Anderson (1994), in which they examined 30 innovations in academic and administrative areas at 238 institutions, showed that the average time for adoption of an innovation within institutions of higher education was 25 years. The time needed for adoption differed according to discipline, with innovations in computer and library science diffusing faster than other fields. The rate of diffusion of innovations in higher education in computer and library science was similar to the rate of innovation diffusion in industry.

No aspect of the process occurs in a vacuum. The social system of the individual or institution exerts influence upon the entire process. Within organizations, such as higher education institutions, the diffusion of innovation is related to the internal and external characteristics of the institutional structure and the characteristics of the individuals within the institution (Getz, Siegfried & Anderson, 1994). The social structure of the system—within which the individual perceives the innovation and the communication channels developed within the system—greatly influences the number of individuals who adopt an innovation and the length of time it takes for the individual to adopt or reject the innovation (Rogers, 1995).

Institutional Background

The University, established in 1839, became a land-grant institution in 1870 under the Morrill Act of 1862. Although the University was predominantly a residential campus composed of 18 schools and colleges, and more than 20,000 students, there was also a strong emphasis on continuing education and outreach.

In 1980, the campus technology services were mainly mainframe computers allowing administrative access to information. By 1990, as a result of increased demand and technological changes, the system included connectivity to remote sites and network segmentation. As the technology grew, services to support the technology were maintained at the departmental level. Due to differences in commitment and funding, departments provided differing levels of support for technology. Some departments provided little support while other departments built their own separate networks.

Over the past five years, the institution has made both fiscal and written commitments to the integration of technology into the curriculum. The official institutional technology plan listed as a major goal the integration of instructional technology programs throughout the university curriculum, and over $25,000,000 was budgeted for this purpose. Projects developed to achieve the goal included upgrading of the library technology system, participation in innovative technology development, and increased infrastructure. This strength of administrative commitment at this institution appeared to contradict much literature, which indicated a lack of commitment and administrative support as one major barrier to incorporation of technology in classroom instruction (Albright, 1996; Bryon, 1995; Geoghegan, 1994; Knapper, 1988).

During this time period, several changes occurred on the campus relative to the use of technology. For students the changes included automatic e-mail accounts upon enrollment, the requirement of several hours of classroom instruction in courses that were considered technology enhanced, and the increased accessibility of on-line support services. For the faculty, an instructional technology teaching and support group was formed to provide new avenues of access to learning about how to use technology in the classroom. In some cases, grants were provided to faculty for development of technology-enhanced instruction. Also, for the students, faculty, and staff, a desktop replacement program was initiated and computer labs were upgraded. Administratively, the leadership in the information and computing services division changed and a new committee structure was initiated to increase participation in planning.

The University had several specialized centers for the support of faculty who desired to use technology in their classroom instruction. One center provided support to faculty and students through such services as the help desk, specific training programs, and hardware support and repair. Another center for faculty support provided services such as equipment rental, media materials preparation, and audiovisual supplies (such as audio and video equipment). A third source for faculty support was a center composed of faculty, staff, and students. This center was one of the primary sources of faculty support for the integration of technology into classroom instruction. Programs included faculty training institutes, workshops, and a faculty-mentoring program.

Faculty Perspectives on the Use of Technology

According to Clark (1987) and Austin (1990), university faculty operate within four overlapping, yet distinct, cultures: (1) the academic profession in general, (2) the individual disciplines, (3) the specific institution as an organization, and (4) institutional type. These four cultures provide the framework for a discussion of the findings of this case study on the diffusion of technology for classroom instruction at this institution.

Faculty who were using technology agreed that the use of technology in the classroom provided some benefits that encouraged them to continue to explore the use of technology in their classroom teaching. They stated that the use of technology in their classrooms enhanced student learning, and faculty and student interactions, leading to increased empowerment of students. Additionally, faculty felt that the use of technology had increased their awareness of teaching principles and forced an examination of the way they teach. Another benefit, according to the faculty that were using technology in their classroom instruction, was that the development of materials and the determination of what to use had led them to consider the pedagogy of their classroom instruction. One faculty member said:

[It is] rethinking the way we teach anything. Because...a typical college professor, they went to school, they did well under the system. So they get their PhD, they come and they use the system that they learned under. And so, lectures, three lectures a week, a laboratory room, write a paper, turn it in. Technology doesn't lend itself to that.

Another faculty member explained reasons to incorporate technology as such:

I chose this profession not just to become a researcher. I chose the profession also because I wanted to teach. ... I wanted to learn about the psychology of teaching. I wanted to learn about teaching methodology. ... I just wanted to improve the teaching process. ... So I was thinking, well, how would you put some of these things [technology being used] ...integrate them into education.

One issue that participants perceived as very important was the return to learning for the faculty member. Faculty who reported using technology in teaching viewed themselves as able to learn from their students in a new and different way. They indicated that the empowerment of the students had changed the student-faculty relationship and now, although the faculty member was still the expert, the students and faculty members have become participants in a collaborative learning community.

The following was one professor's description of how electronic mail, listserves, and the World Wide Web had changed the communication in the classroom and thereby the faculty role and the role of these students:

My role has changed. Everybody is talking. It has moved from me doing all the talking, to working with the student on something that they want to do, which I love. It allows me to take a class of 15 or 20 students and essentially collaborate with every one of them. And then they talk to each other about what they are doing. So the learning moves from me telling you, to me working with you, and then us telling everybody...everybody in the class. And that has set a very high standard.

All of the interviewed faculty, whether they used technology in classroom instruction or not, were concerned with teaching and the effect of technology on the profession and on student learning. Every individual considered him or herself a good teacher and researcher and committed to academe and the traditional institutional mission of a Research I institution. This commitment indicated strong support for Austin's (1990) academic cultural value of the "...notion that the purpose of higher education is to pursue, discover, produce and disseminate knowledge, truth, and understanding" (p. 62).

Faculty who were using technology in their instruction still felt that the professional autonomy of others who did not use technology must be respected and maintained. The continual pursuit of knowledge and dissemination of knowledge within the autonomy and freedom of the academic institution were values of all of the faculty. Their support of the conservative diffusion of technology in education and their assertion that faculty should not be pushed to use technology, unless it is essential to the content of the course, indicated that they value this aspect of the culture of the profession.

The Individual Disciplines

Clark (1980) stated that the power of the disciplines is the strongest for faculty. It is easier to change institutions than to change disciplines. The individual faculty member has spent years being socialized into the particular discipline as a student and faculty member. Special organizations in each discipline increase the sense of belonging to the discipline on a national or international basis and thereby enhance the individual self-identity as a member of the discipline.

In the use of technology in instruction, several differences were evident among the various disciplines. Disciplines, such as journalism and veterinary medicine—in which the use of technology was a specific component of the curriculum—were more heavily involved in using technology such as multimedia and Web-based interactions in classroom instruction than were disciplines for which the use of technology was not a component of the curriculum, such as English or social work. Faculty from disciplines considered a "hard paradigm," such as chemistry, indicated greater acceptance of using technology, such as specialized software programs, in instruction than did participants who were from disciplines considered a "soft paradigm," such as history. In addition, disciplines, like chemistry, in which students would be required to use technology in their careers, were more supportive of the incorporation of technology, such as Web-based instruction, into classroom instruction than disciplines, like languages, in which students might not have to use technology in their careers.

Another disciplinary difference was evident when faculty discussed support for technology in general. Faculty in disciplines that were well funded indicated they received higher levels of fiscal support from their departments whereas faculty in disciplines that were less well funded found it difficult to obtain departmental support. As one faculty member said:

I have never had to want for expendables, hardware, and software. Now, that is an important point because I am probably the exception. Probably a lot of teachers really don't have the resources that they need.

Several other faculty members in other disciplines who stated that they could not obtain the equipment they needed supported this view. One faculty member actually stated that many of the hardware and software items that were used for classroom instruction were purchased with personal funds because the department did not have the necessary funding. Another faculty member gave the departmental rationale for refusing the request for portable equipment. This faculty member was told that getting a laptop would be supporting personal work and that "...the computer might be used for consulting or something..." and therefore the department could not purchase such an item.

The Specific Institution

Despite the institutional technology plan and the fiscal commitment by administration, faculty described a number of major problems related to the institution and the use of technology in the classroom. Among the issues was a perceived lack of coordinated effort at the institutional level to support faculty use of technology. A faculty member who did not use technology in classroom instruction saw the lack of technology standards across campus as a major issue. Although a number of auditoriums and classrooms across campus were capable of supporting the use of various forms of technology, such as multimedia presentations, what worked in one room might not work in another. This faculty member indicated that since the professor was responsible for using the equipment in the classroom, each individual would have to learn several operating systems and be prepared to provide several types of equipment, such as a variety of connector cables.

A connected issue was the lack of assurance that a classroom would have the necessary capability for using a certain form of technology in instruction. One professor who was incorporating multimedia technology into instruction described the process of using this form of technology in a non-multimedia configured classroom in a building on campus that belonged to another discipline.

I had to pick up a portable computer, video projector ... and haul it all over there all the way from .... I used my luggage cart because they won't deliver the video projector unless somebody over there will sign for it. And since we are not a part of [that department] .... There is a lab right next door [to the classroom], a dedicated undergraduate computer lab, and of course we could not use it.

Another professor who was not using technology in teaching said that this issue was a major reason for not using technology in general:

My attitude is, if the university wants me to use technology, they better guarantee me that its going to be there for me. And I don't think I can get that.

Another faculty member who was using multimedia technology was frustrated because, although the classroom equipment and connections were available, there was no one available to teach one how to use it. This faculty member stated that no one in the department had the skills to use the equipment and no training was available, so everyone was on their own to learn. Additionally, if something suddenly did not work, faculty had no idea who or where to call for help. The process had become very frustrating for faculty and students. This faculty member further stated that as a result of this frustration, only two faculty members in the entire department were using technology in their classroom instruction.

This problem was echoed in another area that also, according to the faculty member, had only two faculty in the entire department using technology in the classroom. One of these two faculty members described it thus:

It isn't routine and standard yet and people don't understand. So, if you want to teach with technology, you have to become an expert, I find, in connections, wiring, and you have to spend time teaching yourself because not many people can help you.

One faculty member who had used Web-based technology in classroom instruction for a couple of years stated:

[When I began] we didn't have anybody to answer the basic questions of where do you start, what do you do first, what do you do second. There was no one. ... I think now the support team is fragmented. I still can't seem to find out where, if I have a question, where I need to go with it.

Rogers' (1995) theory of innovation diffusion stated that the communication channels that promote the diffusion become individual channels as awareness increases. As stated in the literature on the current status of the use of technology in education (Ely et al., 1992; Green, 1996; McCollum, 1998; Olien, 1998), faculty were aware of the use of technology in education. However, the participants in this study indicated that the personal communication channels were not well developed. Individual faculty, although generally aware of the use of technology in education, did not have access to the communication channels that, as Rogers (1995) stated, are essential to the diffusion of an innovation.

The Institutional Type

Another major issue for faculty at this institution was the lack of incentives and rewards for incorporation of technology into classroom instruction. One of the faculty members who began using technology, such as computer simulations and listserves, before receiving tenure stated:

[...] A person who is on the tenure track needs to be focusing on research and creative activity. I wouldn't encourage them, if they didn't already have the skills to learn enough about it, to get into technology and instruction. I just wouldn't do it.

Most of the participants indicated that while including the use of some form of technology in evaluation criteria was an issue that was discussed, opposition to including criteria related to the use of various forms of instructional technology in the evaluation process was strong. One of the faculty members who was untenured stated that using technology in classroom instruction was perilous at this career point:

[But] even though it doesn't count for tenure decisions, if I use the information here and don't make tenure, there are a number of schools that will want me.

One explanation given by a number of the faculty members for the lack of incentives and rewards was that teaching itself was not highly valued institutionally. They indicated that as this institution was a Research I institution, the highest value was on research and it was research that was rewarded.

Analysis

The participants in this case study indicated that core values within academe might affect their use of technology in classroom instruction. The beliefs and values of the academic profession culture emphasize learning, dissemination of knowledge, and autonomy in teaching. The continual pursuit of knowledge and dissemination of knowledge within the autonomy and freedom of the academic institution were values of all of the participants. It was evident from the data collected that these beliefs and values were supported by the incorporation of technology into classroom instruction for those faculty who are using technology. Those faculty who were not using technology in classroom instruction also shared these beliefs and values but were asking for proof that the use of technology did provide support for these cultural values. Their support of the conservative diffusion of technology in education and their assertion that faculty should not be pushed to use technology, unless it is essential to the content of the course, also indicated that they value this aspect of the culture of the institution.

Additionally, the findings supported the cultural differences among disciplines. The participants in this study acknowledged that there are major differences in funding and support for technology among schools and departments, and that these differences affect their ability and desire to use technology in teaching. Since the wealth of the department determines whether or not the equipment is even available, it was obvious that this aspect of the individual disciplines had a strong effect on the diffusion of technology into classroom instruction. Additionally, disciplines in which the use of technology was part of the culture of the discipline showed greater involvement in using technology in classroom instruction.

Interviewees indicated that general attitudes and the climate toward the use of some form of technology for instruction were different depending on discipline. Further, despite the potential described in the literature for doing so, the participants in this study have not crossed disciplinary boundaries through the use of technology, either in research or teaching, but have remained well within their institutional, national, and international disciplinary boundaries. It is perhaps this continued disciplinary perspective that has supported the faculty viewpoint of isolation and lack of support for their efforts.

The official workload for tenure evaluation of faculty at a Research I institution is roughly 40 percent teaching, 40 percent research, and 20 percent service.

Faculty, at this particular institution, felt that the lack of incentives and rewards for using technology was the result of the lack of emphasis on teaching and higher emphasis on research. The general perception was that to achieve tenure, it would be wiser for a faculty member to concentrate on research and not on using technology in teaching.

Conclusion

Despite the campus technology plan and the strong fiscal support from the administration, faculty saw several institutional issues that slowed the diffusion of technology in classroom instruction. One was the lack of campus-wide technology standards, which forced faculty to learn different operating systems and equipment. Another was the lack of coordination of effort to provide support for faculty who wished to learn how to use technology. It was perceived as especially difficult for faculty members to learn to use the technology, since, although the equipment might be available, they did not know where to seek help and few in a given department could help.

This case study has not only provided support for the literature, but also provided findings on the diffusion of technology into the classroom instruction that may increase understanding of diffusion of this innovation in higher education. These findings included: (1) the development of a more collaborative learning environment through the use of technology provided a potential for increased learning for faculty as well as students; (2) personal communication, essential to the diffusion of technology, was fragmented across disciplines and across the institution; (3) the faculty perception of lack of support contrary to administrative perceptions of commitment leads to difficulties in the institutional communication process; and (4) the value of teaching relative to research was low.

Results of this study indicated that faculty and students experienced enhanced classroom learning when technology was incorporated, which supported the values of the academic profession in general. The results of this case study indicated that at this particular institution, incongruities in the values and beliefs reflected by the administration and the perceptions of the faculty were barriers to the increased use of technology in instruction. Finally, as a Research I institution, faculty indicated that the emphasis that was reinforced by the current promotion and tenure system was on research rather than teaching. This emphasis further hindered the diffusion of technology in classroom instruction.

Discussion Questions

1. What could the institution/faculty do to promote the diffusion of technology into classroom instruction?
2. What might be the effect of culture on the diffusion of technology at other types of higher education institutions, such as community colleges?
3. What other aspects of higher education might explain the slowness of diffusion of technology?

References

Albright, M.J. (1996, February). *Instructional technology and higher education: Rewards, rights, and responsibilities.* Keynote address, Southern Regional Faculty and Instructional Development Consortium. (ERIC Reproduction Service No. ED 392 412).

Alvarez, L.R. (1996, May/June). Why technology? Technology, electricity and running water. *Educom Review*, *31*, 3. Available *http://www.educom.edu/web/pubs/review/review/Articles/31324.html*

Austin, A. (1990). Faculty cultures, faculty values. In W.G. Tierney (Ed.), *Assessing academic climates and cultures* (pp. 61-74). San Francisco: Jossey-Bass.

Byron, S. (1995, December). *Computing and other instructional technologies: Faculty perceptions of current practices and views of future challenges.* (ERIC Reproduction Service No. ED 390 338).

Cartwright, G.P. (1993). Part one: Teaching with academic technologies. *Change*, *6*(November/December), 67.

Clark, B.R. (1980). *Academic culture* (Report No. YHERG-42). Higher Education Research Group, Institution for Social and Policy Studies, Yale University. (ERIC Document Reproduction No. ED 187 186).

Clark, B.R. (1987). *The academic life: Small worlds, different worlds.* Princeton, NJ: Carnegie Foundation for the Advancement of Teaching.

Clinton, W.J. (1996, November). Introduction: Achieving the goals — Goal 5 - First in the world in math and science technology resources. Available *http://www.ed.gov/pubs/AchGoal5/intro.html*

Ely, D.P., Foley, A., Freeman, W., & Scheel, N. (1992, June). *Trends in educational technology.* ERIC Clearinghouse on Information Resources, Syracuse University, Syracuse, NY.

Geoghegan, W.H. (1994, July). What ever happened to instructional technology? Paper presented at the *22nd Annual Conference of the International Business Schools Computing Association*, Baltimore, MD. Available *http://w3.scale.uiuc.edu/scale/library/geoghegan/wpi.html*

Getz, M., Siegfried, J.J., & Anderson, K.H. (1994). *Adoption of innovations in higher education.* Vanderbilt University, Nashville, TN.

Gilbert, S.W. (1995, September/October). Technology & the changing academy: Symptoms, questions, and suggestions. *Change*. Available *http://contract.kent.edu/change/articles/sepoct95.html*

Green, C. (1997). Past, promise and potential: Tracking change via the campus computing project. 1997 TLTR Summer Institute presentation. Available *http://www.wilpaterson.edu/aahe/si97/cg/sld.htm*

Green, K.C. (1996, January). The 1995 national survey of information technology in higher education: Technology use jumps on college campuses. *The Campus Computing Project*. Available *http://ericir.syr.edu/Projects/campus_computing/1995/index.html*

Green, K.C. (1996, November). The 1996 national survey of information technology in higher education: Instructional integration and user support present continuing technology challenges. *The Campus Computing Project.* Available *http://ericir.syr.edu/Projects/campus_computing/1996/index.html*

Heterick, R.C., Jr. (Ed.) (1993). Introduction: Reengineering teaching and learning. *CAUSE Professional Paper Series #10*. Available *http://cause-www.colorado.edu/information-resources/ir-library/text/pub3010.txt*

Katz, R.N. (1993). Silicon in the grove: Computing, teaching, and learning in the American research university. R.C. Heterick, Jr. (Ed.), *CAUSE*

Professional Paper Series #10. Available *http://cause-www.colorado.edu/information-resources/ir-library/text/pub3010.txt*

Knapper, C.K. (1988). Technology and college teaching. In R.E. Young (Ed.), *College teaching and learning: Preparing for new commitments. New directions for teaching and learning, 33* (pp. 31-47).

Laurillard, D. (1993). *Rethinking university teaching: A framework for the effective use of educational technology*. New York: Routledge.

Lee, J. (1996). *Information technology at the gate: Faculty perceptions and attitudes about technology-mediated instruction innovation in higher education.* Doctoral dissertation, University of California, Berkeley. Available *http://wwwlib.umi.com/dissertations/fullcit?170476*

Leiner, B.M., Cerf, B.G., Clark, D.D., Khan, R.E., Kleinrock, L., Lynch, D.C., Postel, J., Roberts, L.G., & Wolf, S. (1998). A brief history of the Internet. Available *http://www.isoc.org/internet-history/brief.html*

Lever-Duffy, J.C. (1991, November). *Strategies for empowering educators with technology: A presentation for the League of Innovation.* (ERIC Document Reproduction Service No. ED 387 168).

Mason, J. (1996). Building an overview: Fitting information technology (IT) into the educational setting. Available *http://sunsite.unc.edu/horizon/mono/CD/Change_Innovation/Mason.html*

McCollum, K. (1998, March 20). Information technology: 'Ramping up' to support 42,000 student computers on a single campus. *The Chronicle of Higher Education*, A-27-29.

Miles, M.B. (1964). Innovation in education: Some generalizations. In *Innovation in education* (pp. 631-662). New York: Bureau of Publications, Teachers College, Columbia University.

Molnar, A.R. (1997). Computers in education: A brief history. *T.H.E. Journal*. Available *http://www.thejournal.com/SPECIAL/25thani/0697feat01.html*

Neal, E. (1998, April). AAHESGIT73: Faculty skepticism & judgement vs. laziness. Discussion list *aahesgit@list.cren.net*

Olien, D. (1998, February). New technologies bring challenge in dealing with governors and state legislatures. *NASULGC Newsline, 7*, 2.

Plotnick, E. (1996). Trends in educational technology. *1995 ERIC Digest. ERIC Clearinghouse on Information and Technology*. (ERIC Document Reproduction Service No. ED 398 861).

Ringle, M. (1996, May/June). Why technology? The well-rounded institution. *Educom Review, 31*, 3. Available *http://www.educom.edu/web/pubs/review/review articles/31324.html*

Rogers, E.M. (1995). *Diffusion of innovations* (4th ed.). New York: The Free Press.

Saettler, P. (1990). *The evolution of American educational technology.* Englewood, CO: Libraries Unlimited, Inc.

Timeline: 50 years of computing. (1997). *T.H.E. Journal.* Available *http://www.thejournal.com/SPECIAL/25thani/0697feat01.html*

Walsh, S.M. (1993). *Attitudes and perceptions of university faculty toward technology-based distance education.* Doctoral dissertation, University of Oklahoma.

Whitaker, G.R., & Ekman, R. (1998, February). Initiative on the cost-effective uses of technology in teaching: The Andrew W. Mellon Foundation. Available *http://ww.mellon.org.cutt.html*

This case was previously published in Case Studies on Information Technology in Higher Education: Implications for Policy and Practice, pp. 144-156, edited by L.A. Petrides, published by Idea Group Publishing (2000).

Chapter XII

Wiring Watkins University: Does IT Really Matter?

Andy Borchers
Kettering University, USA

Executive Summary

This case describes the "wiring" of Watkins University (a fictional name for a real Midwestern university) between 1997 and 2003 as the university responded to competitive pressures in the higher education market. After describing the University and the competitive challenges it faced, the case takes the student into a strategy session between the organization's CFO, CTO and Provost as they review progress on four key initiatives: Web based teaching, student laptop program, a Web based ERP implementation and a proposed "one card" system. Questions are raised as to acceptance of the technology, the impact of these initiatives on the organization's strategic posture and competitiveness, IT budget planning, and future steps for the organization to take.

Introduction

This case describes the "wiring" of Watkins University as a response to competitive pressures. The case is set in a strategy session as management reviews four key initiatives: Web based teaching, student laptop program, Web based ERP implementation and "one card" system. Questions addressed include acceptance of technology, the impact on the organization's strategic posture and competitiveness, and IT budgeting.

This case is based on the experience of a real university from 1997 to 2003. The name of the school, as well as enrollment and financial information, has been disguised to preserve the institution's anonymity. The general trends illustrated in the data, however, are consistent with real events.

Organizational Background

"It is time to convene the IT steering committee," said Loran Woodward. The executive conference room comfortably held the three members of the Watkins University IT steering committee and any invited visitors. Loran Woodward, a lifetime academic and engineer by training, served as Provost of the school and was responsible for the academic programs the school conducted. Lawrence Johnston was the school's Chief Technology Officer. He recently had left the IT industry to work for Watkins. Although he had earned a PhD in engineering many years ago, he was relatively new to the academic world in general and Watkins in particular. Johnson Lee was the Vice President of Administration. A veteran academic, Lee held a PhD in educational leadership and was a CPA. All three committee members dressed in dark suits, consistent with the conservative nature of the school.

It was late March of 2002 and winter had not left the campus yet. As the members of the committee shook off the cold, they faced the prospect of making hard choices on the school's 2003-2004 IT budget. There were many more IT initiatives than the school had funds to budget. Their challenge was to determine which initiatives and staffing decisions could help Watkins succeed in the increasingly competitive higher education marketplace. The school had recently hit a 15-year low in attendance and was just starting to turn the corner in the marketplace. The school's President and Board of Trust were eager to hear from the steering committee about positive changes in the IT arena that could help the school succeed.

University History and Organization

Watkins University has a long history of providing technology-focused education to students from the major U.S. metropolitan area where the school is located and throughout the Midwest. First established as a private institution of higher learning in the early 1930s, the school developed a local reputation in the fields of engineering, architecture, science, and, later on, management. Conveniently located on a 200-acre campus in a suburban area, the institution is organized in four schools as shown in Figure 1. The four schools evolved through the institution's history, largely as a response to the needs of local employers and the needs of its largely commuter student population.

Figure 1. University organization

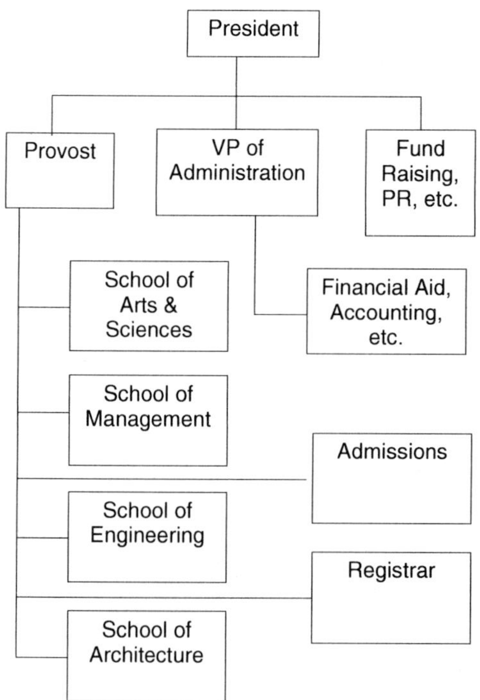

Enrollment Trends and Challenges

One of the grim realities that the steering committee faced was that Watkins was struggling with enrollment. After growing to a peak enrollment of nearly 6,000 students in the 1980s, Watkins faced a steady drop until bottoming out in 1997 at approximately 3,600 students. Table 1 shows enrollment trends for Watkins and its major local competitors—a private urban university, two suburban state universities and one urban state university.

Enrollment and graduation trends in engineering programs, the traditional heart of the university, were equally disturbing. Watkins was well known to employers as a source of entry-level engineers. Even considering declining enrollment and graduation data at a national level, Watkins was losing significant market share. Table 2 shows the number of engineering graduates per year for each of five competing institutions and the U.S. as a whole.

Many explanations were offered for the decline in enrollment and graduations. First, Watkins as a private institution had to significantly increase tuition to cover its costs during the 1990s. Tables 3 and 4 demonstrate this trend. Even with aggressive tuition discounting, at times as high as 20%, Watkins struggled to maintain enrollment.

Second, as Table 2 illustrates, the national trend in engineering enrollment through the 1990s was declining. Watkins was particularly hard hit since it

Table 1. Total enrollment

	Watkins	Urban Private	Suburban State A	Suburban State B	Urban State A	Total	Watkins %
1989	5,481	8,010	7,579	12,323	32,315	65,708	8.3%
1990	5,551	7,871	7,799	12,586	34,380	68,188	8.1%
1991	5,233	7,824	8,021	12,467	33,744	67,289	7.8%
1992	4,959	7,498	8,245	13,264	35,469	69,435	7.1%
1993	4,480	7,426	7,846	12,831	34,109	66,691	6.7%
1994	4,252	7,573	8,234	13,362	33,400	66,820	6.4%
1995	4,132	7,486	8,098	13,532	31,988	65,237	6.3%
1996	3,975	7,393	8,366	14,162	31,653	65,549	6.1%
1997	3,627	6,894	8,230	14,307	30,575	63,633	5.7%
1998	3,725	6,725	8,234	14,485	31,671	64,840	5.7%

Source: nsf.caspar.gov (disguised)

Table 2. Number of engineering graduates

	Watkins	Urban Private	Suburban State A	Suburban State B	Urban State A	Total	Watkins %	U.S. Total
1990	463	87	175	106	219	1,050	44.1%	64,677
1991	423	83	170	122	205	1,003	42.2%	62,156
1992	407	69	154	103	162	895	45.5%	61,898
1993	302	63	151	114	190	821	36.8%	62,670
1994	355	59	144	115	147	820	43.3%	62,962
1995	344	61	132	103	163	804	42.8%	63,330
1996	242	63	138	100	184	727	33.2%	63,029
1997	188	55	148	146	164	701	26.8%	62,310
1998	261	63	125	102	148	698	37.4%	60,881
2000	179	66	138	128	150	662	27.1%	59,396

Source: caspar.nsf.gov (disguised)

focused on fields like civil and mechanical engineering that suffered the most declines and did not offer majors in emerging fields such as biomedical engineering. Third, Watkins saw a significant decline in enrollment at the freshman and sophomore level. Students discovered that they could attend local community colleges at a much lower cost and simply transfer to Watkins for their junior and senior years.

Finally, Watkins found itself surrounded by branch campuses of its traditional competitors and new entrants such as the University of Phoenix. These schools offered students degrees that could be more quickly earned than Watkins' offerings. Watkins' distinctiveness was not fully appreciated by many adult

Table 3. Annual tuition (in $000)

	Watkins	Urban Private	Suburban State A	Suburban State B	Urban State A
1994	6.2	11.3	3.5	3.3	3.4
1995	8.2	11.8	3.7	3.6	3.6
1996	8.8	12.4	4.0	3.6	3.7
1997	9.4	13.0	4.1	3.7	3.8
1998	9.4	13.6	4.3	4.0	3.7
2000*	8.7	14.7	4.5	3.8	3.6

Source: caspaqr.nsf.gov (disguised)

* *Note: Watkins changed its formula for reporting tuition in 2000.*

Table 4. Tuition per credit hour for junior/senior engineering students

	Watkins	Urban Private	Suburban State A	Suburban State B	Urban State A
2003	$524	$600	$250	$189	$197

Source: Institutional Web sites (disguised)

Table 5. School of management enrollment

	Watkins
1994	255
1995	362
1996	435
1997	450
1998	566
1999	688
2000	755
2001	809
2002	902

Source: school data, disguised

learners that simply needed a college degree with any major for career advancement. There were also seemingly invisible entrants from "virtual" universities such as Capella University that had no physical presence in the metropolitan area. Some of these competitors are for-profit schools that operate with radically different business models than Watkins had. Differences included high levels of marketing expenditures, total reliance on adjuncts and a strong focus on making programs easily accessible to students.

There was one bright spot in the enrollment front at Watkins. The School of Management, after years of declining enrollment, began to grow again (Table 5). These increases were achieved by adding new graduate degree programs, increased marketing of existing programs and the creation of branch sites. Growing enrollment in Watkins' management programs masked declines in others areas.

Although welcomed by the administration, this growth came with some risks. First, competing schools were adding management programs at branch locations or online. Literally all a competitor needed was some office space and a few adjunct instructors. Second, graduate business programs are of a relatively short duration compared to four-year (or more) undergraduate programs. This made Watkins dependent on constant recruiting and led to the possibility of enrollment declines.

Financial Position

During the 1990s and early 2000s Watkins' financial position was solid due to conservative budgeting by the institution. Unfortunately, however, nearly 80% of the school's funding came by tuition payments from students. Tuition revenue was driven by enrollment, which remained uncertain for Watkins. Further, the school's ability to increase tuition was limited given its price disadvantage compared to competing public schools. Gains in endowment during the 1990s were offset by losses in the stock market in the early 2000s and in any case provided relatively little income. Finally, note that Watkins' administrative ratio (18.4%) was quite high compared to similar private schools of its size and type. Many benchmark schools operated with administrate ratios under 10%. Watkins' finances are summarized in Table 6.

Table 6. Watkins financials (2002)

Revenue			%
Contributions		$2,180,332	6.1%
Government Grants		4,358,319	12.2%
Program Services		28,177,617	78.9%
Investments		988,183	2.8%
Total		$35,704,450	100.0%
Expenses			
Program Services		$26,342,183	73.8%
Administration		6,562,949	18.4%
Other		1,497,868	4.2%
Total		$34,403,001	96.4%
Net		$1,301,449	3.6%

Source: www.guidestar.com (disguised)

Strategic Planning

Several simultaneous events led to a turnaround in fortunes at Watkins University in the late 1990s and 2000s. First, with the support of the University's Board and Administration, the institution began a broad based strategic planning effort in late 1998. The plan brought together various constituent groups and generated a number of planning initiatives shown in Table 7. This initiative was quite new for Watkins. The organization had traditionally been quite conservative and operated in a "top-down" fashion. The planning process was one of the first efforts to function in a more collaborative and cross-functional way.

The impact of the initiatives in Table 7 on IT can be considered in the context of critical success factors (CSFs), an idea originally suggested by John Rockart (1979). Based on this approach, management needs information systems that can provide key indicators of how the organization is doing in achieving its goals. For one, the President and Board had long focused on enrollment as a critical factor for the school's financial health. This is quite reasonable in that tuition provides 80% of the school's revenue. To monitor enrollment, however, requires an effective admission system that can monitor applications and deposits throughout the annual recruiting cycle. Also, the school needs accurate data regarding student retention. Both of these needs were not being met effectively by the current legacy administration system. Although the Watkins administration did not introduce the concept of CSFs in their strategy sessions, the list in Table 7 and subsequent actions by the IT steering committee suggest that they may have implicitly thought in CSF terms.

Table 7. Watkins strategic initiatives

Watkins University Strategic Initiatives
Growth and Market – focused on reaching a goal of 5,000 students
Program and Delivery – focused on developing distinctive programs
Constituency Centered Culture – focused on service delivery
Educational Campus Environment – focused on capital projects to build the University's infrastructure, both physical and technology
Institutional Reputation and Support – focused on fund raising

Source: school Web site

Although the titles of these initiatives sound fairly lofty, there were several practical action plans that emerged and led to changes in the institution. As noted, the School of Management, and to a lesser extent other Schools, aggressively began pursuing new programs and branch locations. A stronger constituent focus took hold of the organization. Administrative groups, for example, were reorganized to better focus on customer service to students. Watkins also began to advertise more heavily in their local market, and a major capital campaign was launched. Finally, Watkins began to seriously address the institution's infrastructure, both in terms of physical buildings and laboratory and computer technology. The latter, detailed in a later section, included four major initiatives: a Web based teaching and student laptop initiative designed to change the learning process of the school, a Web based ERP implementation designed to reform the school's business processes and a proposed university one card system intended to offer enhanced services to the student body.

Setting the Stage

IT Infrastructure

Watkins University had a long tradition of using computer technology. After an initial implementation of an IBM mainframe in the 1970s, the school settled in the 1980s on a single vendor strategy, standardizing on digital equipment computing platforms. The school employed DEC VAX/VMS and PC based systems exclusively for all computing needs. The DEC VAX/VMS systems ran a collection of custom developed and purchased administrative applications. They also were employed as e-mail and Web servers. When the administration applications were developed in-house in the late 1980s they had many features, including student access to online registration, transcript and account status, that were quite advanced for their time. However, during the 1990s the University's administrative systems were found to be increasingly inflexible and difficult to maintain. The University's auditor, for example, had difficulty auditing the organization's financial records. The one purchased application, a financial system, only ran on a DOS based server and was not being supported by the original vendor. The student information system used a relational database, but had no referential integrity or user-friendly query interface. Further, the administrative system was written with VT character mode terminals as the primary user interface. Given their age the administrative applications had no Web interface and retrofitting a Web interface was perceived to be prohibitively expensive. This situation was addressed in 2002 with the implementation of a Web based ERP, described in the next section.

In terms of academic computing the IT organization maintained tight control of computer labs, much to the frustration of students and faculty. For example, through much of the 1990s the IT organization insisted that in order to provide consistent support all lab PCs had to boot off of network drives and have all applications installed on servers. Hardware was sourced strictly from DEC (and later Compaq). One particularly ill-fated venture was made to install a large group of Alpha chip based PCs, despite limited vendor support and complaints from faculty. The PC software selected by the IT staff focused on products such as Word Perfect and Borland's Quattro Pro up until 1998 when the organization switched to Microsoft Office. Academic needs such as AutoCAD and math programs were supported, but often with dated releases. This situation was addressed with the implementation of a PC lap initiative in the fall of 2000 as described in the next section.

IT Organization

The IT organization evolved over the years and by 2003 was organized as shown in Figure 2. In this figure the notation of "T," "t," "P," and "p" is based on Wysocki and DeMichiell's (1997, pp. 32-33) notion of "Information Enabled Managers". "T" denotes managers with strong technical skills, while "t" denotes managers with limited technical knowledge. "P" denotes managers with strong process knowledge, while "p" denotes managers with limited process knowledge.

The Banner support team under Tom Jancek installed, implemented and maintained Banner, a packaged ERP system developed by SCT Corporation. This package was commonly used at schools throughout the United States including three of Watkins' closest competitors. It included modules for HR, finance, admissions, student information (grades, registration, etc.), and financial aid. Tom's team of six included three technical people (Tp) that supported the Compaq hardware (located in the Data Center), Oracle database software and system interfaces and three analysts (tP) that worked with user groups to implement the package and generate custom reports.

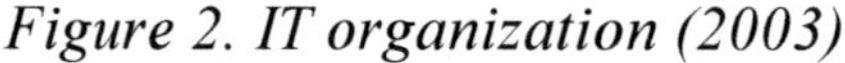

Figure 2. IT organization (2003)

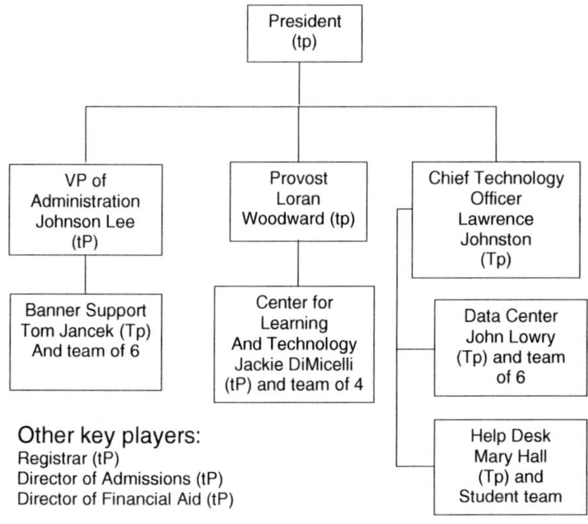

Jackie DiMichiell headed The Center for Technology and Learning (CETL). This five-person team focused on implementing instructional technology for the school. The group operated their own LINUX based servers running BlackBoard, a commonly used Web-teaching tool, in their own office area. CETL worked directly with faculty in implementing the PC laptop initiative. One staff member in this group provided technical support (Tp), while the balance of the staff focused on instructional support and, hence, could be characterized as "tP" where the process in question was education.

John Lowry, a long-term employee of Watkins, headed the Data Center. The Data Center operated the main computer room, the campus data and voice networks and the Compaq VMS servers used for e-mail and Web serving. The group also supported Microsoft NT servers located throughout campus and handled laptop hardware and software associated with the school's laptop program. All of the employees in this area were strong technically (Tp).

The help desk was a relatively new area, headed by Mary Hall. The intent of the group was to provide support to users across campus with various IT services. The group was new, however, and the Banner and CETL groups continued to provide significant user support on their own. Further, the registrar's office provided the first level of support for students, faculty and staff using the Student Information portion of the Banner system.

The various IT organizations were given direction by an IT Steering Committee that consisted of three members: Johnson Lee, Chief Financial Officer, Lawrence Johnston, Chief Technology Officer and Loran Woodward, Provost. On occasion the President of the institution joined in the committee sessions as well. The group typically met on a monthly basis to discuss overall IT direction and to receive briefings from IT staff regarding future specific projects.

IT Budget

Table 8 summarizes the 2002-2003 IT budget for Watkins University. Expenditures in IT constituted about 5.6% of the institution's revenues. Although viewed as strategic for the organization, there was considerable concern among administrators as to whether this level and mix of expenditure was right for the institution.

Table 8. IT budget

Banner Support			
	Salaries		$ 490
	Vendor Support		107
	(Software, hardware)		
Total			$ 597
Center for Technology & Learning			
	Salaries		$ 350
	Vendor Support		70
	(Software, hardware)		
Total			$ 420
Data Center			
	Salaries		$ 490
	Vendor Support		237
	(Software, hardware)		
Total			$ 727
Help Desk			
	Salaries (inc. student)		$ 108
Grand total			$ 1,852

Case Description

In the spring of 2003 the IT Steering Committee held a key meeting to consider a future IT direction for Watkins. Overall, Watkins had made significant headway in turning the institution around in the prior three years. Enrollment had slowly risen from a low of 3,600 in 1997 to about 4,000 in 2002. A major advertising campaign had reinvigorated the school in the marketplace. A major fund raising campaign had brought in some $30 million dollars to fund the construction of new buildings and building up the endowment.

The questions the IT Steering Committee had to consider were where to allocate scarce IT resources and which IT initiatives to emphasize. The trio was keenly aware that technology was a battleground in the higher education market. However, to a large extent competing schools had matched Watkins' IT efforts. Each, for example, had implemented Web based teaching and ERP initiatives. Watkins was alone with laptop and wireless network initiatives, but the significance of these efforts was unclear. Could a strategic advantage be found through IT? How could IT help the school achieve its five key strategic goals (see Table 7)? In particular, should additional resources be deployed to the three major initiatives undertaken to date: laptop computing, Web based teaching, and Web based ERP? Or should there be a reallocation of resources within the IT function? Also, the school had considered implementing a cash card system as a way to offer improved student service. Should a "one card" system be implemented? Finally, the trio had to wonder if there were other initiatives that should be pursued. Emerging technology in PDAs, tablet PCs, P2P networks and other technology were tempting.

Laptop Initiative

Loran Woodward, the Provost, had been a strong advocate of the laptop initiative since its inception in 1998. The process the school undertook to begin this effort focused on identifying the best hardware vendor possible to provide the school with laptop computers. After careful consideration of several major vendors (including Compaq and IBM), a local vendor was selected to provide a private label unit. Only after hardware was selected were faculty asked to recommend software to include with the units. With some level of disagreement and apathy from faculty, the IT staff created a set of four disk images, one per

School. This allowed each School to include the software that it felt was appropriate for its students.

The laptop initiative was implemented first with freshman students in the fall of 2000, followed a year later by sophomores. By 2003 all undergraduate students were included in the program. Coupled with a campus wide wireless network, Watkins had a solid marketing advantage over competing schools as the only school in the metropolitan area with a laptop and wireless network offering for all students.

There were many concerns, however, with the implementation of the laptop program. Initially, the school charged students $660 per term for the rental of a laptop and use of university licensed software. Many students rebelled, claiming that they could acquire this technology for lower cost. Watkins insisted that all students participate, even if they had their own equipment or if they attended only part-time. Student outrage at this approach softened in 2002 when laptop fees were "bundled" into tuition rates.

Although some faculty integrated laptop technology in the curriculum (notably, the School of Architecture), other areas languished. Given Watkins' use of adjuncts to provide about two-thirds of all instruction, it was difficult to get all faculty to make full use of the technology. Some faculty members struggled to find reasons to use laptops in their classes. Casual visits to campus showed that laptops were in frequent use by students, but often for listening to music, instant messaging and other non-academic tasks.

Web Based Learning

The Web based teaching initiative had a similar mixed record of success. Watkins had purchased and implemented BlackBoard, a popular Web based teaching tool. Beginning in 1999 with just a handful of classes, by 2003 all Watkins classes had BlackBoard online classrooms. The CETL had instituted a complete set of faculty training sessions and strongly supported the product. Although many Watkins faculty members used BlackBoard to post some course material and perform other tasks, such as posting grades, the tool was significantly underused. Students, however, had become comfortable with the tool and expected faculty to use it. They noted differences in utilization: "Professor X uses BlackBoard for lots of things while Professor Y hardly uses BlackBoard at all!" The administration had mandated its use, but had no way to ensure faculty actually made beneficial use of the package.

Online teaching presented certain challenges for the degree offerings of Watkins. Management courses, for example, are frequently offered online at other schools. Indeed, there are over 200 regionally accredited schools in the U.S. that offer totally online MBA programs. Watkins' School of Management wondered if they could offer any distinctiveness in a totally online environment, however, particularly given their relatively high tuition. Watkins' other major areas of instruction, namely architecture and engineering, faced different challenges. Architecture is traditionally taught in long studio sessions with faculty. Engineering typically requires significant lab content. There are no professionally accredited distance education programs in architecture or engineering in the U.S.

As of 2003 none of the Schools at Watkins had offered any totally online degree programs. Although Watkins had spread branch campuses around the metropolitan area and in select international locations, there was uncertainty as to whether the school would ever offer virtual degrees. BlackBoard was used, however, to augment traditional on-ground courses, in a handful of online courses and in some "blended" delivery classes with a mix of online and on-ground components.

Web Based Administrative Systems

Watkins made a major commitment to replace its legacy administrative system in mid-2000. The decision on what path to take was made by two groups. First, a team of users and IT personnel undertook an involved selection process to identify and evaluate ERP software. The group created selection criteria and then selected Banner after reviewing software offerings from a number of vendors of academic ERP software. Second, a separate group determined what hardware to run the Banner system on. The group finally selected a UNIX server for administrative computing only after turning down an impassioned plea from the Data Center to continue using the VMS platform with which they were familiar. As a compromise, Watkins shifted from VMS to UNIX, but continued to use Compaq hardware.

The implementation of the Banner system took over two years. The school enlisted a project team with key personnel from each functional area affected (Admissions, Registrar, HR, Finance, Financial Aid and Academic departments). After using outside consultants from a national consulting firm for several months, Watkins hired additional IT staff to run the project in-house.

The team's approach was to implement Banner in a "vanilla" implementation, which is to say without any modifications to the software. The effort did require significant configuration and report writing, but no coding changes to the system.

After starting in late 2000, the finance and payroll functions went live in January of 2002. Watkins implemented the Student Information portion of Banner in the spring of 2002 with pre-registration for the fall 2002 term. The project was significantly over budget with total cost of nearly $3 million and took longer than anyone had originally envisioned.

As implemented in 2002, the Banner system provided for the basic transaction processing needs of the University and offered a Web interface for students and faculty. There were definite benefits to Watkins from moving to the Banner system. Notably, Watkins was able to implement Web based applications and registration, improved tracking of applicants, Web based credit card payment, Web based time entry for payroll and an auditable financial system. Further, the system significantly sped up the processing of financial aid to students and enabled electronic links to student loan vendors. For example, with Banner the University collected $4 million in financial aid for the fall 2003 term by the end of September 30, at least 60 days earlier than usual. There was significant functionality in the Banner system, however, that Watkins did not implement in 2002. Of particular interest were additional Web modules for financial reporting and a workflow automation module that could be used to automate business processes.

One-Card System

Starting in late 2002, Johnson Lee, the VP of Finance, considered the possibility of adding a one-card system to the campus for identification, micro payment and debit card use. The administration was interested in providing enhanced students services as a way to counter competitive threats from area schools. A second motivation for a one-card system was an interest in capturing some "financial" action on cash flows that the university passed on to students. The school dispensed millions of dollars in student loan refunds and payrolls to students each year.

During the summer of 2002 a number of key pieces fell into place. After being rebuffed by their traditional banking partner, officials at Watkins were approached by an FDIC insured Internet bank with the idea of implementing a

Figure 3. Anywhere card proposal

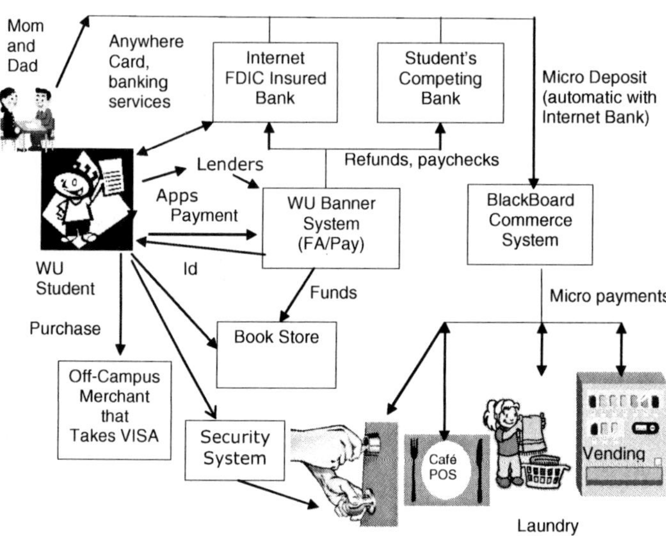

one-card system with debit card capabilities. The BlackBoard Web-teaching platform had a commerce module that could support micro payments and other one-card initiatives. The administration considered a one-card system pictured in Figure 3.

The key features that the Internet bank offered were two-fold. First, the bank offered the ability to periodically query the student's micro payment account in BlackBoard and "reload" it to a pre-set spending amount. Second, the Internet bank offered the idea of "sharing" transaction fees (typically 1.5%) from debit card transactions as an incentive to Watkins to implement their proposal.

Examination of the proposal, however, identified a number of concerns. First, the Internet bank was interested in having the university "encourage" students to deposit refunds from student loans and paychecks directly into accounts at the Internet bank. Watkins would then share in transaction fees as student spent this money. This raised an ethical concern—should a university steer students to a bank that they had a financial interest in?

Table 9. One card implementation cost

One-Card Implementation Cost
Purchase VTS (Value Transfer Station) - $12,000
License add-on to BlackBoard - $7,500/yr
Vending machine modification - $9,000
New cafeteria equipment - $12,000
Door modification - $4,500

Second, Watkins officials became concerned with their ability to deliver service, both from a technical and an administrative perspective. What sounded like a "technological edge" could become a customer service disaster if not implemented well. On the technical side, the architecture shown in Figure 3 is dependent on the University's network infrastructure. The infrastructure was designed to support an academic endeavor, not financial transactions. If the infrastructure failed, students could not open doors, purchase meals, do their laundry or other tasks. The Business office was concerned about the staff needed to service student complaints, especially on trivial transactions. Further, administrators feared they were backing an Internet bank with no track record of success and without branches or staff to serve students. Would the Internet bank stay around? What was their profit potential? For all of these reasons there was a potential negative impact on student satisfaction if services were done poorly.

Third, the cost to implement the system above was not insignificant. An estimate placed the cost at $45,000 to start (Table 9).

Further, beyond these immediate costs significant staff time would be required to implement and operate the system. Vendors, such as the cafeteria and laundry, would have had to cooperate as well and, given the dollar volumes involved, there was little advantage to them.

Fourth, the question of student acceptance came up. Watkins served a diverse student population. While some students were traditional, full-time residential students, Watkins served a large commuter population. Further, over the past 10 years the school has increased graduate enrollment to the point that one-third of the students are mid-career adults. Hence, Watkins' students on the whole are quite sophisticated. Many come to campus with their own debit cards and banking relationships. What advantage would a Watkins "anywhere" card offer students? Off-campus it would function as an ordinary debit card—the same sort of card that most students already had. Would having a single card offer significant benefits over holding two or more cards? On campus, would the convenience of not having to have change for laundry or vending really outweigh tying up funds on a campus card?

Research by one of the faculty in the School of Management highlighted this concern. Using the framework of Davis (1989), the faculty member studied the "perceived ease of use" and "perceived benefit" of a one-card system. Davis's model states that the likelihood of one using a given technology is positively related to these two factors. When surveyed, Watkins students showed a high degree of comfort using the Internet and rated the "perceived ease of use" of such a card high. However, when asked about the "perceived benefit" of such a card, student reaction was apathetic. In fact, a sizable number of students indicated that while they were heavy Internet users, they were strongly opposed to using a campus one-card system. The faculty member was puzzled about this group of "e-commerce resistant students". Were they suspicious of the school's ability to operate the system? Or did they feel that were already too heavily indebted to the school to trust their personal finances to Watkins?

Fifth, Watkins' relatively small size also comes into play. With only 4,000 students, and many of these commuters, there were only a limited number of places to use a one-card system. The school only has one cafeteria, one laundry facility, one bookstore and several dozen vending machines. Metcafe's law, the widely accepted idea that the value of a network is proportional to the number of nodes on it, applies to this situation. The only saving grace to the proposal was the idea of incorporating a debit card into the one-card solution to provide universal use. But many Watkins students already had debit cards from their own banks. If few students went with the debit card feature, Watkins would be stuck handling micro payments with little profit potential from transaction fees and a major potential for customer service problems.

Current Challenges/Problems

As the IT Steering Council began to meet the members realized that they had to make some tough choices. The President was unlikely to approve significant increases in overall funding levels without very convincing evidence. Reallocation between initiatives was possible, but which initiatives should receive more money? Which initiatives should receive less money? Beyond the initiatives, the IT infrastructure had to be supported, but could they cut here and still be able to run the University? Further, they were not sure which, if any, of the initiatives would help the institution in its overall strategic position in the marketplace. As a private school with relatively high tuition, Watkins had to be able to demonstrate customer value and distinctiveness in order to get students to enroll. At the same time, the conservative culture of the school did not encourage risk taking and placed a high penalty on failure.

The laptop initiative had gone through two hardware generations by 2003. The school had over the years acquired a fleet of some 1,500 used laptops. These units had 400 and 800 MHz processors that rapidly were becoming obsolete. New state-of-the-art units could be purchased for about $1,200. But how many units should be purchased? If units were purchased, how could the faculty be engaged so as to use the laptops in the classroom? Or should the school discontinue the laptop program and allow students to acquire their own client devices? The school could continue to provide network connectivity (via wireless and wired connections) without the expenditure for new laptops. This might create support problems, however, for the fledgling helpdesk. Moreover, if the laptop program were discontinued, how would Watkins communicate the reduced value to students? Should tuition be reduced?

As for Web based teaching there were two issues to consider. First, Watkins had resisted the notion of offering academic programs online. Should they reconsider this? A significant move into online education would require additional IT staff, perhaps two employees, plus significant work by faculty to design programs and staff to market them. Second, Jackie DiMichiell asked to add to two additional staff members at an approximate cost of $130,000 (including benefits) to lead curriculum development projects. These additional staff members would focus on working with faculty to develop custom courseware for use in Watkins classes. Should Watkins commit to adding staff to a support function like CETL? Is the development of custom courseware a strategic area for Watkins to invest in? Should Watkins undertake such an effort if the school elected to offer (or not to offer) distance education degree programs?

The Banner system implementation was now complete and some benefits had accrued. However, the organization was far from paperless and many administrative processes still need major reform. Further, most of the school's competitors had implemented the same software package and had achieved most of the same benefits. Should Watkins continue to invest in their ERP implementation? Or should the ERP team be reduced to a maintenance crew of four employees to reduce expenses? Although benefits could be obtained through further automation, Watkins was a fairly small institution with only 350 employees. How much automation made sense? Besides automating transactions, could the ERP system be leveraged to provide better information for decision makers? Can the ERP system address any of Watkins' Critical Success Factors?

The VP of Finance developed the "one card" proposal with some reluctant assistance from the Banner team. A potential Internet bank had been identified to team up with Watkins. Should Watkins invest $50,000 in software acquisition and a significant amount of existing staff members' time in this project? Will students find the system sufficiently useful and easy to use to warrant its use? What are the potential downsides to such a proposal?

Were there other initiatives that Watkins should be considering? The school had focused on several of the "hot button" issues that other universities were focusing on and vendors were selling solutions to. But were there any "silver bullets" that Watkins could use to boost the institution's competitive position and take a competitive lead? Are there emerging technologies that Watkins could use to be distinctive in the marketplace?

A more basic, underlying question is: "What is the value of IT to Watkins? How central is IT to the success of the institution?" Should the steering council fight for more funding from a reluctant president? Or should they attempt to manage down the cost of IT?

References

Brown, J., & Hagel, J. (2003, June). Does IT matter? An HBR debate. *Harvard Business Review,* 2-4.

Carr, N.G. (2003, May). IT doesn't matter. *Harvard Business Review,* 5-12.

Davis, F. (1989). Perceived usefulness, perceived ease of use, and user acceptance of information technology. *MIS Quarterly, 13*(3), 319-340.

Kern, H., Galup, G., & Nemiro, G. (2000). *IT organization: Building a worldclass infrastructure.* Upper Saddle River, NJ: Prentice Hall.

Porter, M. (1979, March). How competitive forces shape strategy. *Harvard Business Review.*

Porter, M. (2001, March). Strategy and the Internet. *Harvard Business Review,* 62-78.

Rockart, J. (1979, March). Chief executives define their own data needs. *Harvard Business Review.*

Wysocki, R.K., & DeMichiell, R.L. (1997). *Managing information across the enterprise*. New York: John Wiley & Sons.

This case was previously published in the Journal of Electronic Commerce in Organizations, 2(4), October - December 2004, pp. 30-46.

Chapter XIII

Challenges of Complex Information Technology Projects:

The MAC Initiative

Teta Stamati
University of Athens, Greece

Panagiotis Kanellis
University of Athens, Greece

Drakoulis Martakos
University of Athens, Greece

Executive Summary

Although painstaking planning usually precedes all large IT development efforts, 80% of new systems are delivered late (if ever) and over budget, frequently with functionality falling short of contract. This case study provides a detailed account of an ill-fated initiative to centrally plan and procure, with the aim to homogenize requirements, an integrated applications suite for a number of British higher education institutions. It is argued that because systems are so deeply embedded in operations and organization and, as you cannot possibly foresee and therefore plan for environmental discontinuities, high-risk, 'big-bang' approaches to information systems planning and development must be avoided. In this context the case illustrates the level of complexity that unpredictable change can bring to an information technology project that aims to establish the 'organizationally generic' and the destabilizing effects it has on the network of the project's stakeholders.

Organizational Background

Located on the western edge of London, Isambard University received its Royal Charter[1] in 1966 and since then enjoys a considerable reputation for research and teaching in the science and technology fields in which it specializes. Close connections with the public sector, industry and commerce characterize Isambard University. These links were built through a commitment to the thin sandwich[2] undergraduate degrees which made the University's graduates among the most employable in the country and, by its distinctive competence in applied and strategic research. As a direct result, Isambard University is popular with undergraduates, while its earnings from contract research per member of academic staff are significantly above the national average in most of the cost centers in which it is active.

In the beginning of the 1990s the Higher Education (HE) sector in the UK started to experience dramatic changes. The Secretary of State invited comment on the scale, purpose and structure of HE, and the Government made its views clear through the introduction of numerous policy changes affecting universities' funding, teaching and research. Those were followed by the merger of the Ministries of Education and Employment, and the move of the Office of Science and Technology to the Ministry of Trade and Industry, signifying an increased requirement for public spending on HE to have a demonstrable effect on employment and national economic growth. For example, in November 1995, a 7% overall reduction in universities funding for 1996 was announced, including a 31% fall in capital funding, meaning that over a six-year period the unit of funding for teaching each student would have had to be reduced by 28%. Direct financial support for students was also reduced. The previous students' allowance scheme was terminated, with the balance between student grants and loans moving even more deterministically towards the latter, with the Government signaling its adamant intention to fundamentally review the funding mechanisms.

It was against this background of environmental turbulence that Isambard University, as indeed every other academic institution of HE, operated. Another one of the key environmental changes was the Government's plan to double the number of undergraduate students, from one million to two million, over a 25-year period beginning from 1989. In the medium term this was to be achieved through a strategy of 'expansion with greater efficiency'. Hence, a major challenge for Isambard University was to determine a plan and assure that the necessary infrastructure was in place for participating in this program of expansion in a way that would build upon and strengthen its distinctive characteristics. Associated with this change was the Government's decision to abolish the Council for National Academic Awards (CNAA[3]). Institutions with degrees validated by this body were now required to seek alternative means of validation, either through the acquisition of chartered status, or through association with an existing chartered institution. Opportunities to validate the awards of other institutions were therefore available for Isambard University.

Isambard University's strategy of actively seeking growth and diversity, by merging and fostering links with other institutions, came into fruition in February 1995, when the West London Institute of Higher Education was incorporated into the University as Isambard University College. This amalgamation marked the beginning of significant restructuring as the College departments had to be molded into a unified faculty structure. By the end of 1995, the Departments of Education from the two institutions were brought together into a single School of Education, and the Department of Design joined the Faculty of Technology. Furthermore, there were plans involving the splitting of the College Department of Human and Environmental Sciences into a Department of Sports Sciences and a separate Department of Geography and Earth Sciences. In addition, Isambard was for the first time planning to establish an Arts Faculty. This re-organization was the cause of considerable instability.

Adding to these was the intensification of the competition for research funding. Changes in the Funding Council's allocation model were directed towards greater selectivity in the use of research funding and an increased emphasis on research quality and proven research success. For these reasons, Isambard was experiencing a shift in its funding arrangements and had to obtain external funding to compensate for a reduction in central funds through the Higher Education Funding Council for England (HEFCE). Whereas in the past there were one or two revenue streams to be maximized, now there were at least five.

These included:

- Central funding from the HEFCE based on a series of assessments (for example Research Assessment Exercise)
- Project-driven funding from UK research councils and from the European Community
- Collaborative and contract research for industry and commerce
- Overseas student fee income
- Conference accommodation and catering income

Hence it was towards the end of the '80s and the beginning of the '90s that Isambard University found itself exposed to an operating environment that in many respects was borrowing the business — like characteristics of the commercial sector. In the Vice Chancellor's own words:

The only cloud on our horizon as we start the new year is the uncertainty of the environment in which we will be seeking to put those values [to continue to be a mixed teaching and research university which is financially sound; and to be characterized by teaching and research which is of relevance to its user community] into practice. 1995 entered with less clarity about the future of the UK Higher Education system than most of us working in it have ever known. (Sterling, 1995, p. 16)

Setting the Stage

Information systems played a critical role at Isambard University. Its orientation towards engineering and sciences dictated a high level of interest in, and use of such systems, among other high technology facilities. Since the mid-eighties its systems infrastructure developed from a central multi-user mainframe with islands of computation in the various departments, to a distributed computing system linking central and departmental resources and providing user access at required locations, via terminals, PCs, and workstations. Teaching and research staff, partnering with their close links to industry and commerce, demanded 'state-of-the-art' computing at industry standards. The following elements constituted the framework for the University's computing infrastructure:

- UNIX for main service operating systems
- Networks based on X.25 and Ethernet
- IBM compatibility for PCs
- Adoption of UNIX- based workstations
- Application software of industry standards
- Centralized file service

It was also recognized that all administrative work ought to be underpinned with effective information and management systems. Historically, the administrative computing capability had been developed to service the central administrative functions. As management and administrative tasks and activities by departments and faculties increased, so did the need for support in those areas. This change in responsibility brought about the development, within some departments and faculties, of local systems to support their management and administrative activities and needs. In parallel with this, there was an increasing demand from departments and faculties for management information from central administration and support, in terms of access to system facilities. In 1988, it was observed that in terms of hardware, the host machine supported about the maximum number of peripherals it could, and was utilized beyond the normal expected level. This meant that any further expansion of support was not feasible without increasing computing power and capacity. In addition, the terminal access of administrative systems for individual departments provided via the University's network did not provide an adequate response to those remote users, and the service level did not always fulfill their needs. It was not necessarily the case that the information held within the systems was inadequate, but barriers existed which prevented or hindered its use by the departmentally base staff that needed it. There were also issues associated with the data itself, and it was felt that they could probably be resolved by developing new hardware and software architectures to support the differing needs of the users. In summary, the main issues were:

- **Format and structuring:** Data was not formatted and structured so that it could be presented to the user in a useful and meaningful way.

- **Access:** There was limited access to the data caused primarily by technical constraints.
- **Currency:** Data was found to be current for one set of users but out of date for others, due to differences in need and timescale.
- **Ownership:** There were areas where lack of ownership definition and responsibility had resulted in a lapse in maintenance of the data. Where ownership was at the center, but data was derived from other sources, there were problems in maintaining it. An example was customer records where ongoing information was provided from many sources, but there was no area responsible for collecting the data and no means of distributed input. Any breakdown of communication resulted in central and departmental information being different.
- **Completeness:** There was a wealth of information in all subject areas held by individual departments and within the faculties, which was not captured effectively. The necessary mechanisms (i.e., coordinated and integrated systems) did not exist to enable this to happen.

The software applications processing this data had been developed over the last 12 years. Their development had been tailored to the specific needs of the users that applied at the time of development or subsequent amendment. As management and administrative roles and responsibilities were undergoing change, new users were bringing in a new set of needs to be satisfied. Similarly, changing circumstances—unpredictable demands from the Universities Funding Council (UFC)[4] and changing rules for allocating funds—and pressures were bringing about different needs. During the period of 1988-1990 it became clear that while the existing systems satisfied many of the central administrative requirements, new needs in both the management and administration of the university arose.

Case Description: Management and Administrative Computing Initiative

The UFC's Management and Administrative Computing (MAC) initiative was announced in September 1988. The aim of the initiative was to promote the introduction of more effective and sophisticated systems to support the increasingly complex decisions that faced universities and colleges (Kyle,

1992). In addition, the systems were to provide the UFC with the information needed for allocating funds more effectively across the pool of universities. The cost of institutions 'doing it alone' was estimated at £ 0.5 million or more for each. To avoid this, the Universities Grants Committee (UGC[5] — precursor to the UFC) commissioned a study to develop an information/data specification or 'Blueprint', which aimed to cover 80-90% of the needs of any single institution. A Managing Team was formed, and an initial study based on direct input from five universities and contributions from 20 more was completed. The team, comprising senior computing staff and university administrators, was chaired by the Vice Chancellor of the University of Nottingham.

The UFC decided that they would only fund information technology developments for MAC that were organized to suit 'families' of universities. The objective was to group institutions into five or six families with similar computing requirements. Whilst geographic proximity was helpful in promoting frequent contact between the family members, it was not to be the only consideration. Others included similarity in size, structure, type of institution, existing collaboration (for example on purchasing), and computing development needs.

The Initial Phases

The Blueprint undertaken by Price Waterhouse (now PriceWaterhouseCoopers) delivered at the end of 1988. The five main participants were Manchester University, Strathclyde University, Newcastle University, University College London and Isambard University.

In March 1989 the blueprint was sent to all universities, together with a request that each university prepare a 'migration strategy' report. This would have to include each university's present administrative computing situation, both in terms of its computing hardware and its existing applications, and of its development priorities and requirements for the future and additionally:

- A comparison of the information needs of the University with the generalized blueprint and an identification of gaps between the two
- The identification of the characteristics of the institution in order for the Managing Team to classify it
- The development of an outline strategy for migration from the University's existing systems to the outline architecture in the blueprint

Isambard's migration strategy was prepared with the assistance of two consultants from Ernst and Young and emphasized the importance placed by the University on the provision of management as well as operational information. There were also two additional features that were highlighted: one was the need to conform to the University's own Information Technology strategy[6]; the other was the fact that a new development platform had to be selected for any future systems, as the existing systems were coming to the end of their useful life. The preparation of Isambard's migration strategy for MAC took place at about the same time and led to a decision to integrate management and administrative computing systems. This decision for integration was one of the principal factors that led to a commitment to the Oracle database platform as it was the one supported by the University's computing services. This migration strategy was sent to the UFC in July 1989.

The Formation of Families

The MAC Managing Team used the migration strategies submitted by all universities as the basis for the formation of different 'families'. A consultant from the National Computing Center (NCC) assisted in analyzing the strategies. As a result of his analysis and at a meeting held in September 1989, it was proposed that the families should be formed around the four main relational database products available at that time and in use in universities, as the universities believed it to be the most important factor regarding their future systems development. In addition it was thought that this would enable them to achieve the objective of developing a common code to run on their hardware. The products were *Oracle*, *Ingres*, *Powerhouse* and *Secqus*. Each university was then asked to choose which family it wished to join, with the UGC hoping "that, in time, all members of any one family will be using the same administrative computing software which they will develop and maintain jointly." The process of forming the families took place during October 1989 and Isambard joined the largest one—the Oracle Family—which represented a wide variety of universities. Other reasons for this were the size of the family itself—the bigger the family, the smaller the contribution Isambard believed it would have to make—and the viability of the supplier; in terms of sales, Oracle was by far the largest of the four as well as the most 'open'.

In October 1989, the Family was simply a collection of universities that agreed to cooperate on systems development using a particular product. A constitution and *modus operandi* had to be drawn up for the Family in addition to a plan of its activities. This was necessary in order to obtain funding from the UFC. The constitution established a Management Board in which each university had one representative and one vote. A Chairman was elected from among those representatives, and the Family incorporated as a limited company known as Delphic Ltd.

The Board also decided to form a number of what they called *Application Groups*, one for each area of the management and administrative systems identified in the Price Waterhouse's Blueprint. This did not mean that the groups had to undertake the development of the systems themselves, but that they were to be responsible for working directly with the commercial contractors employed by the Family. Each member of the Family had to be a member of at least one group, and Isambard took the decision to join the Management Information Application Group.

The Analysis, Design and Delivery Phases

In February 1990, it was decided to contract Mantis UK to undertake the analysis stage of the Family's systems development program. This involved the production of the functional analysis and data dictionary of the members' requirements, under the sections covered by the six Applications Groups set up by the Management Board: Students, Staff, Finance, Research and Consultancy, Physical Resources, and Management Information. The work on this contract commenced in February and ended in June 1990. It involved several consultants from Mantis UK plus many staff from all the member universities of the Family and was supervised by a Project Manager employed on a consultancy basis, together with a small group[7] chaired by the administrative computing manager of Bristol University.

The result of all the work—a huge coordinated effort between Mantis UK and the Family members—culminated in an enormous document running into several hundreds of pages which contained everything one ever wanted to know about management and administrative computing requirements in UK universities. It was made up of two main parts. The first was the analysis of all the management and administrative functions that universities needed the systems to help them carry out (the *Function Hierarchy*). The second identified all the data items required by these functions and the relationships between them (the *Entity Relationship Model*). These were followed by proposals concerning the development of the required systems. The document therefore comprised the deliverables from the analysis stage on the basis of which the system was to be designed and built.

The next stage was to commission someone to design and build the systems software on the basis of this analysis and data dictionary. An initial description of the work to be tendered was issued by the NCC on behalf of the Family at the end of April 1990, and expressions of interest in receiving a full tender document were invited. The formal invitation to tender was issued in June to three companies expressing interest. These were Mantis UK, Hoskyns and Price Waterhouse. The Family received the three tenders on August 7, 1990, and spent the rest of the month assessing them. A detailed scoring system was used to evaluate the three tenders against a whole range of factors. This evaluation process was followed by a period of intense negotiation over the costs with each of the suppliers and significant reductions over the original tender price were eventually achieved.

The outcome was that Mantis UK was offered the contract to develop the full set of management and administrative systems. The recommendation was formally accepted by a meeting of the Management Board in September 1990, and a contract was subsequently drawn up with Mantis UK with the assistance of specialist legal advice. The complexities of the negotiations over the contract were such that it was not formally signed until May 1991, although the work itself started and continued during the negotiation period.

Although the MAC system was designed as one closely integrated system, its software was to be made available in phases (see Appendix). All applications, with the exception of payroll, would use *SQL Forms V.3* with pop-up windows etc. as part of the user interface. The Finance application was based on Mantis's own accounting package that was to be enhanced to cater for the additional functionality requested by the Family. Whenever the Mantis development team finished writing and testing a release of software, this was to be passed over to the appropriate Application Group for them to run their own acceptance tests on it. It is important to note that the '80/20' rule applied here. A small part of the system was left to the discretion of the programmers working at each of the universities, who after an Mantis software release and in close cooperation with Mantis developers, would attempt to 'tailor' the system to the specifics of the sites (Pollock, 2001). If an institution was encountering problems in running the software, the 'Delphic Support Desk' had to be contacted. This would assess the problem and then pass the solution back to the institution responsible for the particular application. If the problem could not be resolved, it was forwarded back to Mantis which had to redesign and rebuild the application.

Management and Administrative Computing Initiative Outcome for the Delphic Family

Towards the end of 1994 and with the funding for the MAC Initiative nearing its termination date of March 31, 1995, the Delphic members were experiencing severe delays concerning the delivery of the main application packages. The Anticipated Availability Schedule (see Appendix) shows the time slippages. Kyle (1994) summarized some of the main causes for the delays as follows:

1. The design of the Student Structure was found to be flawed, and had to be redone.
2. Mantis's decision to merge its development team responsible for its own Finance package with the one responsible for the MAC's Finance module.
3. The loss of senior Mantis development staff, particularly during critical design stages.
4. The introduction of a new stage: implementation by a test (lead) institute between the end of acceptance testing and the release of an application in its supported state.
5. The decision of Delphic to make modules available in 'baskets'. This meant that the first module accepted had to wait until the acceptance of the last module in the basket before it could be implemented.

Complementary to the above a number of observations can be made regarding this state of affairs concerning the initiative.

Price Waterhouse's approach for conducting the initial feasibility study (i.e., the Blueprint) was considered hardly appropriate for as complex a system as MAC was. On the basis of the knowledge they had acquired about university administration from developing information systems for Durham and Leeds Universities, and because time was of essence, they adopted a 'drive the user base instead of letting the user base drive you' approach. This meant that Price Waterhouse as in effect designing the Blueprint based on its assumptions of what was needed, and then presenting it to the representatives from a cross-sample of universities, inviting them to comment.

However, the representatives did not have the blueprints in advance to study and to comment interactively with the consultants—they were given to them at the meetings, where at the end a decision had to be made. This, coupled with the large size of the project and its 'open' structure, resulted in some areas being overlooked and others not being looked at in sufficient detail. The final Blueprint was a huge and complicated technical document, and by large the universities did not check it out as they ought to have done. It was of a hierarchical structure cut down to functions described in little detail, which made it difficult for systems personnel to understand, let alone explain it to their line managers and get the much-needed feedback. The fact that this approach was problematic became evident when the families started their own individual developments. They found out that the result was not as much of the Blueprint as they had thought it to be.

The application of the '80/20' rule mentioned in the preceding section meant that the finalization and successful implementation of the various modules was heavily reliant on the skills and efforts of the programmers who were working the code so as to make it compatible to the specifics of each site. But they were tasked to work with the system only in certain ways, as Mantis wanted to ensure that the code would only be modified in the ways they deemed appropriate. In a sense they were "...attempting to configure the local programmers as their users..." (Pollock, 2001, p. 7) and this gave rise to a lot of friction. The following excerpt from a final report to the Delphic Support Desk regarding an issue illustrates this:

...As you may know, [the University] migrated from [MAC] 1.3 to 1.4 last week and encountered some problems which we helped with. We also advised them to migrate to 1.5, as 1.4 was no longer supported. This they did over the weekend and again had some problems, which I have mentioned in the log. They contacted me on Monday morning and I have been looking at the problem(s) over the last day and a half. We have carried out a few checks and offered some advice on overcoming some of the problems, but it would appear that the problem lies in the data that they are working with and not a problem in any of our code... Quite simply, I cannot justify any more time on this problem as it does not appear to be a problem with our software, rather a problem on site which may well require a great deal of time to identify... Their current work-around is to use the basket 4 forms against the basket 5 database. I have expressed my concern over this and warned them that this is unsupported but they

appear to be confident that they have an adequate work-around. (Pollock, 2001, p. 14)

Arguably, the causes for the delays mentioned above can be experienced in any project of MAC's scope, scale and complexity. However, the first one on Kyle's list draws one's attention, as it was the result of an environmental discontinuity that could have not been anticipated—that of semesterization8. It was felt as something that was clearly overdue, a departure from a rigid and inflexible academic structure that originated in the beginning of the last century to a more open and clearly cost-effective scheme. As a result of semesterization, Isambard, for example, was able to increase considerably its student numbers by offering a wider range of choice regarding the structure of its courses, rather than only the four-year thin sandwich course option. This change affected mainly the Student Module. The fact that in 1994 parts of it had not been contracted (see Appendix), although the initial delivery date for the completed module was July 1992, shows clearly the magnitude of the effect that this change had.

The Student Module was driven by what was called "*Program Structures*"—schemes of study. "Program Structures" was designed in such a way that in an attempt to provide for integration, every single module was required to know what the structure was when dealing with student administration. For example, the Student Registration, Student Finance, and the Assessment and Degree Conferment modules related first of all to the Program Structure and its maintenance, and in effect were totally dependent on it. This module's development had to start virtually from scratch again because of semesterization, and it was estimated that its delivery had to be put back by a year to 18 months.

Twenty-six months later and there was still no definite delivery date, although an estimation was that a 'formal' deliverable had to wait for another two years. Needless to say, no member of the Family could afford to bear the cost of a product that had not been proven to work, and in which acceptance tests had to take place throughout a whole academic year and be evaluated against the annual cycle of activities. The metaphor of the old lady who is trying to cross the road and waits for someone else to do it first, in order to see if he gets run over, illustrates the case. Angela Crum Ewing, deputy registrar at Reading University (a member of the Delphic Family), said after they decided to hold onto their in-house applications, rather than implement a MAC solution: "MAC is in a position of transition. We did not want to commit to a new, untried system, when we had our own in-house systems which worked well" (Haney, 1994).

A 'sneak preview' of the modules by Family members resulted in a lot of skepticism about the future, stemming from the fact that continuous disappointment would mean dissatisfied stakeholders who will not stop placing pressure in favor of project abandonment. The effect of semesterization had major repercussions not only on Mantis UK as the system developer, but on all members in the Family who were counting on the deliverables and had already made their migration plans. For Isambard University, only the quantifiable costs amounted to the region of more than £50,000—two extra man-years of further systems development work that no one had anticipated.

Current Challenges/Problems Facing the Organization

In September 1994, after almost six years of systems development and six months before the termination of the funding, only one of the Delphic modules that were to be made available was finally adopted by Isambard University (Figure 1).

The state of affairs regarding the seven main areas was as follows:

- **Students:** Although at the time Isambard's existing system infrastructure could hardly accommodate semesterization, the administration of the University, tired of waiting for Delphic to come up with a deliverable, was pushing persistently for a new system. In November 1993, after 'shopping around' for any Mantis-based student system in use that could be able to satisfy Isambard's own requirements, a decision was made to consider the system of the University of Liverpool. After some time it was found out that for a number of reasons, this was not the solution either. Firstly the system was designed to meet Liverpool's own requirements in a very specific way and it was never developed as a package for other universities to use. Isambard's own requirements were completely different to theirs. Secondly, it was developed on an older version of Mantis. This meant that its blind adoption would pose problems in the future concerning its integration with any Delphic deliverables. On the other hand, an attempt to modify it would mean

Figure 1. MAC modules adopted by Isambard University after almost six years of systems development

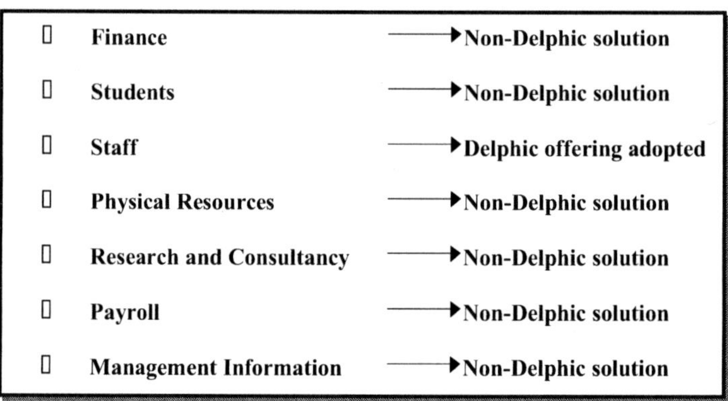

major overhead. Finally, from a technical point of view, the system was not documented—a 'black box' in the systems team's own words. Isambard had no alternative but to develop and design its own in-house student system whose first phase went live in the first week of October 1994 to coincide with the beginning of the new academic year. The system covered the Registration process, but no project was under way regarding the two other main areas—Student Finance and Student Accommodation.

- **Finance:** The development of the Finance module which was a base offering from Mantis UK and which had been enhanced to meet the extra requirements, was also off schedule. As a result, an Mantis quasi-commercial accounting package was adopted and implemented. The package had nothing specific to offer to universities, and if there were a choice, it would have not been taken on board by Isambard. It was developed by Mantis UK (in much the same way as Price Waterhouse delivered its MAC Blueprint) in an attempt to quickly capture a slice of the off-the-shelf software market when it had decided to enter it a couple of years ago. This meant that several enhancements were necessary and it took more that 200 person hours alone to determine whether or not it could replace the existing system. Subsystems to deal with the maintenance of research contracts, and to allow for the issuing of monthly statements of accounts to heads of departments and senior researchers, were designed, and eventually the system went 'live' in August 1994—the beginning of the new financial year.
- **Staff:** Following the installation and assessment of the pre-release version of the first module from Delphic (Posts, People, Appointments and Organiza-

tion), the implementation team agreed and the old system was subsequently discontinued in September 1993. It was replaced by this and the second module (Skills, Recruitment and USR Return). However, at that time (September 1993) Delphic still had not provided any documentation for the system.

- **Physical Resources:** The initial Delphic offering proved to be an 'overkill' for Isambard's requirements. It provided more than was actually needed, and two key areas had already been covered by in-house-developed Mantis systems. One area was the administration of the University's own housing facilities and the people who occupied them, and the other was an inventory system for mobile equipment. The Delphic offering still held some level of attraction to Isambard's Management Services team, but only when used in conjunction with the Delphic Finance Module, as it offered the facility the option to debit directly a departmental account at a store as soon as an item was issued out. The Stock Control Module was at the time running at test mode, but as these two packages were designed to be highly integrated, there was a deadlock situation as the Finance module had not been delivered. Moreover, as mentioned above, a commitment had been made to the in-house-developed finance system, which was unlikely to be replaced for at least two years.
- **Research and Consultancy:** No view had been formed about this module as there had not been a delivery. Supposedly it provided the ability to maintain profiles of staff and possible customers who could require applied research to be undertaken by the University on their behalf. An in-house-developed Mantis system was then in operation centered around publications of Isambard staff and information on customers. The accounting side (e.g., the recording of costs against research projects) was partly accommodated by the core finance system. Again, it was rather like Physical Resources—nothing particularly attractive given the overhead in implementing either of the Delphic modules that tended to be reasonably sophisticated for Isambard requirements.
- **Payroll:** A bureau service from a leading UK bank catered for the payroll function at Isambard. The consensus of the Director of Financial Services was that it was adequate, and therefore he was cautious and opposed any change. What were however lost by this decision were the integration and the economies, such as saving in paperwork and clerical time that came with the Delphic module, and that were associated with raising the cost of various processes between the two interconnected functions—payroll and personnel. However, the high level of integration offered between Delphic's Pay-

roll (not delivered at that time) and Staff modules were attractive to Isambard, as it had implemented the latter. After some careful consideration it became clear that its adoption was very unlikely to happen, as at the outset it seemed a very general package; again, many enhancements would have been necessary. This was a significant requirement considering the size of Isambard's Management Systems Team and its constrained time scales.

- **Management Information:** Similarly, no 'final' view was formed. There had been a development where Management Information was considered to be the 'Cinderella' module—the sort of one where by residing within the other modules, management information requirements at a strategic level could be easily accommodated. In September 1994, only statistics of various sorts could be generated for Government use, and those with considerable difficulty. In order to cure the problem, Delphic bought the rights for individual universities to acquire *Holis*—a powerful expert system, as there was general consent that Mantis UK was delivering 'textbook' systems. This meant that they had gone too far in terms of splitting down to tables for the database, without considering that most legacy systems already in place at universities were hierarchical, thus operating with one table. This transition posed a considerable challenge. It required a lot of effort and man-hours for the Management Services team that had to undergo the process, as *Holis* was not available when the initial design decisions were made. *Holis* was generally looked upon as the solution in gluing and running the whole of the independent databases together as it could accommodate any set of computerized data-like spreadsheets and flat files which did not necessarily have to follow Delphic's database format.

The MAC Initiative was funded from 1988 to 1995 and a total of 11 million were invested in those seven years. "Universities snub software policy," read a headline in *Computing* (September 22, 1994)—a professional trade magazine. "UK universities are going their own way to buy core administrative software after finding a government-sponsored scheme out of touch with their business needs," the article continued. Birmingham and Reading Universities both confirmed in September of that year that they were moving outside the MAC initiative for their latest developments, and the University of Sussex being dissatisfied with the delivered software for Undergraduate student admissions eventually chose a separate system. With the funding for MAC running out in July 1995, similar moves from other institutions were being planned, as there was no other viable alternative.

The outcome was that although Families continued to exist in a rather informal way, MAC-related activity slowly came to an end after the central funding terminated. The Delphic and Mantis UK Management Boards agreed and concluded their contract at the end of April 1996. The agreement was to deliver all remaining software in an 'as-is' state at the end of January in order to be tested at the University of Liverpool. The software was to be accepted at the end of February, with any 'bugs' to be remedied under the warranty agreement. Delphic was to make no further development demands on Mantis (Philips, 1996). It is without doubt that many interpretations can be given regarding the final outcome, and in retrospect each Family managed to achieve the objective of producing software to cover a number of the Data Blueprint areas. Some of these systems did run quite successfully in a number of institutions (Hillicks, 2002). What must be noted, however, is the fact *that no University managed to achieve the initial objective of using only the MAC modules exclusively.*

The ending of the contract meant that Delphic was in total control of the situation rather than having to work through Mantis, and in 1996 MAC was a far cry from the initial objective for an integrated information system where all the functional subsystems could be seamlessly linked so that one would not end up with a collection of disjointed and ineffective systems (Kanellis & Paul, 1995; Kanellis, 1996). For Isambard University in particular, the main attraction in joining the Delphic Family was the integrated solution that they were offering. Graham Kyle, manager of the Management Services team, summarized eloquently the situation: "...as you can observe, the way we are staggering here at Isambard, there is no sign of integration as far as we are concerned." One feature of Delphic that did not apply to any of the other families was that from day one the deliverable was designed as one system. It caused Mantis UK problems because, when the first major slippage occurred (the Students Module), Mantis had to respond to pressure from the Delphic representatives who demanded some deliverables." This meant that Mantis had to unbundle the system by separating and redesigning the links, a major cause for MAC's failure to meet deadlines. Almost all deliverables were at least two years late, according to the dates quoted by Mantis UK in the original specification, and this caused considerable stress and frustration to Isambard, which had to decide which route to follow regarding its infrastructure: to wait and see how Delphic would handle the situation after the termination of the contract with Mantis, to see how to integrate the various probable solutions described in the beginning of this section or to make a fresh beginning abandoning all previous investments? Difficult choices indeed and hardly the type one expects to be faced with at the end of an information technology development project that started with the best of expectations.

References

Haney, C. (1994). Universities snub software policy. *Computing,* (September 22), 14.

Hillicks, J. (2002). *Development Partnerships between HE and Vendors: Marriage made in Heaven or Recipe for Disaster?* Online: www.jiscinfonet.ac.uk/Resources/external-resources/development-partnerships/view

Kanellis, P. & Paul, R.J. (1995, August 2-5). Unpredictable change and the effects on information systems development: A case study. In W.A. Hamel (Ed.), *Proceedings of the 13th Annual International Conference of the Association of Management* (pp. 90-98). Vancouver, BC: Maximilian Press Publishers.

Kanellis, P. (1996). *Information Systems and Business Fit in Dynamic Environments.* Unpublished PhD Dissertation, Brunel University, UK.

Kyle, G. W. (1992). *Report on the UFC MAC Initiative.* London: Brunel University.

Kyle, G. W. (1994). *MAC Situation Report.* Brunel University, UK.

Philips, T. (1996). *MAC Progress Report.* Online: www.bris.ac.uk/WorkingGroups/ISAC/13-2-96/i-95-10.htm

Pollock, N. (2001). The tension of work-arounds: How computer programmers. Paper submitted to *Science, Technology & Human Values.*

Sterling, M. (1995). *Vice-Chancellor's Report to Court.* Brunel University, UK.

Endnotes

1. Royal Charters have a history dating back to the 13th century. The original purpose was to create public or private corporations and to define their privileges and purpose. Nowadays, Charters are normally reserved for bodies that work in the public interest and can demonstrate pre-eminence, stability and permanence in their particular field. Many older universities in England, Wales and Northern Ireland are also chartered bodies.

2 Sandwich courses involve a period of work in industry or a commercial organization. On a 'thick' sandwich course, the student spends the third year working away from university. The 'thin' sandwich course has placements lasting six months each calendar year.

3 The CNAA was founded by Royal Charter in 1964, with the object of advancing education, learning, knowledge, and the arts by means of the grant of academic awards and distinctions.

4 UFC became the Higher Education Funding Council for England (HEFCE) which was established following the Further and Higher Education Act 1992. A principal feature of the legislation was to create one unified higher education sector by abolishing the division between universities and polytechnics.

5 Under the education Reform Act of 1988, the University Grants Committee (UGC) was replaced with the Universities Funding Council (UFC) which in turn was replaced by the Higher Education Funding Council for England (HEFCE) to conform to the Further and Higher Education Act 1992 which made provision for a single system of higher education, with a unified funding structure and separate funding councils for England, Scotland and Wales.

6 It was during 1989 that Isambard University was required to prepare a renewed internal information technology strategy to support its bid to the UFC's Computer Board for funds related to academic computing from 1990 onwards. The principal objective of the strategy was to make available a range of integrated computing facilities to staff and students throughout the University using an infrastructure of distributed computing based on campus networking.

7 Members comprised of the chairmen of the six Applications Groups, plus a couple of other members nominated by the Management.

8 A standard of measurement in higher education used to group weeks of instructional time in the academic calendar. An academic year contains a minimum of 30 weeks of instructional time. An individual semester provides about 15 weeks of instruction, and full-time enrollment is defined as at least 12 semester hours per term. The academic calendar includes a fall and spring term, and often a summer term.

Appendix

Delphic Family Schedule of Deliverables

(a) DELPHIC family initial schedule of deliverables

1990/1991	1991/1992	MARCH 1993
STUDENT REGISTRATION, FEES, EXAMINATIONS	FULL STUDENT SYSTEM	MANAGEMENT INFORMATION & ALL SYSTEMS
FINANCE PHASE 1	FINANCE PHASE 2	
PAYROLL PACKAGE	PERSONNEL PHASE 2	
INTERIM PERSONNEL PACKAGE	RESEARCH AND CONSULTANCY 1	
	PHYSICAL RESOURCES PHASES 1,2,3	

(b) DELPHIC family schedule of deliverables (as at 30.09.1994)

Module	Applications	Design	System Test	Acceptance Test Signed- Off
FINANCE	Sales Document Input	11/91	2/92	10/92
	Purchase Document Input, Budgets & Commitments	11/91	2/92	10/92
	Sales & Purchase Ledgers	4/92	3/93 **(1)**	4/93
	Nominal Ledger	2/93	5/93 **(1)**	(3)
	Payroll Integration	1/93	3/93	(2)
STUDENTS	Program Structures	5/92	8/92	1/93 **(3)**
	Registrations	11/92	12/92	**(3)**
	Student Finance	10/92	3/93	**(3)**
	Admissions	10/92	3/93	7/94
	Assessments	10/92	8/93	**(3)**

(b) (cont.)

Module	Applications	Design	System Test	Acceptance Test Signed-Off
PERSONNEL	Degree Conferment	3/93	8/93	**(3)**
	Timetabling	**(4)**	**(4)**	**(4)**
	Accommodation	**(4)**	**(4)**	**(4)**
	Alumni	**(4)**	**(4)**	**(4)**
	Posts, People, Appointments & Organisations	11/91	3/92	6/92
PAYROLL RESEARCH PHYSICAL RESOURCES	Skills & Recruitment	12/91	7/92	1/93
	Absences & Occupational Health, Committees, Reviews	15/1/93	12/3/93	7/93
	Superannuation	11/92	3/93	6/94
	Integration			
	Stand Alone	-	10/92	**(3)**
	Integrated	6/92	3/93	**(3)**
	Project Application	2/93	3/93 **(1)**	**(3)**
	Research Projects	2/93	3/93 **(1)**	**(3)**
	Asset Register & Allocation	10/91	4/92	6/92
	Stores Control & Management	10/91	10/92	2/93
	Job Progress & Costing	6/92	1/93	3/94

(1) Denotes specific dates agreed by Mantis; (2) Denotes acceptance test failed; (3) Denotes awaited; (4) Denotes not yet contracted

This case was previously published in the Journal of Cases on Information Technology, 7(4), October - December 2005, pp. 46-62.

Chapter XIV

A Case of an IT-Enabled Organizational Change Intervention: The Missing Pieces

Bing Wang
Utah State University, USA

David Paper
Utah State University, USA

Executive Summary

This case study documents an organizational change intervention concerning the implementation of a novel information technology at a university-owned research foundation (URF). It evidences the disparate expectations and reactions by key actors toward the change event, marking a mismatch between a new paradigm required by the new technology and existing information technology practices. Drawing upon change management and management information systems (MIS) literature, we discuss the perceived change management issues hindering the change process at URF. Our discussion is tempered by a theoretical lens that attempts to integrate the literature bases drawn upon in this research. In particular, resistance from in-house IT specialists was observed as the strongest force obstructing the novel IT implementation. This study offers a forum to stimulate both researchers and practitioners to rethink the necessary elements required to enact change, especially with respect to novel IT implementations.

Organizational Background

The information technology (IT) enabled change process reported in this case is being implemented in a university-owned research organization (hereafter, the parent organization will be referred to as the *university* and the research organization will be referred to as *URF*). URF was formally incorporated in 1967 as a not-for-profit corporation with its origin as a space science and technology research laboratory that was created in 1959. URF was established primarily to provide an organizational structure for the management and physical support of applied research, the discovery of new ideas, and the advancement of new technologies. Since its establishment 40 years ago, URF has expanded from supporting a single-disciplinary research base to a multidisciplinary research base in space science and technology, small molecular systems, water science and technology, and associated information technologies; from owning one research laboratory to over 15 research facilities and laboratories; from having two university professors who started the first research laboratory to employing more than 400 scientists, engineers and administrative staff. Over the years, URF has evolved into a distinct research institute with international recognition as an associated reputation as a world-class research facility. URF not only provides research administration, management, and stewardship of funds for university-wide research projects, but also undertakes much of its renowned research activities in space, water and bio-molecular science and technologies via its various research units.

URF currently has three research units and one technology commercialization office: the Space Unit (SU), the Molecular Unit (MU), the Water Unit (WU), and the Commercialization Office (CO). Each unit is characterized by its own identity in terms of management style, culture, finance, and research capacity. SU, as one of 10 university affiliated research centers (UARCs) in the nation, is the largest unit within URF and generates 94% of total URF research funding.

The sources of funding by agency include: Ballistic Missile Defense Organization (BMDO) 39.7%, Air Force 20.6%, Navy 18.6%, NASA 15.5%, Private 2.0%, other Department of Defense (DoD) 1.5%, other Federal 1.4%, National Science Foundation (NSF) 0.4%, and state funding 0.4%. A board of trustees provides oversight and direction for the policies, procedures and development of the organization. There are currently 16 members on the board with backgrounds in academia, industry and government. The president of the university (the parent organization) appoints URF's directors with approval from the existing board.

Until about five years ago, URF was managed and administrated under the auspices of a university model in all operational aspects such as finance, human resources, and research/business development. The vice president of research for the university had played a key role in the management and administration of URF. A major portion of URF research funding was contract and grant-based and its financial structure followed A21—a university accounting scheme.

However, during the past five years, URF has experienced tremendous growth that demanded transformation from a university-oriented organization to a business-oriented corporation. Moreover, the increased scrutiny by federal government audits required URF to move to a more independent business environment. As a result, the accounting scheme has recently moved from A21 to A122, a not-for-profit protocol, to reflect the standard adopted by many other major federal and industrial scientific laboratory operations. Also, the role of the vice president for research changed from active to inactive in terms of URF management responsibility. Instead, URF appointed a CEO to lead the organization. An orchestration of changes has thereby been enacted—namely changes in leadership, financial structure, organizational structure, business process management, and IT. Due to the rapid expansion of the organization, the contracts and grants URF procures with federal and private entities demands an even higher level of research, ideas, and competence to compete with other major scientific and private laboratories. In fact, 94% to 96% of the research dollars generated by URF are contract dollars, unlike in the past where grant-based dollars were more significant. The difference between contracts and grants is important. Contract procurement must be competed with private industry and a good or service must be delivered. Grant procurement is only competitive on the front-end. That is, once a grant is procured there are no deliverables, and thus no competition exists on the back end.

Setting the Stage

The slowdown of the global economy, shrinkage of federal funding available for basic and applied research programs, and increasingly more stringent regulations in federal defense research contracts during the past several years have greatly impacted the ability of URF to compete. Such environmental change has seriously challenged the viability of the URF research and management practices that had been exercised successfully in the past. Taking on that challenge, URF top management launched a large-scale organizational transformation designed to revitalize URF and enable it to continue to grow. It was hoped that URF would be able to reposition itself as a cutting-edge player in the increasingly competitive environment by transforming into a true business-oriented corporation. One overriding strategic goal of the transformation was to ensure better management of intellectual properties (discoveries/technologies) to further secure and expand its business base and continuously increase its capability to compete with other scientific and industrial laboratories.

To facilitate this goal, a novel IT (BATON technology) was introduced into the organization with the purpose of streamlining/automating core management processes related to intellectual property and discovery protection. An outside consulting team was secured to lead the IT implementation.

Utilization of BATON literally enforces change in the manner in which managers use IT to create (and utilize) contract management processes, identify/secure new ideas and discoveries, and monitor contract/project progress. Consequently, effective utilization of BATON requires a significant change in current practices of the IT department. That is, the IT department must adapt to administer IT in the way that effectively supports newly created management processes.

Four key groups were involved in the initial planning and implementation of BATON—top management (essentially the CEO), external IT consultants, business managers, and in-house IT specialists. Each group (excluding the CEO) was assigned roles and responsibilities within each phase of the BATON implementation process. As the case unfolds, it will be made clear how each group reacted to the changes accompanying the novel IT implementation.

Case Description

Managing change is frequently cited in the organizational development (OD) literature. Traditionally, three phased elements — envisioning change, implementing change, and managing reactions to change — have been reported in the OD literature as enabling change (Jick, 1993). We use these phased elements as a theoretical lens to frame the IT intervention described in this case. As such, we explore the change management issues occurring in each of the three phases based on the perceptions of change actors. To provide a theoretical foundation that will help readers better understand our case (within an integrated context of OD and MIS), we first introduce the theoretical phases we followed.

- **Vision Issues.** The foundation of any successful change process rests on a clear vision of how change can be desirable to the future of the organization and how it can be directed and shaped to reach anticipated outcomes (Tichy & Devanna, 1986). However, as suggested by many researchers, not enough effort has been afforded to properly communicating said vision and educating people to share in this vision given that it is intended to stimulate and guide organizational change (Jick, 1993). Without a systematic structure to communicate and translate vision into reality (Graves & Rosenblum, 1987), visionaries will likely encounter skepticism and other negative reactions to change. Moreover, the seeming inconsistency between vision articulation and action by visionaries in leading the change effort merely increases confusion and cynicism among organization members (Richards & Engle, 1986).
- **Implementing Change.** Issues involved in implementing change often encompass three elements—supporting structure, change consistency, and the power to bridge the gap between the change strategist's vision and organization reality (Oden, 1999). To enable change, there must be a supporting structure in place that facilitates the creation of an environment in support of useful and innovative action leading toward realizing the vision (Richards & Engle, 1986). At the same time, consistency in change techniques employed during the process, as perception becomes reality, is crucial to enhance the enthusiasm and morale of the change actors. That is, if what is perceived as strength from one constituency is greeted with more ambiguity from another, the overall perceptions of the change intervention will be negatively influenced (Jick, 1993). Finally, change implementers often bemoan their frustration due to insufficient power to overcome the resistance they encounter

to transform the organization into a new paradigm as called for by the change vision (Beckhard & Harries, 1987). Without considering such issues during the implementation process, there exists the potential to derail the course of change (as demonstrated by the consultants' experience described later).

- **Managing Reactions.** Managing reactions to change is probably the most challenging and unpredictable element in a change process. Receptivity, resistance, commitment, cynicism, stress, and related personal reactions must be considered within the framework of planning and implementing an organizational change, as researchers come to realize that organizations, as open systems, depend on human direction to succeed (Armenakis & Bedeian, 1999). Cases about unsuccessful change programs reported in many studies have exemplified that change without considering the psychological effect on others in the organization, particularly those who have not been part of the decision to make the change, is a major concern (Jick, 1993). OD researchers further point out that if the reactions to change are not anticipated and managed, the change process will be painful and perhaps unsuccessful (Beer et al., 1990).

In the MIS literature, managing reactions to change is also cited as a challenging and unpredictable element. Traditionally, IT managers often take a *technological imperative* perspective (Markus & Benjamin, 1996). As such, "technology is seen as a primary and relatively autonomous driver of organizational change, so that the adoption of new technology creates predictable changes in organizations' structure, work routines, information flows, and performance" (Orlikowski, 1996, p. 64). Change strategists trapped within this perspective largely neglect the social issues involved in technology-based organizational change. The *techno-centric* lens offered by this perspective often limits their focus on technological issues and away from human issues such as affective impact of technology on change recipients, behavioral reactions to change, and attitudinal shifts that may occur during a change process (Berney, 2003). However, as the studies on IT-enabled change continue to reveal the importance of the human element in this process, MIS researchers have come to realize that the technological imperative model is not sufficient to effectuate change (Orlikowski, 1996). The most current paradigm of IT-based organizational change intervention, in which organizations employ technology as a mechanism to enact and institutionalize intended change, requires change strategists to heed human issues and respond effectively to the various reactions triggered by the intervention (Jick, 1990).

Furthermore, IT specialists are frequently referred to as change agents because they identify psychologically with the technology they create or support (Markus & Benjamin, 1996). Ironically, IT specialists that are stereotyped as being in love with technical change and seem to benefit the most from an IT-enabled change resist such desirable change implementation (Orlikowski, 1994). This paradox has inspired a new stream of research that attempts to monitor/analyze behavioral reactions of IT specialists and explores forces/barriers precipitating resistance to change. Among this research are Markus and Benjamin's (1996) study classifying organizational beliefs and behaviors of stereotyped groups of IT specialists. Their interpretation suggests that many IT specialists fear that new technologies in the hands of users may threaten their professional credibility and self-esteem. As they explain, "new technology makes these IT specialists vulnerable: unless they know everything about it, they will look technically incompetent when users inevitably experience problems. Further, even when a new technology's problems are known and tractable, the shakedown period increases their workload and working hours" (Markus & Benjamin, 1996, p. 391).

Framed within the foregoing theories, the reminder of this case description articulates the research methodology and our story. The story includes the CEO's vision that initiated the IT-enabled change intervention, the external IT consultants' implementation issues, and the resistance from in-house IT specialists toward change. We organize our story chronologically to explain what happened during the intervention process and discuss the change management issues critical to the IT-enabled change intervention.

Research Methodology

This case study explores an organizational phenomenon—namely a change intervention enabled by IT and the reactions by various constituencies towards the changes during the intervention process. As such, we adopt an in-depth qualitative case study approach to explore the context within which the phenomenon occurred. The procedures for the data collection and analysis process are interwoven within an iterative cycle consisting of interview-analyze-refine-interview.

- **Data Collection.** The data were collected mainly through unstructured and semi-structured interviews. Interview participants spanned across different levels and different functionalities of the organization, including the CEO, deputy directors, external IT consultants, business managers, in-house IT specialists, and research engineers. A contact summary sheet was designed and used for every interview session to keep track of respondent information. Each interview lasted approximately 60 to 90 minutes and was recorded and carefully transcribed. Necessary clarifications with interview participants were made to ensure the reliability and validity of the data collected. Also, we supplemented interview data with on-site observations as well as various written documents (i.e., annual reports, mission statements, and meeting notes). Our data collection goal was to capture actors' perceptions of the intervention and the associated consequences of their actions as the change unfolds. This process of data collection proved to be efficient as it emphasized problems and issues that emerged during different phases of the change process.

- **Data Analysis.** To ensure rigorous data analysis, the case study approach as advocated by Creswell (1998) and Yin (1994) was utilized. Data analysis was integrated with data collection throughout the entire research process. Analysis centered on classifying data into coherent constructs (by identifying both surface and latent change issues), relating findings to existing OD and MIS literature, and generating/refining interview questions based upon the data obtained through prior interviews. Such an iterative cycle of data collection and analysis allowed us to organize new insights, accommodate emergent constructs, refine interview questions, and adjust the research focus accordingly.

We began data collection and analysis for this case study in the summer of 2003. The process during which we iteratively interviewed, transcribed, resolved data discrepancies, and synthesized such information had a duration of over seven months. Such a longitudinal approach is critical to investigating change intervention as it helps researchers capture multiple perceptions/perspectives of change as it unfolds and enables them to develop a cogent lens for better understanding organizations and people (Garvin, 1998).

CEO's Vision

Five years ago, the former executive director of URF retired and a new CEO (the current CEO) was appointed to lead the organization into the future. His mission was to develop and implement a strategy of growth to better compete in a changing business environment. The current CEO can be characterized as an *entrepreneurial-type* of leader because his history is one of founding and launching new organizations. His *leadership by vision* style is new to many people at URF.

An excerpt from the CEO's vision states: "URF has reached a fundamental turning point in the way it does business and performs research, paving the way for future cooperative success." It later continues with, "URF will further its efforts to a successful future via the management and commercialization of intellectual properties." To facilitate this fundamentally new way (process) of doing business, the CEO announced at the project introduction meeting with his business managers that "a new information technology has been evaluated and chosen to assist managing the transfer of intellectual properties into the commercial arena. This technology, known as BATON technology, will be implemented to the benefit of URF, the University, and the community."

Consistent with his vision and our interviews, the CEO believes that the successful implementation of the BATON technology will not only streamline, automate, and document the intellectual properties management process, but more importantly, it will change the culture of people by promoting a new way to manage the process of discovery. In an interview, the CEO explained:

In the grant area, it's very much the case that your white paper constitutes your discovery. While you're delivering goods ([which is the case within URF]), not a white paper, you're not revealing your discoveries. [As such] we have developed a very poor habit across the University and in URF, simply to ignore discovery. Now for every contract we have, we are to identify the intellectual property [the discoveries] in order to report those discoveries and inform the federal government what they have earned through their investment, not only in the goods or services received, but also in the discoveries identified. By doing so, it is to change the culture of our people, to realize that they are having discoveries that have value internally, and identifying our critical areas of contribution is important. The discovery is our future. I contend that in the future, if we don't do an effective job of that, we will lose the ability to compete with the big guys who can just redo our ideas and cut us out of opportunity.

However, such vision had not been widely advertised and championed to other members of the organization because the CEO believes that change takes time and therefore should be communicated in a subtle manner. As a result, the vision was not universally shared among organization members, as evidenced in interviews with business managers at URF. "I know [that] many other managers do not see that vision," said a deputy director of a unit at URF, "I know where he [the CEO] wants us to go, but without a roadmap of how to get there is a question [shared] by many people."

It is also important to note that the vision's promise to value people's ideas and discoveries and bring new opportunities to the organization did not seem to stimulate them (with the exception of the external consultants). Rather, it was seen as another wave of new leadership manifesting as, "I guess this is a different management style," "we just do what we are supposed to do," "as long as we get things done, it is all right, I think." Such are the perceptions of senior engineers that we interviewed. Even the consultants who worked closely with the CEO on the intervention project and understood the vision well enough to implement it had frustration. "I thought this was a pet-project of his, but it didn't really turn out to be the case because I didn't see [the CEO] put it as his top priority." Without consistent support from top management, the consultants felt powerless and concerned: "in spite of the fact that we are leading this project, there is no structure, and we have no power to push what we know needs to change."

Intervention Begins with BATON Technology

The existing IT system, as explained by the CEO, did not include standard procedures to assist principle investigators (PIs) in documenting and reporting research activities, new ideas, and by-product discoveries. In fact, each PI used their own spreadsheet and other *non-centrally-controlled* software to manage research projects and/or contracts. Even data pertaining to a single project/contract were scattered across the enterprise without a central repository to consolidate financial, human resource, and project progress for said project/contract. The management and reporting of such scattered information for all projects/contracts at the organizational level was recalcitrant. The same was true with intellectual protection of discoveries.

Moreover, the legacy system was not built to accommodate ever-changing regulations imposed by government agencies for regulating research and development of sensitive defense technologies. Without a mandated contract management process and a centralized system that supports said process, absolute compliance with regulations and procedures for each contract was difficult and challenging to say the least, especially as URF strives to grow and compete with other major industry laboratories.

Building a centralized process and the associated IT system that optimally rectifies such problems, however, is not an easy endeavor. Given the weaknesses of the traditional IT paradigm in dealing with rapid system development and expansion (i.e., tremendous time and resources required), BATON was considered because it was designed to support dynamic modeling and deployment of management processes in accordance with IT. One of its important merits is that it allows non-technical people such as business managers to map and manage business process logic, and build their own management processes for each contract or research project directly into the IT architecture. Such mapped processes are automatically translated into the system with database interactions and programming tasks that are completed by system designers (see appendix A for an example). BATON-facilitated designs thereby drastically shorten system development cycle times and reduce interference from IT specialists in the process mapping arena. That is, it limits the time (and workload) required of managers and system designers as they attempt to understand each other's domain knowledge. It allows them to more easily transform such knowledge into effective IT support for each individual contract. With BATON, management processes pertaining to project/contract operations can be centrally streamlined and thereby effectively reflect specific contract regulations because the responsible manager, who understands said regulations and processes, actually maps such processes into the system through a graphical user interface (GUI).

Once a process is established, all those involved in a particular contract or research project have no choice but to follow the basic structure of the mapped process. For example, a business manager can create a set of memos of a process as he/she sees it, and these memos, in turn, are negotiated until a consensus is reached by all responsible parties. The memos are then recorded into BATON with help from IT specialists. Each memo contains process steps that describe workflow. Each step is associated with a process-key and each process-key has a unique operational definition (see Appendix B for an example).

All process keys are stored in BATON as libraries of process logic trees that allow valid users to navigate said trees. Process keys are really just sophisticated indexes that point to different locations in an overall process that is stored in the BATON system. The logic of a process is defined with a hierarchical tree structure. This *tree* (as conceptually realized by a manager) is finally translated by system designers into BATON. An integrated system is thus created because the tree represents a process that, once recorded into the system, must be followed by all users of the system.

In mid 2002, the CEO decided to hire two IT consultants to facilitate the realization of his vision. He charged the consultants with leading implementation of the BATON technology at URF. BATON was chosen because of its innovative nature and process capability. Such features convinced the CEO that BATON was a good choice because it offered potential to alleviate many of the difficulties inherent in existing process management at URF, and in particular, the intellectual protection process.

Charged with the responsibility of BATON, the consultants began the implementation process as well as other required changes. Their initial plan was to present the project to business managers to get them excited about how BATON can help their business. The hope was that the managers would become enthused so that they would rally further support within the organization. The managers quickly came on board because BATON obviously offered them a way to better manage their processes and obtain data when and where needed. The next target group was the in-house IT specialist, because the consultants needed access to systems and data controlled by these people. In addition, the IT specialists would have to be the long-term custodians of BATON after the consultants leave. With assistance from the in-house IT specialists, the consultants expected to complete the implementation within months.

Consultants' Expectations

During August and September of 2002, the consultants carried out their plan with business managers as expected. They frequently met with business managers to familiarize them with the technology and convince them of the advantages offered by BATON, such as the ability to quickly and easily build their own processes. For this constituency, the consultants knew that managers do not want to be presented technical complexities, only how an IT can help them. They therefore attempted to sell managers on the ease of use and usefulness of BATON. To get managers to buy-into the BATON system and assure successful implementation of said system, the consultants carefully prepared their presentation and material in such a way as to demonstrate the business impact and how BATON works. Following are some of the most salient presentation points:

BATON is a tree-based system development tool, and it is the most feasibly efficient solution for URF in its current situation.

Using trees, it enables managers and research scientists to conceptually design logical structures that automatically generate the necessary Java code, coordinate with relational databases, and work with directory services with the goal of building a complete application.

No IT background is needed for managers and research scientists. With only limited assistance from IT specialists, managers and research scientists will be able to layout basic structure of an application within a few days, and by a week, they can incorporate a complete set of complex logical elements.

Such elements will then constitute the architecture of a new application in BATON, within weeks; a resulting application can be built and tested.

During the presentation, there was some skepticism, but once BATON was demonstrated the business managers were generally encouraged by the notion of what the technology can do and how it can do it. The consultants also had a few managers actually design a simple process structure after the presentation. This exercise helped to greatly reduce any remaining skepticism. Within a few days of preliminary training, managers were prepared to readily accept the technology and facilitate their part in implementing it.

The consultants felt very positive at this point in time and believed they had an important first victory toward disseminating a positive attitude toward the intervention. As a result, the consultants anticipated a smooth transition to the next step of the process — gaining cooperation with the in-house IT specialists to set up a pilot infrastructure for the new system. This anticipation seemed reasonable because, after all, the in-house IT specialist would be managing the new technology and should readily appreciate its advantages.

Current Infrastructure and Practices in the IT Department

By October, after examining the existing IT infrastructure, the consultants noted that the legacy system built and maintained by the IT department for the past 15 years had many inherent problems such as lack of integration, redundant processes, redundant code, redundant data, and no apparent coordination. In retrospect, one of the consultants noted:

Data is not stored in one place, that is, there is no centralized repository. This means that it is difficult to retrieve information on a project or contract on an ad hoc basis (via SQL). Data on a project or contract may be stored in several locations owned by more than one IT person (the DBA may have user information, the network person the same and so on). Data is not stored logically and/or consistently. There was no database structure or strategy (e.g., overall ERD) that could be found. We were never shown an ERD for human resources, IT or any other part of the business.

As for system security which is a big thing for IT, the IT department does a lot of firefighting, that is, they fix a problem without thought of an overall schema to help identify the root cause rather than a symptom. For example, if security needs to be heightened, IT builds a new firewall (or firewalls) to deny malicious access. The problem again is that there is no overall security strategy, just band-aids. At least we never noticed anything that explicitly verbalized or documented. Servers are everywhere with no seeming strategy for coordinating IT resources.

"There is a method to the madness, I suppose," said one of the consultants in an interview with us, "but it was not possible for us to determine their IT security, network, database or other management strategy because they are either not documented as such or they do not exist at all."

Moreover, the culture of the IT department was such that "you do what you have to do to make it work." There was no standard in terms of system development and data access. Each IT specialist developed and controlled a piece of a stand-alone application as his or her own property. Decisions about which additional applications needed to be built and how they should be built were usually made separately by individual owners. One of the consultants told us that "[the CEO's] goal with BATON is to reduce these *ad hoc* applications. Some of these applications may do the same thing, but are never shared because nothing is integrated." Also, the ability of business managers to obtain access to project data depended mostly on their relationship with individual owners. That is, personal connections with system administrators and developers determined who got what data, rather than access to data being determined by a general data access policy.

Since the organizational culture from the past few decades was family-oriented, administration of the IT department from top management was relaxed. As a result, IT specialists had great power over how they operated their supporting functionalities. Furthermore, IT specialists, guarded by *techno-babble* (technical jargon), were able to easily shield themselves from any attempts to question their practices or motives in order to defend their turf. According to one consultant, "since most managers do not know IT in any detail, it is not difficult to SCARE people away from potentially poor practices!" The consultants' perception was that *technology intimidation* was used as a defense mechanism because business managers are not normally IT literate and are thereby easily intimidated.

One of the consultants reflected that "when the company was small, this [lack of macro management] was probably not a problem, but the tremendous growth of URF in the past five years has made it almost impossible to operate IT support in this way."

In spite of the discovered poor IT practices, however, the consultants were still confident that implementation was possible: "By implementing this new IT-project, we hope to change the existing IT infrastructure and make it into an integrated one. Also we anticipate that there will be a good chance for us to bring in a new paradigm of integrated and coordinated business practices."

Consultants' Frustration

With some effort, in November, the consultants moved the BATON project into the IT department and got it started. They talked with each IT specialist in the department in an effort to understand their corresponding responsibilities and the overall structure of the existing system architecture. At first the project seemed to be going well, but as events unfolded the consultants began to feel frustrated.

It seemed to the consultants that the in-house IT people simply did not care about the project. It also seemed that the IT people were not willing to carry out their given responsibilities to make the project a success. In fact, the assistance that the consultants expected from the IT department turned out to be resistance:

IT controlled all the databases and systems. As a result, we had to go through the DBA to get access to the database and subsequent access to the data inside the database. However, access was not easily forthcoming. It literally took a month for us just to get an account on the real system. Actually, we were never really sure that the account that we were given was really on the real system. We suspected that it was a dummy *account with non-production data. Of course, this set us back months because we had to figure out what was going on.*

It seemed that at almost every step the consultants took to move the project forward, the IT department induced obstructions of some kind. "We had the same problem with network security. To connect to a database server, we asked the network administrator to open a port for us. Again it took weeks for us to really get one." When the consultants needed to prototype the new system somewhere, they again became frustrated: "we needed a machine to host our system, but we were turned away because our project was not included in their routine operation." In spite of enormous efforts expended by the consultants, the project was not making progress with IT.

Unable to push IT forward, the consultants turned to the CEO for support and hoped that he would help the effort. According to one of the consultants, however, the CEO was ambiguous in answering their request. "I think, although we were delegated by the CEO to lead the project, we didn't really have the power to push IT in any real direction. Hence we could not make change which was crucial to implement the project." One of the consultants also noted: "The CEO shared the vision but didn't actively help us." Although business managers had sponsored the project, they did not feel that it was their responsibility to push IT to change. Without a supporting structure to facilitate the change, the consultants felt alone and powerless to overcome resistance from IT. "We really wished that people from all levels had joined us and to create an environment that would pressure IT [for change]. To date, this hasn't happened."

By early 2003, what really concerned the consultants was that they were losing sponsorship from business managers. It was obvious that the new system could not be built and tested for production without costing another year in implementation time. The consultants revealed to us that what they promised in terms of project timelines was not being met. Having perceived the problems in implementation in IT, business managers began pulling back, doubting that the technology would really work.

As obstacles to the IT implementation continued to mount, the consultants started to realize that the project was facing serious challenges and that they were trapped between the vision and the reality. Powerless and helpless, the consultants noticed that their enthusiasm was fading.

IT Reactions to Change

Finally, in March of 2003, one of the consultants resigned and the database administrator (DBA) from the IT department was appointed to lead the BATON project. By the time we finished our first round of interviews at URF, one and half years had passed since the project began and the system still had not been moved into production. Business managers had gone back to using their original IS applications to manage their processes the way they had prior to BATON.

What had really gone wrong? Wondering about this question, we interviewed (for the second time) the consultants. "Basically, IT had strongly resisted the implementation because they feared that they would lose power over controlling the data and systems." "This is the power that IT doesn't want to lose," according to one of the consultants.

As further pondered by the consultants:

IT traditionally controls everything that is technology related. With that power, IT is able to operate as they see fit. Since most of the IT specialists have worked at URF for many years (and were responsible for creating the culture over time), they are content with the loose *culture that exists at both IT and URF. At the same time, non-IT people have become accustomed to the IT practices. That is, no one has ever challenged how IT should provide expertise to support the organization.*

The consultants also pointed out that "... being unfamiliar with BATON may cause IT to resist the implementation of this technology." One of the consultants confided that the level of resistance from IT was somewhat of a surprise. "I thought that IT people would love this technology since it is novel and eventually it should free them from tedious application development. But this turned out to be just a misconception on our part."

From the consultants' story, it may seem that IT is resisting good change with no regard for progress or the business. However, there is another side to the story. The major BATON programmer (who has been on the project from the beginning) did not really resist implementation and actually has become a champion of the project. We now relate some of his perceptions:

I don't really think people [within the IT department] really envisioned a purpose as much as [the consultants] did. I think they [other IT specialists] were there just because they had to be there. As far as purpose goes, I don't even know what it did at the beginning [how BATON worked when he first began the project].

Nobody really knew what the technology was for [at the beginning]. I think they [other IT specialists] were just busy with other projects. I guess they just figured it wasn't their problem either.

I think it's hard for them [other IT specialists] to take [consultants] seriously, because [one of the consultants] often said the tool [will] basically replace all [other] IT tools. And their experience was that they had never seen anything [that] would do this in the first place. So it's hard to take [the consultant] seriously. I think they [other IT specialists] just figure more like it's impossible.

Also, the programmer revealed that the CEO was just so busy that he could not become actively involved in the implementation. Although the DBA was assigned to lead the project, she was also busy with her routine work, and did not really care about the project anyway. The programmer concluded, "... basically there is no lead on this project now."

Admittedly, the consultants, reflecting upon their experience with the IT department, commented that they had not been consistent in educating across all groups concerning the new technology and the potential benefits to the organization in the long term. Neither had they made as much effort as they should have to rally sponsorship from IT people and prepare them for the intervention. "I guess we did not spend as much time and energy with the IT department as we did preparing business managers for the new technology. We could have spent more time with IT prior to pushing for implementation." The consultant went on to say that "... without laying the groundwork for a change at the IT level, we underestimated the difficulties in implementing the project, [and] were unable to make the intended change to a new paradigm within IT." The reason given by the consultants was that the tool is really for business managers, not IT. However, "IT is central to the plan. We should have anticipated this. We didn't mean to underestimate IT. We just thought that they would do as directed by the CEO."

Current Challenges/Problems Facing the Organization

The major challenge facing successful implementation of BATON is the mismatch between the legacy IT culture within URF and the paradigm shift inherent in the novel technology. Adding to this challenge is the imperative of effectively managing the change process, particularly resistance to change. Unfortunately, URF management never recognized the urgency to systematically re-examine the change intervention. The next subsection provides additional analysis of the case to help readers understand the critical problems facing the organization so as to develop a more informed plan of rectification.

Mismatch

Historically, the culture at URF was rooted in that of a small, family-owned business. With fewer contracts and grant projects, the level of managing IT support in business process management was relatively low. Such low levels of control on the IT department and a lack of an overall IT strategy from top management made the IT department a self-indulgent (and relatively independent) entity that possessed undue power in controlling processes. This translated into an inability to share data across independent systems, and created practices based upon personal connections rather than standard IT procedures and policies. As the organization expanded in size and number of contracts over the past decade, the existing IT culture did not fit. Instead, the expansion of the organization as well as the changing business environment demanded increased strategic planning of overall process management, efficient utilization of IT resources, and standardized IT operations. That is, top management believed that a high level of strategic control on IT would be necessary to match the continued expansion of URF.

To illustrate, the new technology (BATON) allows business managers to implement their own processes without direct interference from IT. Implementation of BATON induces a radical departure from the existing culture within IT. That is, IT was used to dictate how information is to be supplied to processes rather than managers dictating how and when they need information to support their businesses. With BATON, IT actually has to do less work because they only have to translate the management-established process into the system infrastructure. However, this also implies that IT will no longer be able to control the processes to the extent that they had in the past. Furthermore, a process management system built with BATON technology is, by default, centralized and shared so that it can be used across all levels of the organization to meet disparate needs. The artifactual boundaries set by individual IT owners are thereby broken. "Do me a favor" requests are replaced by standard IT procedures and policies if BATON is successful. This new paradigm contrasts significantly with the existing non-standardized culture and practices within IT and thereby demands drastic changes in policies, procedures, and attitudes.

The mismatch (between nonstandard IT practices and BATON requirements), however, had not been fully recognized by top management during planning of the change intervention. Moreover, top management (and the consultants) underestimated the challenges (change management issues) of implementing the new technology in a provincial IT culture. Hence, top management faces a dilemma. They must reconcile the mismatch to save the project from failure by creating a better estimate of crucial change management issues as they relate to the IT culture. Therefore, the reader should begin thinking about ways that URF can reconcile this mismatch. In addition, the reconciliation should take into account the following change management issues that are still hindering progress.

- *Communicating/sharing the vision of change.* As the case revealed, there was insufficient energy from top management to communicate and promote the vision to lower levels of the organization (i.e., programmers and other IT specialists). Further, the CEO's vision was well established, but it did not include specific objectives and plans to guide realization of the vision. Only informed by an abstract vision, organization members had limited understanding of how the change initiative would really affect them. This was clearly demonstrated by the fact that IT specialists were unaware of the purpose of BATON when it was first implemented in their department. As a result, they did not buy into the project (from the beginning), and as change unfolded, their resistance to the change escalated. The absence of a concrete and consistent articulation of the change vision, that should be communicated and shared by organizational members, created an early obstacle to a successful change intervention.

- *Managing the change process.* In spite of the fact that the external consultants were hired to lead the implementation of BATON, they were seen by organization members as outsiders with no influence or power. Further, responsibilities for enacting change were not clearly assigned to those involved in the change (i.e., business managers, PIs, in-house IT specialists). Without such clear responsibilities, the normal management structure was not sufficient to support the change effort given that managers are already busy. As indicated from analysis of the case, consultants lost political sponsorship from other actors (i.e., managers and PIs) to a great extent in that they were unable to overcome the resistance they encountered when attempting to bring IT into the change effort. This insufficient management of the change process has contributed greatly to the problems encountered with BATON implementation within the IT department. Indeed, researchers have purported that "it is not the results management is managing, but the processes that achieve results" (Jick, 1993, p. 171).
- *Resistance to change.* It seems apparent that the CEO took a technological imperative perspective in attempting to realize his vision with respect to intellectual property protection and process management. That is, he and other top management implicitly assumed that implementing BATON would automatically enable expected changes in work routines, information flows, and performance. While such assumptions appear to be reasonable for business managers because the benefits are apparent, they fail when dealing with IT department resistance because it is more difficult for IT people to understand how such change benefits them. The IT department was used to controlling business processes, data, systems, and was seldom challenged by management to change such practices. As a result, it was difficult to convince them that BATON offered any real benefits because management ne-

glected the existing IT culture developed over the years. As the change process unfolded, IT was pressed to rethink almost every aspect of their culture, and a sense of being questioned about their current practices emerged among IT specialists. As such, IT was immediately defensive about BATON and resisted because they wanted to maintain their comfortable way of life. In contrast, business managers were not as deeply affected (in a perceived negative sense) as their IT counterparts. Thus business managers were less resistant to changes brought about by BATON. The challenge facing top management concerns what can be done to be more proactive in diffusing IT resistance.[1]

References

Armenakis, A.A., & Bedeian, A.G. (1999). Organizational change: A review of theory and research in the 1990s. *Journal of Management, 25*(3), 293-315.

Beckhard, R., & Harries, H.R. (1987). *Organizational transactions* (2nd ed.). MA: Addison-Wesley.

Beer, M., Eisenstat, R.A., & Spector, B. (1990). Why change programs don't produce change. *Harvard Business Review, 68*(6).

Berney, M. (2003). *Transition Guide: How to Manage the Human Side of Major Change.* Washington, DC: Federal Judicial Center.

Creswell, J.W. (1998). *Qualitative Inquiry and Research Design: Choosing Among Five Traditions.* London: Sage Publications.

Garvin, D.A. (1998). The process of organization and management. *Sloan Management Review, 39*(4), 33-50.

Graves, P., & Rosenblum, J. (1987, December). Rolling out the vision. *OD Practitioner.*

Jick, T.D. (1990). The recipients of change. *Harvard Business School Case N9-491-039.*

Jick, T.D. (1993). *Managing Change: Case and Concept.* Columbus, OH: The McGraw-Hill Companies.

Markus, M.L., & Benjamin, R.I. (1996). Change agentry – The next IS frontier. *MIS Quarterly, 20*(4).

Oden, H.W. (1999). *Transforming the Organization: A Social-Technical Approach.* Westport, CT: Greenwood Publishing Group.

Orlikowski, W.J. (1994). The contradictory structure of systems development methodologies: Deconstructing the IS-user relationship in information engineering. *Information Systems Research, 5*(4).

Orlikowski, W.J. (1996). Improvising organizational transformation over time: A situated change perspective. *Information Systems Research, 7*(1).

Richards, D., & Engle, S. (1986). After the vision: Suggestions to corporate visionaries and vision champions. *Transforming leadership: From vision to results.* Alexandria, VA: Miles River Press.

Tichy, N.M., & Devanna, M.A. (1986). *The Transformational Leader.* West Sussex, UK: John Wiley & Sons.

Yin, R.K. (1994). *Case Study Research: Design and Methods.* Thousand Oaks, CA: Sage Publications.

Endnote

[1] Names of the organization, its parent organization, units, and members have all been disguised.

APPENDIX A

Illustration for Mapping Business Processes

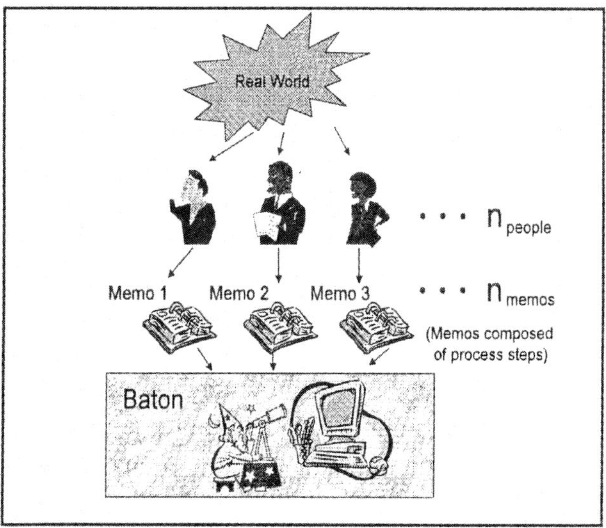

This case was previously published in the Journal of Cases on Information Technology, 7(1), January - March 2005, pp. 34-52.

Chapter XV

Discussion Questions for the Case Studies

Amy Scott Metcalfe
The University of British Columbia, Canada

The case studies presented offer several perspectives from which to better understand knowledge management in higher education. The questions provided below may be used with any of the case studies, or the chapters contained in this book. When asking students to answer the questions, it may be helpful for them to consider similar issues in their own institutions.

1. From a knowledge management perspective, what kinds of issues were presented in the case? Were the issues resolved effectively? If so, how? If not, why?
2. What "problem" is discussed in the case study? Who identified this problem? Could there have been alternative perspectives that were not considered?
3. What are the knowledge assets presented in the case? Who owns or has jurisdiction over those assets?
4. How does the case illustrate the unique characteristics of higher education organizations?

5. What economic, political, or social factors contributed to the situations presented in the case?
6. Would these factors be barriers to KM implementation? If so, how might these factors be addressed?
7. Who were the key players in the case? What role did each individual play?
8. What subgroups are presented in the case, and what are their roles?
9. Are there tensions between subgroups? How would relations between groups affect KM projects in that organization?
10. Who was not "at the table," and would their contributions affect the outcome if they had been involved?

Teaching Strategies

1. **Problem-based learning:** Divide students into groups. Assign each group to use one of the case studies. Each group will act as a consulting company that has been asked to develop a knowledge management or information systems proposal for their particular case study institution. The proposal should address the main issues presented in the case, but permit the students to elaborate on the case if necessary. Depending on the nature of the course you are teaching, the proposals can be technical in nature or come from an organizational consulting perspective. Have each group present their proposals to the class.
2. **Research paper:** Using the case studies as examples, assign a research paper in which each student identifies an economic, social, or political barrier to KM implementation that is occurring or has occurred on his or her campus. Students should approach the problem from a theoretical perspective, using a framework from one of the case studies or chapters in this book or another you have presented in class. Research for the papers may include interviewing individuals on campus, examining documents, statistical analysis, or other appropriate methods.

Section V

Resources

Appendix A: Resources

KM Journals

Electronic Journal of Knowledge Management
http://www.ejkm.com/

International Journal of Knowledge Management
http://www.idea-group.com/journals/details.asp?id=4288

Journal of Information & Knowledge Management
http://www.worldscinet.com/jikm/jikm.shtml

Journal of Knowledge Management
http://miranda.emeraldinsight.com/vl=2588674/cl=64/nw=1/rpsv/jkm.htm

Journal of Knowledge Management Practice
http://www.tlainc.com/jkmp.htm

Knowledge Management Research & Practice
http://www.palgrave-journals.com/kmrp/

Knowledge Management Review
http://www.km-review.com/cgi-bin/melcrum/eu_content.pl?docurl=pub%20kmr%20home

Knowledge, Technology, and Policy
http://www.moted.org/kt&p/

KM and Higher Education Resource Centers

HigherEd.org, Inc.
http://www.highered.org/

Institute for the Study of Knowledge Management in Education
http://www.iskme.org/

KM Information Sites

Destination KM
http://www.destinationkm.com/

KM World
http://www.kmworld.com/

Knowledge Management Resource Center
http://www.kmresource.com/

CIO.com's Knowledge Management Research Center
http://www.cio.com/research/knowledge/

Knowledge Management News
http://www.kmnews.com/

KM Magazine
http://www.kmmagazine.com/

KM Central
http://www.icasit.org/km/

Appendix B: Selected Bibliography

Ahrens, K., Chung S.F., & Huang C. (2003). Conceptual metaphors: Ontology-based representation and corporate driven mapping principles. In *Proceedings of the ACL Workshop on the Lexicon and Figurative Language*. Accessed October 26, 2004, from *http://acl.ldc.upenn.edu/acl2003/lexfig/pdf/Ahrens.pdf*

Anderson, M. S. (2001). The complex relations between the academy and industry: Views from the literature. *Journal of Higher Education, 72*(2), 226-246.

Andrews, W. (2003). Visionaries invade the 2003 search engine magic quadrant. Gartner Research. Retrieved November 7, 2004, from *http://www3.gartner.com/mq/asset_50500.jsp*

Angele, J., & Sure, Y. (2001). Whitepaper: Evaluation of ontology-based tools. Workshop presentation at the *13th International Conference on Knowledge Engineering and Knowledge Management*. Retrieved October 26, 2004, from *http://www.aifb.uni-karlsruhe.de/WBS/ysu/publications/eon2002_whitepaper.pdf*

Anonymous. (2001). Resurveying the terrain: Refining the taxonomy for the postsecondary market. *Change*, *33*(2), 53.

Arbaugh, J. (2002). Managing the on-line classroom: A study of technological and behavioral characteristics of Web-based MBA courses. *Journal of High Technology Management Research, 13*(2), 203-223.

Ausiello, K., & Wells, B. (1997). Information technology and student affairs: Planning for the twenty-first century. *New Directions for Student Services, 78*, 71-81.

Banks, S.P., & Riley, P. (1993). Structuration theory as an ontology for communication research. In S. Deetz (Ed.), *Communication yearbook* (Vol. 16, pp. 167-196). Newberry Park, CA: Sage.

Barley, S. R. (1986). Technology as an occasion for structuring: Evidence from observations of CT scanners and the social order of radiology departments. *Administrative Science Quarterly, 31*(1), 78-108.

Barley, S. R. (1996a). Technicians in the workplace: Ethnographic evidence for bringing work into organization studies. *Administrative Science Quarterly, 41*(3), 404-41.

Barley, S. R. (1996b). *The new world of work.* London: British-North American Committee.

Barratt, W. (2001). Managing information technology in student affairs: A report on policies, practices, staffing, and technology. Paper presented at the *Annual Conference of the National Association of Student Personnel Administrators,* Seattle, March 17-21.

Bates, A. W. (2000). *Managing technological change: Strategies for college and university leaders.* San Francisco: Jossey-Bass.

Becher, T. (1989). *Tribes and territories: Intellectual enquiry and the cultures of the disciplines.* Philadelphia: Society for Research into Higher Education and Open University Press.

Becher, T., & Trowler, P. (2000). *Tribes and territories: Intellectual enquiry and the cultures of the disciplines.* Philadelphia: Society for Research into Higher Education and Open University Press.

Becker, H. (2001). How are teachers using computers in instruction? The Center for Research on Information Technology and Organizations. Retrieved February 12, 2004, from *http://www.crito.uci.edu/2/pubdetails.asp?id=292*

Beninger, J. R. (1990). Conceptualizing information technology as organization and vice versa. In J. Fulk & C. Steinfield (Eds.), *Organizations and communication technology* (pp. 29-45). Newbury Park: Sage Publications.

Beniger, J. R. (1996). Who shall control cyberspace? In L. Strate, R. Jacobson, & S. B. Gibson (Eds.), *Communication and cyberspace: Social interaction in an electronic environment.* Hampton Press.

Benjamins, V. R. et al. (1998). Knowledge management through ontologies. *Proceedings of the 2nd International Conference on Practical Aspects of Knowledge Management.* Retrieved October 26, 2004, from *http://citeseer.ist.psu.edu/benjamins98knowledge.html*

Benjamins, V. R. et al. (1999). (KA)^2: Building ontologies for the Internet: A mid term report. Retrieved October 26, 2004, from *http://citeseer.ist.psu.edu/276747.html*

Bennett, K., & Metros, S. (2001). The promise and pitfalls of learning objects: Current status of digital repositories. Retrieved from *http://itc.utk.edu/educause2001*

Berger, N. (1999). Pioneering experiences in distance learning: Lessons learned. *Journal of Management Education, 23*(6), 684-690.

Bernbom, G. (Ed.) (2001). *Information alchemy: The art and science of knowledge management.* EDUCAUSE Leadership Series #3. San Francisco: Jossey-Bass.

Bijker, W. E., Hughes, T. P., & Pinch (Eds.) (1987). *The social construction of technological systems: New directions in the sociology and history of technology.* Cambridge, MA: MIT Press.

Birnbaum, R. (2000). *Management fads in higher education: Where they come from. What they do. Why they fail.* San Francisco: Jossey-Bass.

Blackler, F. (1995). Knowledge, knowledge work, and organizations: An overview and interpretation. *Organization Studies, 16*(6), 1021-1046.

Bolt, D., & Crawford, R. (2000). *Digital divide: Computers and our children's future.* New York: TV Books.

Borsook, P. (2000). *Cyberselfish: A critical romp through the terribly libertarian culture of high-tech.* New York: PublicAffairs Press.

Bransford, J., Brown, A., & Cocking, R. (2000). *How people learn: Brain, mind, experience, and school.* Washington, DC: National Academy Press.

Breneman, D. W. (1993). *Higher education: On a collision course with new realities.* Washington, DC: Association of Governing Boards of universities and Colleges.

Brown, J. S., & Duguid, P. (1996). Universities in the digital age. *Change,* July/August, 11-19.

Brown, J. S., & Duguid, P. (2000). Balancing act: How to capture knowledge without killing it. *Harvard Business Review, 78*(5), 3-7.

Buckley, D. (2002). In pursuit of the learning paradigm. *Educause Review,* January/February.

Bukowitz, J. R., & Williams, R. L. (1999). *The knowledge management fieldbook.* Upper Saddle River, NJ: Financial Times, Prentice Hall.

Burris, B. H. (1993). *Technocracy at work.* Albany, NY: SUNY Press.

Burton-Jones, A. (1999). *Knowledge capitalism: Business, work, and learning in the new economy.* New York: Oxford University Press.

Carmean, C. (2002). Learner-centered principles. Retrieved March 11, 2004, from *http://educause.edu/nlii/keythemes/lcp/*

Carmean, C., & Haefner, J. (2002). Mind over matter: Transforming course management systems into effective learning environments. *Educause*, November-December, 27-34.

Carnevale, D. (2004, October 1). University of Florida's software upgrade delays payday for teaching assistants. *The Chronicle of Higher Education*, A 35.

Carnot, M. J. et al. (2003). *A summary of literature pertaining to the use of concept mapping techniques and technologies for education and performance support.* Technical Report submitted to the Chief of Naval Education and Training, Pensacola, FL. Retrieved October 26, 2004, from *http://www.ihmc.us/users/acanas/Publications/ConceptMapLitReview/IHMC%20Literature%20Review%20on%20Concept%20Mapping.pdf*

Carnoy, M., Castells, M., Cohen, S. S., & Cardoso, F. H. (1993). *The new global economy in the Information Age: Reflections on our changing world.* University Park: The Pennsylvania State University Press.

Castells, M. (1997). *The power of identity.* Oxford: Blackwell Publishers.

Castells, M. (2000). *The rise of the network society* (2nd ed.). Oxford: Blackwell Publishers.

Cavanaugh, C. (2001). The effectiveness of interactive distance education technologies in K-12 learning: A meta-analysis. *International Journal of Educational Telecommunications,* 7(1), 73-88. Retrieved June 15, 2004, from *http://www.unf.edu/~ccavanau/CavanaughIJET01.pdf*

Cerney, K. (1996). Making local knowledge global. *The Harvard Business Review*, May-June, 22-26.

Chandler, D. (1996). Shaping and being shaped: Engaging with media. *CMC Magazine,* (3), 2. Retrieved June 15, 2004, from *http://www.december.com/cmc/mag/1996/feb/toc.html*

Chase, R. L. (1997). The knowledge-based organization: An international study. *The Journal of Knowledge Management, 1*(1), 38-49.

Chew, P. (1992). Faculty generated inventions: Who owns the golden egg? *Wisconsin Law Review, 2*, 259-314.

Clark, B. R. (1983). *The higher education system: Academic organization in cross-national perspective (Campus no. 368).* University of California Press.

Clark, T. (2001). Virtual schools: Trends and issues. Distance Learning Resource Network and WestEd. Retrieved March 14, 2004, from *http://www.wested.org/online_pubs/virtualschools.pdf*

Clegg, S. R. (1990). *Modern organizations.* Newbury Park, CA: Sage.

Coate, L. E. (1996). Beyond re-engineering: Changing the organizational paradigm. In A. Kendrick (Ed.), *Organizational paradigm shifts* (pp. 1-18). Washington, DC: National Association of College and University Business Officers (NACUBO).

Cohen, A. M. (1998). *The shaping of American higher education: Emergence and growth of the system.* San Francisco: Jossey-Bass.

Colclough, G., & Tolbert, C. M. (1992). *Work in the fast lane: Flexibility, divisions of labor, and inequality in high-tech industries.* Albany: SUNY Press.

Collins, R. (1979). *The credential society.* New York: Academic Press.

Collis, B., & Striker, A. (2003). Re-useable learning objects in context. *International Journal of E-learning, 4*(2), 5- 16. Retrieved October 13, 2004, from *http://dl.aace.org/14190/*

Collis, B., & Winnips, K. (2002). Two scenarios for productive learning environments in the workplace. *British Journal of Educational Technology, 33*(2), 133-148.

Contractor, N. S., & Eisenberg, E. M. (1990). Communication networks and new media in organizations. In J. Fulk, & C. Steinfield (Eds.), *Organizations and communication technology* (pp. 143-172). Newbury Park: Sage Publications.

Convera. (2004a). Mission-critical search & categorization for the enterprise. Retrieved October 26, 2004, from *http://www.ihssolutions.com/canada/documentation_library/index.cfm*

Convera. (2004b). RetrievalWare's advanced categorization and dynamic classification. Retrieved October 26, 2004, from *http://www.convera.com/Products/rw_categorization.asp*

Cook, J., & Cook, L. (1998). How technology enables the quality of student-centered learning. *Quality Progress*, July, 59-63.

Cottey, A. (2003). Open knowledge: A proposed adaptation of open science, focusing on guidelines for knowledge claims. *SGR Newsletter, 26*, pp. 17-8.

Creative Commons. (2004). "Some rights reserved": Building a layer of reasonable copyright. Retrieved April, 15, 2004, from *http://creativecommons.org/learn/aboutus/*

Creswell, J.W. (1994). *Research design: Qualitative and quantitative approaches.* Thousand Oaks, CA: Sage.

Cross National Perspective. Berkeley: University of California Press.

Crow, R. (2002). *The case for institutional repositories: A SPARC position paper.* Washington, DC: The Scholarly Publishing and Academic Resources Coalition.

Crystal, M. E., & Jones, D. P. (1985). *A common language for postsecondary accreditation: Categories and definitions for data collection.* Boulder, CO: National Center for Higher Education Management Systems.

Cuban, L. (1986). *Teachers and machines: The classroom use of technology since 1920.* New York: Teachers College, Columbia University.

Curren, L. (2004). MIT's double-secret hidden agenda. eLearn. Retrieved on June 15, 2004, from *http://www.eLearnMag.org/subpage/sub_page.cfm?article_pk=11125&page_number_nb=2&title=FEATURE%20STORY*

Daday, G., & Burris, B. (2001). Technocratic teamwork: Mitigating polarization and cultural marginalization in an engineering firm. *The Transformation of Work, 10*, 241-262.

Davenport, T. H. (1997). *Information ecology: Mastering the information and knowledge environment.* New York: Oxford University Press.

Davenport, T. H., & Prusack, L. (1997). *Working knowledge: How organizations manage what they know.* Cambridge, MA: Harvard Business School Press.

Davenport, T., DeLong, D., & Beers, M. (1998). Successful knowledge management projects. *Sloan Management Review, 39*(2), 374-84.

Davis, E. (1998). *Techgnosis: Myth, magic and mysticism in the age of information.* New York: Harmony Books.

Delphi Group. (2002). *Enabling electronic communications compliance. Snapshot.* Boston: Delphi Group.

Delphi Group. (2003). *Maximizing organizational 'know how' in government entities. Snapshot.* Boston: Delphi Group.

Demarest, M. (1997). Knowledge management: An introduction. Retrieved on March 1, 2004, from *www.noumenal.com/marc/km1.pdf*

Demarest, M. (1997). Understanding knowledge management. *Long Range Planning, 30*(3), 374-384.

DeSanctis, G., & Fulk, J. (1999) Articulation of communication technology and organizational form. In G. DeSanctis, & J. Fulk (Eds.), *Shaping organizational form: Communication, connection, and community* (pp. 5-32). Thousand Oaks: Sage.

Diaz, V. (2004). *The digitization and control of intellectual property: Institutional patterns of distributed learning behavior and the organizational policy response.* Unpublished doctoral dissertation, University of Arizona.

Diaz, V., & McGee, P. (2004). Policies for success on the new learning object frontier. Presentation at the *National Learning Infrastructure Annual Meeting,* San Diego.

Dillon, M. (2002). Knowledge management: Chimera or solution? *Portal: Libraries and the Academy, 2*(2), 321-336.

Downes, S. (2002). Design and reusability of learning objects in an academic context: A new economy of education? Retrieved June 15, 2004, from *http://www.usdla.org/html/journal/JAN03_Issue/article01.html*

Drucker, P. (1998). The knowledge-creating company. In P. Drucker et al. (Eds.), *Harvard Business Review on knowledge management* (pp. 1-19). Cambridge, MA: Harvard Business School Press.

Duderstadt, J. (2000) *A university for the 21st century.* Ann Arbor: University of Michigan Press.

Duderstadt, J. J. (2000). Can colleges and universities survive in the information age? In R.N. Katz and Associates (Eds.), *Dancing with the devil:*

Information technology and the new competition in higher education (pp. 1-25). San Francisco: Jossey-Bass.

Dutton, W. H. (1999). The virtual organization: Tele-access in business and industry. In G. DeSanctis, & J. Fulk (Eds.), *Shaping organizational form: Communication,connection, and community* (pp. 473-496). Thousand Oaks: Sage.

Ebo, B. (Ed.) (1998). *Cyberghetto or cybertopia? Race, class, and gender on the Internet.* Westport, CT: Praeger Publishers.

El-Khawas, E. (1994). *Campus trends 1994: A time of redirection.* Higher Education Panel Report, no. 84. Washington, DC: American Council on Education.

Epper, R. M., & Garn, M. (2004). Virtual universities real possibilities. *EDUCAUSE Review*, *39*(2).

Etzkowitz, H. (1983). Entrepreneurial scientists and entrepreneurial universities in American academic science. *Minerva, 21*, 198-233.

Etzkowitz, H. (1989). Entrepreneurial science in the academy: A case of the transformation of norms. *Social Problems, 36*, 14-29.

Ewell, P. T. (1999). Imitation as art: Borrowed management techniques in higher education. *Change, 31*(6), 10-15.

EZRO. (2004). Retrieved June 15, 2004, from *http://ezro.devis.com/*

Fairweather, J. S. (1988). *Entrepreneurship and higher education.* Washington, DC: Association for the Study of Higher Education.

Firestone, J. M., & McElroy, M. W. (2003). *Key issues in the new knowledge management.* Amsterdam: Knowledge Management Consortium International Press.

Forsythe, D. E. (1996). New bottles, old wine: Hidden cultural assumptions in a computerized explanation system for migraine sufferers. *Medical Anthropology Quarterly, 10*(4), 551-574.

Frederickson, S., Clark, B., & Hoehner, P. (2002). A primer for the online instructor: Part 1: Getting started. *Learning and Leading with Technology, 29*(6), 6-12.

Frey, B. E. (2002). Reflections. *Educause*, January-February, 8-14.

Friedman, D., & Hoffman, P. (2001). The politics of information. *Change, 33*(2), 50-57.

Fulk, J., Schmitz, J., & Steinfield, C. (1990). A social influence model of technology use. In J. Fulk, & C. Steinfield (Eds.), *Organizations and communication technology* (pp. 117-140). Newbury Park: Sage Publications, 117-140.

Gandel, P. B., Katz, R. N., & Metros, S. E. (2004). The weariness of the flesh: Reflections on the life of the mind in an era of abundance. *Educause Review, 39*(2), 40-51.

Gatz, L.B., & Hirt, J.B. (2000). Academic and social integration in cyberspace: Students and e-mail. *The Review of Higher Education, 23*(3), 299-318.

Getz, M., Siegfried, J.J., & Anderson, K.H. (1997). Adoption of innovations in higher education. *The Quarterly Review of Economics and Finance, 37*(3), 605-631.

Gibbons, H., & Wentworth, G. (2001). Andragogical and pedagogical training differences for online instructors. Paper presented at *DLA 2001*, Callaway, Georgia. Retrieved March 9, 2004, from *http://www.westga.edu/~distance/ojdla/fall43/gibbons_wentworth43.html*

Giddens, A. (1984). *The constitution of society: Outline of the theory of structure.* Berkeley, CA: University of California Press.

Grasel, W. (1999). The reality of brands: Toward an ontology of marketing. *American Journal of Economics and Sociology, 58.* Retrieved October 26, 2004, from *http://ontology.buffalo.edu/brands.html*

Green, K., & Jenkins, R. (1998). *IT financial planning 101: Developing an institutional strategy for financing technology.* NACUBO Business Officer, March.

Griffin, S., & Wason, T. (1997). The year of metadata. *Educom Review, 32*(6). Retrieved October 26, 2004, from *http://www.educause.edu/LibraryDetailPage/666&ID=ERM9763*

Gumport, P. J. (1997). In search of strategic perspective: A tool for mapping the market in postsecondary education. *Change*, November/December.

Gumport, P. J., & Pusser, B. (1995). A case of bureaucratic accretion: Context and consequences. *The Journal of Higher Education, 66*(5), 493-520.

Guskin, A. E. (1994). Reducing student costs and enhancing student learning, Part I: Restructuring the administration. *Change, 26*(4), 23-29.

Hakken, D. (2003). "Knowledge management fatigue syndrome" and the practical importance of the cyberspace knowledge question. In D.

Hakken (Ed.), *The knowledge landscapes of cyberspace* (pp. 55-69). New York: Routledge.

Halstead, D. K. (1979). *Higher education planning: A bibliographic handbook.* Washington, DC: U.S. Department of Education, National Institute of Education.

Halstead, D. K. (1981). *Higher education: A bibliographic handbook (volume II).* Washington, DC: U.S. Department of Education, National Institute of Education.

Hammer, M., Leonard, D., & Davenport, T. (2004). Why don't we know more about knowledge? *MIT Sloan Management Review, 45*(4), 14-8.

Heller, D. E. (Ed.) (2001). *The states and public higher education policy: Affordability, access, and accountability.* Baltimore: Johns Hopkins University Press.

Herbert, S. (2000). Zoning cyberspace. *Studies in Law, Politics, and Society, 20,* 101-123.

Heydebrand, W. (1979). The technocratic administration of justice. *Research in Law and Society, 2,* 29-64.

Heydebrand, W. (1983). Technocratic corporatism: Toward a theory of occupational and organizational transformation. In R. Hall & R. Quinn (Eds.), *Organizational theory and public policy* (pp. 93-114). Beverly Hills, CA: Sage.

Heydebrand, W. (1989). New organizational forms. *Work and Occupations, 16*(3), 323-357.

Higgs, P., Meredith, S., & Hand, T. (2003). *Technology for Sharing: Researching learning objects and digital rights management.* Flexible Leader 2002 Report. Retrieved January, 10, 2003, from *http://www.flexiblelearning.net.au/leaders/fl_leaders/fll02/finalreport/final_hand_higgs_meredith.pdf*

Hilmer, F.G., & Donaldson, L. (1996). *Management redeemed: Debunking the fads that undermine corporate performance.* New York: The Free Press.

Hoover, R. E. (1997). The role of student affairs at metropolitan universities. *New Directions for Student Services, 79,* 15-25.

Hovland, I. (2003). *Knowledge management and organisational learning, an international development perspective: An annotated bibliogra-*

phy, Working Paper 224. Retrieved October 7, 2004, from Overseas Development Institute (ODI) Web site *http://www.odi.org.uk/rapid/Publications/Documents/WP224.pdf*

Hughes, T. (2001). Through a glass darkly: The future of technology-enable education. *EDUCAUSE Review.* Retrieved April 13, 2004, from *http://www.educause.edu/ir/library/pdf/ffp0111s.pdf*

Huysman, M., & de Wit, D. (2004). Practices of managing knowledge sharing: Towards a second wave of knowledge management. *Knowledge Process Management, 11*(2), 81-92.

Inxight. (2003). *Inxight SmartDiscovery: Discover the true value of information.* Sunnyvale, CA: Inxight Software, Inc. Retrieved October 26, 2004, from *http://www.inxight.com/products/smartdiscovery/*

Ives, W., Torrey, B., & Gordon, C. (1998). Knowledge management: An emerging discipline with a long history. *Journal of Knowledge Management, 1*(4), 269-274.

Jackson, M. H. (1996). The meaning of "communication technology": The technology-context scheme. In B. Burleson (Ed.), *Communication yearbook 19* (pp. 229-268). Beverly Hills, CA: Sage.

Jackson, M. H., Poole, M. S., & Kuhn, T. (2002). The social construction of technology in studies of the workplace. In L. Lievrouw, & S. Livingston (Eds.), *New media handbook* (pp. 236-252). Sage.

Jamieson, P., Fisher, K., Gilding, T., Taylor, P., & Trevitt, C. (2000). Place and space in the design of new learning environments. *Higher Education Research and Development, 19*(2), 221-237. Retrieved June 17, 2004, from *http://www.oecd.org/els/pdfs/EDSPEBDOCA027.pdf*

Johnson, L. (2003). *Challenges impeding the learning object economy.* Macromedia White Paper. Retrieved June 15, 2004, from *http://download.macromedia.com/pub/solutions/downloads/elearning/elusive_vision.pdf*

Johnstone, S. M. (2002). Sign of the times: Change is coming for e-learning. *Educause,* November-December, 15-24.

Jordan, T. (1999). *Cyberpower: The culture and politics of cyberspace and the Internet.* New York: Routledge.

Joy, L. (2004). Training versus learning. Retrieved on March 18, 2004, from *http://www.structured-training.com/asp/trainingvlearning.asp*

Kalfoglou, Y. (2002). Maintaining ontologies with organisational memories. Retrieved October 26, 2004, *http://www.ecs.soton.ac.uk/~yk1/kalfoglou-kluwerKMOMbook.pdf*

Karns, J. (1993). Redesigning student services. *Planning for Higher Education, 21*(3), 27-33.

Kasteren, J. van. (2003). Semantic Web should be based on well-founded ontologies: An interview with Nicola Guarino. *DigiCULT: Towards A Semantic Web for Heritage Resources*. Thematic Issue 3, May 2003.

Katz, R. N. (2002). An interview with Neil Gershenfeld, Director for the Center for Bits and Atoms at MIT. *Educause*, March-April, 34-38.

Katz, R. N. & Oblinger, D. (Eds.) (2000). *The "E" is for everything: E-commerce, e-Business, and e-Learning in the future of higher education*. San Francisco: Jossey-Bass.

Kidwell, J. J., Vander Linde, K. M., & Johnson, S. L. (2000). Applying corporate knowledge management practices in higher education. *EDUCAUSE Quarterly, 4*, 28-33.

Kidwell, J., Vander Linde, K., & Johnson, S. (2000). Applying corporate in higher education. *EDUCAUSE Quarterly*. Retrieved June 17, 2004, from *http://www.educause.edu/ir/library/pdf/EQM0044.pdf*

Kidwell, J. J., Vander Linde, K. M., & Johnson, S. (2001). Applying corporate knowledge management practices in higher education. In G. Bernbom (Ed.), *Information alchemy: The art and science of knowledge management* (pp.1-24). San Francisco: Jossey-Bass.

Klein, H.K., & Kleinman, D.L. (2002). The social construction of technology: Structural considerations. *Science, Technology, and Human Values, 27*(1), 28-53.

Kleiner, C. (2004). *Decades of rankings. America's Best Colleges 2004 Edition.* Washington, DC: U.S. News and World Report.

Knowledge Integrity, Inc. (2000). Collecting quality customer data. *Knowledge Management, 3*(2), 78-80. Retrieved October 26, 2004, from *http://www.destinationcrm.com/km/dcrm_km_article.asp?id=226*

Koch, H., Paradice, D., Chae, B., & Guo, Y. (2002). An investigation of knowledge management within a university IT group. *Information Resources Management Journal, 15*(1), 13-21.

Kouzmin, A. (1980). Control in organizational analysis: The lost politics. In D. Dunkerly, & G. Salaman (Eds.), *The international yearbook of organization studies* (pp. 56-89). Boston: Routledge and Kegan Paul.

Kraan, W. (2003). IMS and OKI, The wire and the socket. *CETIS News*. The Center for Educational Technology Interoperability, July 17.

Kumar, V., & Long, P. (2002). *MIT's open courseware initiative and open knowledge initiative.* Transcript from CREN Tech Talks, March 7.

Lamont, J. (2003). Dynamic taxonomies: Keeping up with changing content. *KM World, 12*(5). Retrieved October 26, 2004, from *http://www.kmworld.com/publications/magazine/index.cfm?action=readarticle&Article_ID=1508&Publication_ID=90*

Lape, L. (1992). Ownership of copyrightable works of university professors: The interplay between the copyright act and university copyright policies. *Villanova Law Review, 37*, 223-269.

Laudon, K., & Laudon, J. (1999). *Management information systems: Organization and technology in the networked enterprise.* Englewood Cliffs, NJ: Prentice Hall.

Laurillard, D., & McAndrew, P. (2003). Reusable educational software: A basis for generic e-learning tasks. In A. Littlejohn (Ed.), *Resources for networked learning.* UK: Kogan-Page.

Lea, L., Clayton, M., Draude, B., & Barlow, S. (2001). The impact of technology on teaching and learning. *EDUCAUSE Quarterly, 24*(2).

Leake, D. B. et al. (2003). Aiding knowledge capture by searching for extensions of knowledge models. *Proceedings of the International Conference on Knowledge Capture*. Retrieved October 26, 2004, from *http://portal.acm.org/citation.cfm?id=945655&dl=ACM&coll=GUIDE*

Learning Content eXchange. (2003). A new industry model for the e-learning market. Retrieved June 17, 2004, from *http://www.learningcontentexchange.com/LearningObjectEconomy.pdf*

Leik, R. (1998). There's far more than tenure on the butcher block. *Sociological Perspectives, 41*(4), 745-755.

Leslie, L. L., & Rhoades, G. (1995). Rising administrative costs: Seeking explanations. *The Journal of Higher Education, 66*(2), 187-212.

Loader, B. (Ed.) (1997). *The governance of cyberspace: Politics, technology and global restructuring.* New York: Routledge.

Loader, B. (Ed.). (1998). *Introduction, cyberspace divide: Equality, agency, and policy in the information society.* New York: Routledge.

Luker, M. (1999). Preparing your campus for a networked future. Educause Leadership Strategies Series. Jossey-Bass Publishers, November, No. 1.

Lyman, P. (2001). Knowledge discovery in a networked world. In G. Bernbom (Ed.), *Information alchemy: The art and science of knowledge management* (pp.1-24). San Francisco: Jossey-Bass.

Lyotard, J. (1984). *The postmodern condition: A report on knowledge* (trans. G. Bennington and B. Massumi). Minneapolis: University of Minnesota Press.

Marshall, C., & Rossman, G. B. (1989). *Designing qualitative research.* Newbury Park, CA: Sage.

Massy, W. F., & Zemsky, R. (1990). *The dynamics of academic productivity.* Denver: State Higher Education Officers.

Massy, W. F., & Zemsky, R. (1995). *Using information technology to enhance academic productivity.* White paper, EDUCAUSE National Learning Infrastructure Initiative.

McChesney, R. W., Wood, E. M., & Foster, J. B. (1998). *Capitalism and the information age: The political economy of the global communication revolution.* New York: Monthly Review Press.

McClelland, B. (2001). Digital learning and teaching: Evaluation of developments for students in higher education. *European Journal of Engineering Education, 26*(2), 107-115.

McGee, P., & Robinson, J. (2004). The digital divide: Making a case for open source. Paper published in the *Proceedings of the Education and Information Systems: Technologies and Applications (EISTA) Conference*, Orlando, Florida.

McGee, P., Carmean, C., & Jafari, A. (2005). *Course management systems for learning: Beyond accidental pedagogy.* Hershey, PA: Idea Group Publishing.

McGorry, S. Y. (2003). Measuring quality in online programs. *The Internet and Higher Education, 6*(2), 159-177.

McLaughlin, J., Rosen, P., Skinner, D., & Webster, A. (1999). *Valuing technology: Organisations, culture and change.* New York: Routledge.

McMillen, J. (2001). *Intellectual property: Copyright ownership in higher education, university, faculty, & student rights.* Asheville, NC: College Administration Publications, Inc.

McOmber, J. B. (1999). Technological autonomy and three definitions of technology. *Journal of Communication, 49*, 137-153.

Mentkowski, M. & Associates. (2000). *Learning that lasts: Integrating learning, development, and performance in college and beyond.* San Francisco: Jossey-Bass.

Merriam, S.B. (1988). *Case study research in education: A qualitative approach.* San Francisco: Jossey-Bass.

Metcalfe, A. S. (2004). *Intermediating associations and the university-industry relationship.* Unpublished doctoral dissertation, Center for the Study of Higher Education, The University of Arizona.

Meyer, K. (2002). Quality in distance learning. *ASHE-ERIC Higher Education Report, 29*(4), 1-121.

Milam, J. H. (1998). *The politics of web sites.* Panel presentation at the Annual Forum of the Association for Institutional Research, Minneapolis, MN.

Milam, J. H. et al. (2000). *Concept maps for web-based applications.* ERIC technical report. Retrieved October 26, 2004, from *http://highered.org/docs/milam-conceptmaps.PDF*

Milam, J.H. (2001). Knowledge management for higher education. *ERIC Digest.* EDO-HE-2001-05.

Miles, M.B., & Huberman, A.M. (1984). *Qualitative data analysis: A sourcebook of new methods.* Beverly Hills, CA: Sage.

Mintzberg, H. (1979). *The structuring of organizations.* Engelwood Cliffs, NJ: Prentice Hall.

MIT. (2004). OpenCourseWare. Retrieved from *http://ocw.mit.edu/index.html*

Moneta, L. (1997). The integration of technology with the management of student services. *New Directions for Student Services, 78*, 5-16.

Moore, A. (2002). Open-source learning. *Educause Review*, September-October, 43-51.

Moore, A. (2003). The next big thing... again. KM World supplement. April. Retrieved October 26, 2004, from *http://www.kmworld.com/publications/whitepapers/ECM03/moore.pdf*

Moore, M., & Kearsley, G. (1996). *Distance education: A systems view.* Wadsworth Publishing.

Morey, D., Maaybury, M., & Thuraisingham, B. (Eds.) (2000). *Knowledge management: Class and contemporary works.* Cambridge, MA: MIT Press.

Nass, C., & Mason, L. (1990). On the study of technology and task: A variable-based approach. In J. Fulk, & C. Steinfield (Eds.), *Organizations and communication technology* (pp. 46-68). Newbury Park: Sage Publications.

National Center for Charitable Statistics (NCCS). (2004). National taxonomy of exempt entities – Core codes. Retrieved October 26, 2004, from *http://nccs2.urban.org/ntee-cc/irs_code.htm*

National Center for Educational Statistics (NCES). (2004a). IPEDS Glossary. Retrieved October 26, 2004, from *http://nces.ed.gov/ipeds/glossary/*

National Center for Educational Statistics (NCES). (2004b). IPEDS Finance Data FASB and GASB – What's the Difference? Retrieved October 26, 2004, from *http://nces.ed.gov/ipeds/web2000/gasbfasb.asp*

National Center for Postsecondary Improvement (NCPI). (1998). The user-friendly terrain: Defining the market taxonomy for two-year institutions. *Change,* January/February.

National Learning Infrastructure Initiative (NLII). (2004). 2003 NLII Annual Review. Washington, DC: National Learning Infrastructure Initiative. Retrieved October 26, 2004, from *http://www.educause.edu/nlii/*

National Postsecondary Education Cooperative (NPEC). (1999). Best practices for data collectors and data providers. Washington, DC: National Postsecondary Education Cooperative. Retrieved October 26, 2004, from *http://nces.ed.gov/pubsearch/pubsinfo.asp?pubid=1999191*

Neal, E. (1998, June 19). Using technology in teaching: We need to exercise healthy skepticism. *The Chronicle of Higher Education*, B4.

Nichols, R. (1996). The value of education and training. *Discourse, 2*(1), 13.

Niles, I., & Pease, A. (2001). Towards a standard upper ontology. Paper presented at *FOIS Conference*, October.

Nonaka, I. (1991). The knowledge-creating company. *The Harvard Business Review*, November-December, 96-104.

Norris, D., Mason, J., & Lefrere, P. (2003). *A revolution in the sharing of knowledge: Transforming e-Knowledge*. Ann Arbor, MI: Society for College and University Planning.

Noy, N. F., & McGuinness, D. L. (2000). *Ontology Development 101: A guide to creating your first ontology*. Stanford Knowledge Systems Laboratory Technical Report KSL-01-05 and Stanford Medical Informatics Technical Report SMI-2001-0880, March 2001. Retrieved October 26, 2004, from *http://www.ksl.stanford.edu/people/dlm/papers/ontology-tutorial-noy-mcguinness-abstract.html*

Nylund, A. L. (2000). Finding patterns in a deluge of data. *Knowledge Management, 3*(2), 69-71. Retrieved October 26, 2004, from *http://www.destinationcrm.com/km/dcrm_km_article.asp?id=189*

Oettinger, A.G. (1969). *Run, computer, run: The mythology of educational innovation*. Cambridge, MA: Harvard University Press.

Ogbuji, U. (2003). XML knowledge management flourishes in learning technology initiatives. Retrieved October 26, 2004, from *http://www-106.ibm.com/developerworks/xml/library/x-think21.html*

Olivas, M. (1992). The political economy of immigration, intellectual property, and racial harassment: Case studies of the implementation of legal changes on campus. *Journal of Higher Education, 63*, 570-598.

Olsen, F. (2003, January 17). Giant Cal State computing project leaves professors and students asking, why? *The Chronicle of Higher Education*, A 27.

Olson, F. (2001). Getting ready for a new generation of course-management systems. *The Chronicle of Higher Education, 48*(17), 25.

Open Knowledge Initiative (OKI). (2004). Retrieved from *http://web.mit.edu/oki/index.html*

Open Knowledge Network (OKN). (2004). Retrieved from *http://www.openknowledge.net/*

Open Source Portfolio Initiative (OSPI). (2004). Retrieved from *http://www.theospi.org/*

Orlikowski, W. (2000). Using technology and constituting structures: A practice lens for studying technology in organizations. *Organization Science, 11*(4), 404-428.

Packard, A. (2002). Copyright or copy wrong: An analysis of university claims to faculty work. *Communication Law and Policy, 7*, 275-315.

Papadopoullos, A. (2003). *Meaningful search: Why PET scanners are not about cats & dogs.* Carlsbad, CA: Convera.

Paulsen, E. (1997). What does support really cost? *Support Management*, May-June, 14-22.

Peebles, C. S., & Antolovic, L. (1999). Cost (and quality and value) of information technology support in large research universities. *Educom Review, 34*(5).

Perdue, P. (1994). Technological determinism in agrarian societies. In M. R. Smith & L. Marx (Eds.), *Does technology drive history? The dilemma of technological determinism.* Cambridge, MA: MIT Press.

Petrides, L., Khanuja-Dhall, S., & Reguerin, P. (2000) The politics of information management. In L. Petrides (Ed.), *Case studies on information technology in higher education: Implications for policy and practice* (pp. 118-127). Hershey, PA: Idea Group Publishing.

Petrides, L. A., McClelland, S. I., & Nodine, T. R. (2004). Costs and benefits of the workaround: Inventive solution of costly alternative. *The International Journal of Educational Management, 18*(2), 100-108.

Pinch, T., & Bijker, W. (1987). The social construction of facts and artifacts: Or how the sociology of science and the sociology of technology might benefit each other. In W. Bijker, T. Hughes, & T. Pinch (Eds.), *The social construction of technological systems: New direction in the sociology and history of technology* (pp. 17-50). Cambridge, MA: MIT Press.

Poole, M. S., & DeSanctis, G. (1990). Understanding the use of group decision support systems: The theory of adaptive structuration. In J. Fulk, & C. Steinfield (Eds.), *Organizations and communication technology* (pp. 173-193). Newbury Park: Sage Publications.

Por, G. (1997). Designing knowledge ecosystems for communities of practice. Paper presented at the *Advancing Organizational Capability via Knowledge Management Conference*, Los Angeles. Retrieved February 10, 2004, from *http://www.co-i-l.com/coil/knowledge-garden/dkescop/index.shtml*

Porter, D. (Ed.) (1997). *Internet culture.* New York: Routledge.

Raybould, B. (2002). Building performance-centered Web-based systems, information systems, and knowledge management systems in the 21st century. In A. Rossett (Ed.), *The ASTD e-Learning handbook* (pp. 338-353). New York: McGraw-Hill.

Reamy, T. (2002a). Imparting knowledge through storytelling, Part 1. *Mold, 11*(6). Retrieved October 26, 2004, from *http://www.kmworld.com/publications/magazine/index.cfm?action=readarticle&Article_ID=1306&Publication_ID=73*

Reamy, T. (2002b). Imparting knowledge through storytelling, Part 2. *KMWorld, 11*(7). Retrieved October 26, 2004, from *http://www.kmworld.com/publications/magazine/index.cfm?action=read article&Article_ID=1328&Publication_ID=74*

Reeves, T. (2002). Evaluating what really matters in computer-based education. Retrieved June 15, 2004, from *http://www.educationau.edu.au/archives/cp/reeves.htm*

Reflections on the life of the mind in an era of abundance. (2004). *EDUCAUSE Review, 39*(2), 40-51.

Reingold, H. (1993). *The virtual community: Homesteading on the electronic frontier*. Reading, MA: Addison-Wesley.

Rhoades, G. (1995). Rising stratified administrative costs: Student services' place. In D. Woodard (Ed.), *Budgeting as a tool for policy in student affairs: New directions for student services* (p. 70). San Francisco: Jossey-Bass.

Rhoades, G. (1998). *Managed professionals: Unionized faculty and restructuring academic labor.* Albany: State University of New York Press.

Rhoades, G. (1998). Reviewing and rethinking administrative costs. In J.C. Smart (Ed.), *Higher education: Handbook of theory and research* (Vol. XIII). New York: Agathon Press.

Rhoades, G., & Sporn, B. (2002). New models of management and shifiting modes and costs of production: Europe and the United States. *Tertiary Education and Management, 8,* 3-28.

Rifkin, J. (2000). *The age of access: The new culture of hypercapitalism, Where all of life is a paid-for experience.* New York: J. P. Tarcher/Putnam.

Robson, R. (2001). All about learning objects. Retrieved June 15, 2004, from *http://www.eduworks.com/LOTT/tutorial/learningobjects.html*

Rosen, J. (2002). Blackboard nears profits. *Publishers Weekly, 249*(22), 20.

Rossett, A., & Donello, J. (1999). Knowledge management for training professionals. Retrieved February 3, 2004, from *http://defcon.sdsu.edu/1/objects/km/map/index.htm*

Rossett, A., & Marshall, J. (1999). Signposts on the road to knowledge management. In K. P. Kuchinke (Ed.), *Proceedings of the 1999 AHRD Conference* (Vol. 1, pp. 496-503). Baton Rouge, LA: Academy of Human Resource Development.

Rowley, J. (2000). Is higher education ready for knowledge management? *International Journal of Educational Management, 14*(7), 325-333.

Salisbury, W., Pearson, R., Miller, D., & Marett, L. (2002). The limits of information: A cautionary tale about one course delivery experience in the distance education environment. *e-Service Journal, 1*(2).

Sampler, J. (1996). Exploring the relationship between information technology and organizational structure. In M.J. Earl (Ed.), *Information management: The organizational dimension* (pp. 5-22). Oxford, UK: Oxford University Press.

Saupe, J. L. (1999). The functions of institutional research. In M. W. Peterson (Ed.), *ASHE reader on planning and institutional research* (pp. 211-223). Needham Heights, MA: Pearson Custom Publishing.

Schiller, D. (1999). *Digital capitalism: Networking the global market system*. Cambridge, MA: MIT Press.

Senge, P. M. (1990). *The fifth discipline: The art and practice of the learning organization.* New York: Currency.

Serban, A. M. (2002). Knowledge management: The "Fifth Face" of institutional research. *New Directions for Institutional Research, 113*, 105-111.

Serban, A. M., & Luan, J. (Eds.) (2002). *Knowledge management: Building a competitive advantage in higher education, New Directions for Institutional Research #113*. San Francisco: Jossey-Bass.

Sevcenko, M. (2003). Online presentation of an upper ontology. *Proceedings of Znalosti 2003*, Ostrava, Czech Republic, February 19-21.

Retrieved October 26, 2004, from *http://ontology.teknowledge.com/Sevcenko.pdf*

Sharpe, T., & Hawkins, A. (1998). Technology and the information age: A cautionary tale for higher education. *QUEST, 50*, 19-32.

Shulman, L. S. (2001). *The Carnegie classification of institutions of higher education.* Menlo Park, CA: The Carnegie Foundation for the Advancement of Teaching.

Sieczka, K. (n.d.). Workplace training versus traditional classroom training. Retrieved February 16, 2004, from *http://www.ideamarketers.com/library/article.cfm?articleid=25789*

Simonson, M., Smaldino, S., Albright, M., & Zvacek, S. (2003). *Teaching and learning at a distance: Foundations of distance learning* (2nd ed.). Upper Saddle, NJ: Pearson Education.

Slaughter, S., & Leslie, L. L. (1997). *Academic capitalism: Politics, policies, and the entrepreneurial university.* Baltimore: The Johns Hopkins University Press.

Slaughter, S., & Rhoades, G. (2004). *Academic capitalism in the new economy.* Baltimore: Johns Hopkins Press.

Smallen, D. (2004). *Benchmarks: Helping your president understand IT investments.* Presentation at the EDUCAUSE Annual Conference, Denver, CO, October.

Smith, M., & Marx, L. (Eds.) (1994). *Does technology drive history: The dilemma of technological determinism.* Cambridge, MA: MIT Press.

Smith, N. (2002). Teaching as coaching: Helping students learn in a technological world. *Educause*, May-June, 38-45.

Solmon, L., & Wiederhorn, J. (2000). Progress of technology in the schools 1999: Report on 27 states. Milken Foundation. Retrieved February 12, 2004, from *http://www.mff.org/publications/publications.taf?page=277*

Sowa, J. F. (2004a). Ontology. Retrieved October 26, 2004, from *http://www.jfsowa.com/ontology/*

Sowa, J. F. (2004b). Ontology, metadata, and semiotics. Retrieved October 26, 2004, from *http://users.bestweb.net/~sowa/peirce/ontometa.htm*

Sørensen, K. (1996). *Learning technology, constructing culture: Socio-technical change as social learning.* STS working paper no 18/96,

University of Trondheim: Centre for technology and society. Retrieved June 15, 2004, from *http://www.rcss.ed.ac.uk/SLIM/public/phase1/knut.html*

Sporn, B. (1999). Adaptive university structures: An analysis of adaptation to socioeconomic environments of US and European universities. In M. Kogan (Ed.), *Higher education policy series.* London: Jessica Kingsley Publishers.

Sproulle, L., & Keisler. S. (1991). *Connections: New ways of working in the networked organization.* Cambridge, MA: MIT Press.

Star, S. L. (1995). *The cultures of computing.* Cambridge: Blackwell Publishers.

Star, S. L. (1999). The ethnography of infrastructure. *American Behavioral Scientist, 43*(3), 337-391.

Stewart, T. A. (1991). Brainpower. *Fortune, 123*(11), 44-60.

Strassmann, P. A. (1997). *The squandered computer: Evaluating the business alignment of information technologies.* New Canaan, CT: Information Economics Press.

Strauss, H. (2002). The right train at the right station. *Educause Review*, May-June, 30-36.

Strauss, H., Kerns, C., & Boettcher, J. (2002). *Course management systems and learning tools: Where are we at the end of 2002?* Transcript from CREN Tech Talks. November 7, 2002.

Sullivan, P. H. (2000). *Value-driven intellectual capital: How to convert intangible corporate assets into market value.* New York: John Wiley & Sons.

Tansey, F. (2003). The standard bearers close ranks. *Syllabus Magazine*, March.

Taylor, J. (2001). Fifth generation distance education. *Higher Education Series, 40.* Retrieved June 15, 2004, from *http:// www.dest.gov.au/highered/hes/hes40/hes40.pdf*

Tenner, E. (1996). *Why things bite back: Technology and the revenge of unintended consequences.* New York: Alfred A. Knopf.

Terenzini, P. T. (1993). On the nature of institutional research and the knowledge and skills it requires. *Research in Higher Education, 34*(1), 1-10.

Thomas, C. R. (1971). *NCHEMS data element dictionary.* Boulder, CO: National Center for Higher Education Management Systems.

Thomas, C. R. (2004). *CHESS data definitions* (2nd ed.). Boulder, CO: National Center for Higher Education Management Systems.

Thomas, G., & Home, T. (2004). *Using ICT to share the tools of the teaching trade: A report on open source teaching.* Becta ICT Research. Retrieved April 9, 2004, from *http://www.seeveaz.myschools.net/Bestpractice/OSDDB6.pdf*

Thomas, R. J. (1994). *What machines can't do: Politics and technology in the industrial enterprise.* Berkeley: University of California Press.

Tiffin, L., & Rajasingham, L. (2003). *Global virtual university.* London: RoutledgeFalmer.

Trowler, P. R. (1998). *Academics responding to change: New higher education frameworks and academic cultures.* Buckingham: Open University Press.

Twigg, C. (2000). *Who owns online courses and course materials: Intellectual property policies for a new learning environment.* The Pew Learning and Technology Program, Center for Academic Transformation at Renssalaer Polytechnic Institute.

Twigg, C. A. (1994). The need for a national learning infrastructure. *Educom Review, 29*(4, 5, 6).

U.S. Census Bureau. (2004). North American Industry Classification System (NAICS). Retrieved October 26, 2004, from *http://www.census.gov/epcd/www/naics.html*

Vaira, M. (2004). Globalization and higher education organizational change: A framework for analysis. *Higher Education, 48*(4), 483-510.

Vallas, S. (1998). Manufacturing knowledge: Technology, culture, and social inequality at work. *Social Science Computer Review, 16*(4), 353-369.

Venkata, R. (2002). Taxonomies, categorization, and organizational agility. KM World supplement. Retrieved October 26, 2004, from *http://www.kmworld.com/publications/whitepapers/KM2/venkata.pdf*

Volkwien, J. F. (1999). The four faces of institutional research. What is institutional research all about? A critical and comprehensive assessment of the profession. *New Directions for Institutional Research, 104.* San Francisco: Jossey-Bass.

Webster, F. (2002). *Theories of the information society* (2nd ed.). London: Routledge.

Webster, J., & Hackley, P. (1997). Teaching effectiveness in technology-mediated distance learning. *Academy of Management Journal, 40*, 1282-1309.

Welsh, J. (2000). Course ownership in a new technological context: The dynamics of problem definition. *The Journal of Higher Education, 71*(6), 668-699.

Wescott, E. (2001). The Internet encyclopedia of philosophy. Retrieved March 18, 2004, from *http://www.iep.utm.edu/r/relativi.htm*

West, T. W., & Dagigle, S. L. (1997). The 4-D world of higher education: A new context for student support services. *NACADA Journal, 17*(2), 13-22.

Whitley, M. A., Porter, J. D., & Fenske, R. H. (1992). *The primer for institutional research.* Tallahassee, FL: Association for Institutional Research.

Wiig, K. M. (1993). *Knowledge management foundations: Thinking about thinking: How people and organizations create, represent, and use knowledge.* Arlington, TX: Schema Press.

Wiig, K. M. (1994). *Knowledge management: The central management focus for intelligent-acting organizations.* Arlington, TX: Schema Press.

Wiig, K. M. (1995). *Knowledge management methods: Practical approaches to managing knowledge.* Arlington, TX: Schema Press.

Wiig, K. M. (1997). Knowledge management: An introduction and perspective. *Journal of Knowledge Management, 1*(1), 6-14.

Wiley, D. (2000). Connecting learning objects to instructional design theory: A definition, a metaphor, and a taxonomy. The Instructional Use of Learning Objects: Online Version. Retrieved June 15, 2004, from *http://www.reusability.org/read/*

Wiley, D. (2003). Learning objects: Difficulties and opportunities. Retrieved June 15, 2004, from *http://wiley.ed.usu.edu/docs/lo_do.pdf*

Wiley, D. A. (2000). Connecting learning objects to instructional design theory: A definition, a metaphor, and a taxonomy. Retrieved October 26, 2004, from *http://www.reusability.org/read/chapters/wiley.doc*

Wilson, T. D. (2002). The nonsense of knowledge management. *Information Research, 18*(1), Paper 144. Retrieved October 7, 2004, from *http://InformationR.net/ir/8-1/paper144.html*

Winner, L. (1977). *Autonomous technology: Technics-out-of-control as a theme in political thought.* Cambridge, MA: MIT Press.

Winner, L. (1986). Do artifacts have politics? In *Whale and the Reactor: A Search for Limits in an Age of High Technology* (pp. 19-39). Chicago: University of Chicago Press.

Winner, L. (2001). Where technological determinism went. In S. H. Cutcliffe, & C. Mitcham (Eds.), *Visions of STS: Counterpoints in science, technology, and society studies* (pp. 11-17). Albany: State University of New York Press.

Wolf-Wendel, L. E., & Ruel, M. (1999). Developing the whole student: The collegiate ideal. *New Directions for Higher Education, 105*, 35-45.

Wulf, W. A. (2003). Higher education alert: the information railroad is coming. *Educause*, January-February, 12-21.

Young, J.R. (2002). Designer of free course-management software asks, What makes a good web site? *The Chronicle of Higher Education,* February 8.

Appendix C:
KM Glossary

Campus Wide Information System (CWIS): Also known as "enterprise systems," these computer-based data storage systems encompass the mission functions of an entire higher education institution.

Course Management System (CMS): Software that allows students and faculty to organize electronic materials for a specific course or set of courses.

Data Mining: The process of searching databases for patterns or specific information.

Data Warehouse: An organization-wide database, often utilized by different subunits for various strategic planning efforts.

Explicit Knowledge: Learning that can be codified and transferred.

Learning Management System (LMS): Another term for a course management system; often used in a business training context or other non-credit learning context.

Learning Object: A reusable unit for instructional purposes, usually in an electronic format; can be a web page, digital video, audio file, guided tutorial, and so on.

Metadata: Often described as "data about data;" a keyword(s) or descriptor(s) used to classify and retrieve specific electronic data.

Ontology: A hierarchical data structure used to organize groups of related data.

Subject Matter Expert (SME): Often the traditional role of instructors and faculty, SME are the people who have specific knowledge of a given knowledge domain.

Tacit Knowledge: Learning that is difficulty to codify and transfer.

About the Authors

Amy Scott Metcalfe, PhD, is an assistant professor in the Department of Educational Studies at The University of British Columbia, Canada. She has written and co-authored several publications on the topics of technological change in higher education organizations, intellectual property policy, and faculty issues. Dr. Metcalfe's recent work focuses on the organizational structures of academy-industry-government relationships. Her dissertation, titled *Intermediating Associations and the University-Industry Relationship*, examined the interorganizational networks between the information technology industry and higher education institutions.

***

Bongsug Chae (PhD, 2002, Texas A&M University) is an assistant professor of management information systems at Kansas State University (USA). His current research interests are in the area of large-scale information system and information infrastructure, knowledge management, technology adaptation, decision support systems, and ethics and social theories for IS research. His work also appears in *Decision Support Systems*, *OMEGA: The International Journal of Management Science*, *Information Resource Management Journal*, *Electronic Journal of Information Systems for Developing Countries*, *International Journal of Information Technology and Decision Making*, *Journal of KMCI* and others.

Gary A. Cruz is the interim assistant director of research and assessment for the Department of Multicultural Programs and Services at The University of Arizona. He is currently a doctoral candidate with an emphasis in science and technology policy at the Center for the Study of Higher Education at the University of Arizona. He received his Master's in Higher Education Administration from Texas A&M University. Among his research interests are the digital divide, Latino higher education access, retention, and persistence in science and engineering, and the intersection of student development and information technology.

Veronica Diaz holds a doctorate from the Center for the Study of Higher Education with an emphasis in science and technology and a minor in management and policy from The University of Arizona (USA). Currently, she is the learning technologies manager for the Eller College of Management and also works with the Learning Technologies Center at the University of Arizona. Dr. Diaz studies various areas of distributed learning at both two- and four-year higher education institutions. A second area of her research has focused on intellectual property ownership and control in distributed learning. She also studies higher education policy development behavior in an increasingly technological environment.

Panagiotis Kanellis is currently a program manager with Information Society S.A. in Athens, Greece. He was educated at Western International University in business administration (BSc), at the University of Ulster in computing and information systems (Post-Graduate Diploma), and at Brunel University in data communication systems (MSc) and information systems (PhD). He is a research fellow in the Department of Informatics and Telecommunications at the National and Kapodistrian University of Athens and an adjunct faculty member at the Athens University of Economics and Business.

George S. McClellan is the vice president for student development at Dickinson State University, USA. He received his doctorate in higher education at The University of Arizona and his Master's in Higher Education from Northwestern University. Among his research interests are the effects of computer-mediated communication on student development and the challenges and opportunities presented by the integration of information technology in student affairs.

Patricia McGee, PhD, is a faculty member in the Instructional Technology program in the College of Education and Human Development at The University of Texas at San Antonio (USA). Three summers as American Society for Engineering Education (ASEE) Office of Naval Research Faculty Fellow with the Joint ADL Co-Lab in Orlando and the Defense Equal Opportunity Management Institute has provided her a venue for examining and developing learning objects and related topics. Her work as a 2003 National Learning Infrastructure Initiative Fellow involved researching and writing about learning objects and next generation course management systems resulting in a book on the vision of such systems. As director of a PT3 and Microsoft/AACTE Innovative Teaching grant, she contributes to campus-wide technology initiatives. She develops, teaches, and studies online courses. Currently she is leading an open source ePortfolio project, as well as conducting research about pedagogy within course management system and institutional learning object development and policy-making. Dr. McGee earned a PhD in curriculum and instruction with a concentration in Instructional Technology from The University of Texas at Austin.

Drakoulis Martakos is an associate professor at the Department of Informatics and Telecommunications, National and Kapodistrian University of Athens, Greece. He received his BSc in physics, MSc in electronics and radio communications, and PhD in real-time computing from the same university. Professor Martakos is a consultant to public and private organizations and a project leader in numerous national and international projects. He is author or co-author of more than 50 scientific publications and a number of technical reports and studies.

John Milam, PhD, is executive director of HigherEd.org, Inc. (USA), a consulting firm focused on "Knowledge Management for Higher Education." Dr. Milam has held faculty, administrative, and institutional research positions at the University of Houston, West Virginia University, George Mason University, and most recently the University of Virginia. He has designed a number of KM tools, including the ANSWERS data portal; the IPEDS Dataset Cutting Tool; the GMU Data Warehouse; and Internet Resources for Institutional Research. Dr. Milam has written about numerous KM topics, including concept maps, the costs of distance learning, virtual university models, assessing online education, and organizational learning.

Lilly Nguyen is a research assistant at the Institute for the Study of Knowledge Management in Education (ISKME) (USA). She received her MSc in media and communications at the London School of Economics, where she studied the role of information technologies and organizational learning practices in non-profit organizations. Her research at ISKME has focused primarily on the dynamics of information sharing and knowledge management practices in educational institutions. Her current research interests include information mapping, the social dynamics of information technologies, and how technologies can give shape to identities and communities.

David Paper is an associate professor at Utah State University (USA) in the Management Information Systems (MIS) Department. He has several refereed publications appearing in journals such as *Information & Management*, *Journal of Information Technology Cases and Applications, Information Resource Management Journal, Communications of the AIS*, *Long Range Planning, Creativity and Innovation, Accounting Management and Information Technologies*, *Journal of Managerial Issues, Business Process Management Journal, Journal of Computer Information Systems*, and *Information Strategy: The Executive's Journal*. He has worked for Texas Instruments, DLS, Inc., and the Phoenix Small Business Administration. He has performed IS consulting work for the Utah Department of Transportation (Salt Lake City, UT) and the Space Dynamics Laboratory (Logan, UT). His teaching and research interests include change management, process reengineering, database management, e-commerce, and enterprise integration.

Lisa A. Petrides is the founder and president of the Institute for the Study of Knowledge Management in Education (ISKME) (USA), a non-profit educational think tank that conducts research and offers resources with the goal of helping education institutions increase their capacity to use data and information to improve student and institutional success. She is a former professor at Columbia University, Teachers College, where she coordinated the EdD-MBA joint degree program in education leadership and management offered by the Educational Administration Program and the Columbia Business School. Her publications include a new book, *Turning knowledge into action: What's data got to do with it?*; "The challenges of using external accountability mandates to create internal change," in *Planning for Higher Education*; "Costs and benefits of the workaround: Inventive solution or costly alternative," in *International Journal of Education Management;* "What schools have to teach the corporate world," in *KM Review; Knowledge management in education: Defining the landscape*, a monograph produced by ISKME; and "Knowledge management for school leaders: An ecological framework for thinking schools," in *Teachers College Record.*

Marshall Scott Poole (PhD, 1979, University of Wisconsin) is a professor of information and operations management and of communication at Texas A&M University (USA). He has conducted research and published extensively on the topics of group and organizational communication, conflict management, computer-mediated communication systems, implementation of information systems, and organizational innovation. He has co-authored or edited 10 books including *Communication and Group Decision-Making*, *Research on the Management of Innovation*, *Organizational Change and Innovation Processes: Theory and Methods for Research,* and *Handbook of Organizational Change and Innovation.*

José L. Santos, PhD, is an assistant professor in the Higher Education & Organizational Change Division and an Affiliated Scholar of the Higher Education Research Institute at University of California - Los Angeles (USA). His research interests center on comparative state and institutional policies concerning investments in access and affordability for underrepresented students. He has written on topics such as resource allocation at public research extensive universities, and is also interested in how universities use their information technology and decision support systems for policy-making. He specializes in quantitative methods, having developed such strengths through his background in econometrics and measurement, research methodology, and as a senior institutional researcher.

Lucie Sommer (sommerl@colorado.edu) is an advanced PhD student in the communications department at The University of Colorado, Boulder (USA). She also teaches for the university's Writing and Rhetoric Program. Her most current study project investigates the relationship between the social structures, knowledge frameworks, and communications technologies specific to the higher education setting. In her study of the social construction of knowledge, she draws on scholarship from organizational communication and rhetorical theory.

Teta Stamati is currently a sales manager in Delta Singular S.A. in Athens, Greece. She holds a degree in computing from the Informatics and Telecommunications Department at National and Kapodistrian University of Athens, an MPhil in computing and information systems at UMIST in UK, and an MBA in Lancaster Business School at Lancaster University. She is a research fellow in the Department of Informatics and Telecommunications at the National and Kapodistrian University of Athens.

Richard L. Wagoner received his doctorate in higher education at The University of Arizona (USA). Among his research interests are the changing nature of higher education faculty labor and the challenges and opportunities to both policy and practice in higher education presented by advances in information technology.

Bing Wang is a doctoral candidate in the Management Information Systems (MIS) Department at Utah State University (USA). She worked as a senior executive in a multinational company in Singapore prior to her PhD study, and has offered IT consulting services to the Utah Department of Transportation. She now serves as the assistant program chair as well as a track chair for the 2004 Global Information Technology Management Conference. Her research interests include technology-based organization intervention and change management. She is currently working on a major research project at a university-owned research institute.

Index